D0948306

G 35

Burgess-Carpenter Library
406 Butler
Columbia University
New York, N. Y. 10027

Ben · Gurion
and the Intellectuals

BEN· GURION

and the Intellectuals: Power, Knowledge, and Charisma

 MICHAEL KEREN

WITHDRAWN

NORTHERN ILLINOIS UNIVERSITY PRESS ◆ DEKALB, ILLINOIS

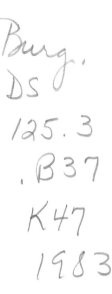

Burg.
DS
125.3
.B37
K47
1983

Library of Congress Cataloging in Publication Data

Keren, Michael.
    Ben-Gurion and the intellectuals.

    Includes bibliographical references and index.
    1. Ben-Gurion, David, 1886–1973—Philosophy.
2. Prime ministers—Israel—Biography.   2. Israel—
Intellectual life.   I. Title.
DS125.3.B37K47   1983   956.94'05'0924   83-17415
ISBN 0-87580-094-7

Copyright © 1983 by Northern Illinois University Press. Published by the Northern Illinois University Press, DeKalb, Illinois
60115. Manufactured in the United States of America. All Rights
Reserved.

Frontispiece courtesy of Dan Taggar

Design by Joan Westerdale

in memory of my father,
Dr. Hermann Horn

cym 84-08-30 117464

Contents

··· ה ···

Acknowledgments

This study is based on David Ben-Gurion's private papers—correspondence, protocols of official and private meetings, diaries and other documents to which I was granted access during my two-year stay at the Ben-Gurion Research Institute and Archives in Sdeh Boker, a small community in the Negev desert where Ben-Gurion lived during the closing years of his life. Additional sources, including personal interviews, have also been used. Unless otherwise noted, all documents cited in the footnotes are located in Sdeh Boker.

I would like to thank Meir Avizohar, director of the Ben-Gurion Research Institute and Archives, as well as Gershon Rivlin, the former director, for granting me access to the previously unpublished material. All members of the Institute's staff, notably Yigal Donyetz and Nechama Milo, were most kind and helpful. I am also indebted to Haim Israeli, Ben-Gurion's former personal aide, and to Shmuel Avi-ad, of Israel's Ministry of Defense, for their valuable assistance and advice.

I wrote this book while on sabbatical leave from Tel-Aviv University, which I spent with the Department of Urban Affairs, University of Wisconsin–Milwaukee. I am indebted to Chava and David Nachmias, who invited me to join the program for a very fruitful year, as well as to Donna Bennett of the Social Science Research Center at U.W.M., who typed the manuscript. During my stay in the U.S., my two excellent research assistants, Yair Goldberg and Reuven Pedhazur, continued to be of great help in conducting interviews and searching for documents following my long distance requests. I would also like to thank all the scholars and public figures who were interviewed: Hanni Bergman (Professor Ernst Bergman's widow), Menachem Dorman, Haim Gevaryahu, Haim Gouri, Dan Horowitz, Yaacov Katz, Ephraim Katzir, Hans Klinghoffer, Moshe Kol, Yeshayahu Leibowitz, Nathan Rotenstreich, Shmuel Sambursky, Ernst Simon, Yizhar Smilanski, and Ephraim Urbach.

Finally, it is my pleasure to thank my good friends and colleagues, Asher Arian, Myron Aronoff, Moshe Czudnowski, Yonathan Shapiro, and Dina Spechler, for their comments on the first draft of this study, and the Faculty of Social Sciences at Tel-Aviv University for its continuing support.

Introduction

in the early 1960s, David Ben-Gurion, a master statesman enchanted by the combined role of knowledge and power in the modern state and skilled in their utilization, found himself in bitter conflict with Israel's leading intellectuals. This confrontation had three unique features. The first concerned the personalities involved. Ben-Gurion, Israel's founder and state-builder, a charismatic leader and towering personality, was fighting a battle of principles with some of the greatest intellectuals in modern Jewish history: Martin Buber, the philosopher and theologian; Jacob Talmon, the historian of ideas; Gershom Scholem, the Kabbalist scholar; and other figures of world fame. Second, the confrontation evolved within a framework of cooperation between the intellectuals and the state. Rarely have intellectuals had such direct access to an important center of power, and the vast exchange of ideas revealed in this study speaks for itself. Third, the intellectuals turned out to be quite effective politically. This was dramatically expressed by a Ben-Gurion supporter following the Prime Minister's resignation: "Don Quixote lies ruined and downcast under the boot of the Knight of the Silver Moon." Reflecting a common disbelief in the power of ideas, he did not fail to add that the Knight— referring, of course, to the intellectuals—"is none other than the barber masquerading as the nobleman."[1]

The immediate context of Ben-Gurion's confrontation with the intellectuals was a political crisis during the years 1960 and 1961 known as the "Lavon Affair" or simply as "The Affair."[2] The crisis was sparked by the question of responsibility for a mishap that had occurred six years earlier. In 1954, a group of young Egyptian Jews was arrested in Egypt for committing arson in several public places, including the American libraries in Cairo and Alexandria. The inexperienced youths, most of whose homemade bombs had not even exploded, had been recruited by an Israeli intelligence officer, a controversial figure who managed to escape unharmed and was later sentenced for treasonable contact with an Egyptian agent. This operation, part of a clumsy scheme to disrupt Egypt's relations with the West, cost the lives of three Egyptian Jews and caused the long-term imprisonment of others. An enquiry commission set up in Israel to investigate the mishap had not reached a firm conclusion as to whether the operation was authorized by the head of military intelligence Benjamin Gibly or by Defense Secretary Pinhas Lavon, a prominent member of Mapai, Israel's then-ruling Labor party. Both men were removed from their posts with some measure of disgrace, although Lavon soon built himself an independent power base as Secretary General of the Federation of Labor.

In 1960, Lavon, armed with what he declared to be "new evidence," approached Prime Minister Ben-Gurion and demanded that he be vindicated. Ben-Gurion, who during the mishap was on voluntary retirement and had little to do with the incident, shrugged a stubborn shoulder. He claimed Lavon was never accused of any wrongdoing, that vindicating Lavon would imply Gibly's guilt, and that only a full judicial procedure could lead to vindication. Lavon, therefore, brought his case before a parliamentary committee, whose proceedings were leaked to the press. In those proceedings Lavon raised severe accusations about a cover-up of the mishap in the defense establishment, hinting at an elaborate conspiracy against him by Ben-Gurion's boys there. This opened a Pandora's box, as every political force in the country was now taking sides over whether a judicial enquiry should be held, as Ben-Gurion demanded, or whether another solution could be found. Mapai's leadership, sensing the beginning of a premature war over Ben-Gurion's inheritance (for which it was not yet prepared), hoped to defuse the crisis by finding a way to vindicate Lavon and to punish him later for breaking the rules of the game. Furious over Lavon's accusations, however, Ben-Gurion refused to go along with this. Tension mounted to unprecedented heights when Ben-Gurion insisted on a "judicial enquiry committee," after a committee of seven compromise-minded members of his own cabinet declared Lavon innocent. The crisis was exacerbated by the ousting of Lavon from his Federation of Labor post—by the same party leadership that had finagled the decision by the "Committee of Seven"— and ultimately resulted in new parliamentary elections, a change of guard in government, and a major split in Mapai.[3]

In January 1961, a public statement was initiated by a group of professors at the Hebrew University in Jerusalem which labeled Ben-Gurion's crusade against the Committee of Seven as a serious challenge to democracy. The statement, signed and supported by dozens of intellectuals all over the country, acknowledged Ben-Gurion's achievements as the founder of the state but rejected the notion, attributed to the Prime Minister's "associates," that the survival of the state depended on "any one individual."[4] This public statement had a far-reaching effect. The scope of the crisis had now spread, and all parties involved— notably Ben-Gurion himself—began to perceive it as a struggle over the foundations of public order and morality.[5] The Affair turned into a gigantic battle between the Prime Minister and the intellectuals, whose voices were heard not only in public meetings and in the press but in many political forums and institutions playing a role in The Affair. The intellectuals, largely siding with Lavon, played a major role in promoting his case as that of an individual facing a tyrannical state apparatus in his quest for personal justice. Although some of them doubted whether Lavon, the political animal, really fitted this image, they turned him into a symbol of the spontaneous, voluntary forces of an open society seeking liberation from the almighty state-builder whose time had come to leave the stage.[6]

Ben-Gurion, for his part, strongly insisted that no justice could be done without the revelation of the whole truth first, and he fiercely attacked the intellectuals for compromising the value of truth which they claimed to cherish. As various scholars have noted,[7] the involvement of the intellectuals in The Affair was a major factor in Ben-Gurion's decision to fight to the bitter end— and bitter it was indeed. Ben-Gurion's final resignation in 1963, and his almost total isolation at the end of his career, were clearly a result of this decision. Till his dying day, Ben-Gurion never got over the surprise and anguish he had suffered as a result of the position taken by the intellectuals. On the surface, their stand was surprising since it could by no means be explained merely by the immediate political context. As many participants in the confrontation had sensed, it had far deeper causes than could be identified at the time.[8] Very fundamental issues in the life of the state—of any state—were at stake.

This study, written from a twenty-year perspective, attempts to explain Ben-Gurion's political conflict with the intellectuals by reference to the sets of ideas that had dominated their relations since the establishment of the state of Israel in 1948. The vast and direct exchange of ideas, as well as its depth and intensity, provides a unique insight into the essence and dynamics of the relationship between knowledge and power in the nation-building process. An effective collaboration between knowledge and power, it is widely agreed, is a requirement for social order and change.[9] It is therefore of great importance to try to understand the nature and limits of that collaboration. Israel's intellectuals were active participants in the nation-building process led by Ben-Gurion, who, for his part, attributed the intellectuals a leading role in this process. Their ultimate confrontation thus reflected deep tensions between knowledge and power as they combine to serve the goals of "nation-building." This term, usually associated with developing societies, is extended here to include every planned effort of rapid socioeconomic change guided by a sense of vision. To those envisioning the future technological society as a major effort of this kind, the confrontation studied here has additional significance. From this perspective, this is a study of an early battle in the war of the modern intellectual against the emerging philosopher-king.

In order to explain the theoretical perspectives of this study, "knowledge" will be defined as the cognitive product of any established branch of science, art, and learning, and "intellectuals" as the acknowledged articulators of ideas based on this knowledge.[10] This definition implies that the inclusion of a person of knowledge as the incumbent of an intellectual elite requires not only familiarity with the world of letters and the articulation of ideas but also some measure of social acceptance.[11] It thus places this study within a relatively new tradition in the political sociology of intellectuals, one which considers the acceptance of ideas as a variable rather than a constant.[12] Within this tradition, the conditions of the communication and diffusion of ideas in society become crucial factors in determining the social role and political behavior of the intellectual.[13]

In the past, the absorption and acceptance of ideas by others received less attention than did the location of the intellectual within certain socioeconomic structures.[14] It was believed that by placing intellectuals within institutional frameworks such as "classes," "roles," or "elites," their political behavior could be explained.[15] And yet the attempt to marry intellectuals to institutionalization had been in Nettl's words: "A shotgun marriage of great therapeutic benefit to the priests but not to the doting couple."[16] In too many instances, especially in critical instances of knowledge-power interaction, the political behavior of intellectuals did not seem to match the institutional location assigned to them. In empirical reality, this behavior often turned out to be more complex than acknowledged by sociological theory, as if the intellectual insisted on playing a free-floating role vis-à-vis the social order.[17] In fact, it has never been easy to categorize intellectuals according to "class," "role," or "elite" status. As is well known, Karl Mannheim in his 1936 treatise, *Ideology and Utopia*, considered intellectuals a classless stratum not too firmly situated in the social order.[18] Talcott Parsons recognized that the intellectual, although performing a complex of social roles, must be defined by the primacy he gives to cultural considerations over social-role considerations.[19] And Suzanne Keller, believing intellectuals to be "members of good standing" among the strategic elites in society, noted, however, in *Beyond the Ruling Class*, that their outlook and values are neither carbon copies of the values of other elites nor reflections of an independent social role.[20] The unique characteristics of the intellectual in the social order make the task of explaining and predicting his political behavior by reference to his social location very hard indeed.

In his study on *Intellectuals and Politics*,[21] Robert Brym ventured to demonstrate that it is only by analyzing the shifting societal ties of intellectuals to various classes and major groups in society that one can arrive at an adequate understanding of their politics. This dynamic notion of the relationship between social conditions and the politics of intellectuals is a refreshing alternative to conceptions predicting intellectuals' political behavior by reference to stable role requirements. Brym criticized three such conceptions—one considering intellectuals to be mere spokesmen of a single class interest, another considering intellectuals to constitute classes in their own right, and a third considering intellectuals as virtually divorced from the class structure. He began by criticizing the "radicalization thesis," which claims that the intellectual's role, defined in terms of his position in the productive process or in the system of social rewards, predisposes its incumbents to adopt a critical stance vis-à-vis society. He argued that radicalism is related to more complex and changing empirical conditions, such as the control over resources of power. He then criticized the famous notion of intellectuals as oligarchs, claiming that fluctuations in the degree to which intellectuals become oligarchs in social movements depend on shifts in power relations between them and other elite and mass groups. Finally, Brym criticized Mannheim's thesis of the modern intellectual as relatively classless. The ideological diversity of intellectuals, which appears to be the consequence of such relative classlessness, is, to Brym, a function of their varied, complex, and shifting attachments to the major groups in society. Brym proposed that the structural location and social identity of the intellectual depends, above all else, on the relative power of society's major classes and groups at any given point in time. He stopped short of the conclusion that it might therefore be worthwhile to search for the structural location and social identity of the intellectual in his relations with government where that power mostly resides.[22]

In his seminal works, Edward Shils offered a frame of reference for the study of intellectuals' relations with government. Shils formulated the research question underlying this study as the question of the sources of tension, which he considered inevitable, between intellectuals and the "laity" and proposed to look at the "traditions" of intellectuals for an explanation. Shils's contributions require some elaboration not only for the useful terminology they offer but also because he constructed a theory of intellectuals' political behavior based on a relatively open and dynamic conception of their interaction with the polity. The concept of "tradition" is central in that theory. Shils defined an intellectual tradition as "a set or pattern of beliefs, conceptions of form, sets of verbal (and other symbolic) usages, [and] roles of procedure, recurrently and unilaterally linked with each other

through time."[23] Every productive intellectual produces his w
under the influence of beliefs, forms, usages, and the etho
procedure and production that he has received and that h
part reproduces. These form the primary tradition to which he is
attached or by which he is dominated. But the intellectual is also
under the influence of traditions not related to particular objects
of his work and its production. These traditions, many of which
concern his relations with authority, are the secondary traditions.

Shils noted that one of the elements in primary intellectual
traditions is that intellectual activity is concerned with fundamental or "charismatic" things. He wrote: "The ethos of intellectual activity has defined the highest performance as being
endowed with charismatic properties. The conception of 'genius,'
the notion of 'inspiration,' both bespeak the charismatic overtones which are oriented to the greatest intellectual accomplishments. Accordingly, intellectual roles of the most creative
intellectuals have been defined as correspondingly endowed with
charisma; their incumbents have been correspondingly perceived."[24] Most of the secondary traditions of intellectuals, being
concerned with authority, also deal with the locus of the charismatic and its institutional manifestations. These traditions assert
that charisma is located in a particular part of society or in a
particular kind of activity.

The belief in the charismatic qualifications of intellectual works
and their producers on one hand and the concern with the location of "charisma" in society on the other brought intellectuals
into "unavoidable contact with earthly authorities."[25] According
to Shils, even if such factors as common class, common social
origin, or mutual need had not been operative, intellectuals
would have been in contact with the "mighty" because they were
fascinated by them. "Intellectual activities are 'serious,' the charismatic is 'serious,' and intellectuals being concerned with the
charismatic have, willy nilly, been drawn into preoccupation with
those in authority because all great, very powerful authority is
believed by those who possess and those who contemplate it to
have a charismatic element resident in it."[26]

At this point some explication of Shils's use of "charisma" is in
order. Contrary to Max Weber's use of the term as referring to a
particular constellation of personality qualities, Shils contended
that the charismatic quality of an individual as perceived by others, or himself, lies in what is thought to be his connection with

"some very *central* feature of man's existence and the cosmos in which he lives."[27] This centrality is constituted by its formative power in initiating, creating, governing, transforming, maintaining, or destroying what is vital in man's life. Thus, "charisma," in this meaning, no longer refers to an extraordinary property of an individual but to a recurrent process whereby the social order is being maintained through the attribution of charismatic qualities.

Attributing charismatic qualities to individuals at vital social positions is part of the process whereby societal power is being legitimized. Shils noted that all effective rulers possess charismatic qualities, i.e., have charismatic qualities attributed to them, unless it is known that they are *fainéants* who have abdicated their responsibilities out of moral weakness or incompetence. This legitimizing process cuts across all political regimes, including those conceived by Weber as "rational-legal," since, to Shils, authority, by its mere existence, calls forth the attribution of charisma.

Shils's conception of "charisma" as a sociological phenomenon related to the functional need for social order, rather than to the occasional intervention by divinely gifted individuals in that order, encourages a new perspective on the societal role of intellectuals. In this conception, intellectuals participate, by nature of their works and traditions, in "the charismatic construction of reality," that is, in the construction of a meaningful social and cultural environment. In this process of construction, elaborated by Eisenstadt as a process involving both symbolic and institutional activities, the intellectual finds himself operating side by side with other social elites. "Symbolic and institutional responses to the quest for the charismatic order," Eisenstadt wrote, "tend to become, in any society, centered in some specific institutional loci that are important from the point of view of the construction of tradition in general and that of the place of intellectuals in it in particular. Among these loci the most important are the so-called centers of society."[28] In such (charismatic) centers, the major spheres of social and cultural identity are crystallized, and the sources of authority and power established and legitimized. Or, as Clifford Geertz phrased it, charismatic centers are "concentrated loci of serious acts" consisting of the point or points in a society "where its leading ideas come together with its leading institutions to create an arena in which the events that most vitally affect its members' lives take place."[29]

This notion provides an important frame of reference for the study of knowledge-power relations, and particularly for the study of the sources of tension between them. An explanation of the sources of tension may now focus on the very competition between various elites engaged in the construction of cultural reality, which implies, as Eisenstadt explained, that each elite poses certain types of questions and answers about the social order, thereby possibly excluding the questions and answers posed by others. Scrutiny of these questions and answers becomes crucial to the explanation and prediction of critical instances of breakdown in charismatic centers and substitutes, to a great extent, for social-role explanations of tension. Such examination adds an invaluable dimension to the existing models of knowledge-power interaction. For instance, Raymond Aron describes the relationship between intellectuals and the ruling classes as "reciprocal."[30] The more remote intellectuals seem to be from the preoccupations of those who govern, the more Aron expects the latter to give vent to their innate hostility and contempt for the "word spinners." The more recalcitrant to modern ideas the privileged classes appear, the more incapable of ensuring the nation's power and economic progress, the more intellectuals incline to dissidence. Such a structural model does not explain why innate hostility and contempt should be expected in the first place or what gives rise to the intellectuals' preoccupation with power and progress, until the dimension of traditions and ideas is incorporated. At the same time, the exchange of ideas in the frame of reference offered here is considered within strict institutional boundaries so as to avoid a return to "the murky waters of traditional intellectual history,"[31] that is, to the tracing of the evolution of ideas with no reference to their social-structural context.

Ben-Gurion's confrontation with the intellectuals constituted a major breakdown in a charismatic center. An analysis of the exchange of ideas between them reveals the dynamics leading to this. Here was a charismatic center by all counts. David Apter, elaborating on the conditions giving rise to charisma in his 1970 study of leadership, suggested that charisma is likely to develop where there exists an attenuated normative situation which, although not challenging preexisting norms directly, allows new combinations, where behavioral situations show a more random basis for the selection of normative alternatives than is presupposed by an institutionalized acceptance of any one particular set, traditional or modern.[32] This was Israel during its nation-building era, beginning with its establishment in 1948 and ending with The Affair. The dominant perception as reflected in almost all memoirs of that period had been one of a new and open phase in the life of the Jewish people, a historic moment offering new hope under circumstances yet to be constructed.

Ben-Gurion's proclamation of the state in 1948 was conceived all over the world as reflecting on 4,000 years of Jewish history, and Ben-Gurion himself became the personification of the nation-building effort conducted in this normative spirit of a meeting between the present and past. His critical decisions were conceived not only as affecting the course of history but as shaping "the institutional and ideational framework of the state and the Jewish people."[33] In this charismatic role, Ben-Gurion compared with other great postwar leaders like Mao, Nehru, Nkruma, Churchill, Adenauer, and de Gaulle, who were all effective in the formation of institutional as well as symbolic reality in critical periods and situations. Ben-Gurion's charismatic role in 1948 has also often been compared to that of Lenin's in 1917.[34] This similarity is striking for the role assigned by both leaders to the intellectuals in the charismatic center.

Ben-Gurion made his views on the role of the intellectuals in the nation-building process explicit in his "call of spirit in Israel" published in the government yearbook of 1951.[35] In that year, Israel was facing severe problems in its efforts to house thousands of immigrants, an immense task even for countries with greater resources and experience. Ben-Gurion realized that the task required the recruitment of extraordinary material and human resources and, like many third world leaders, called for a revolution in all ways of life. "Our former habits of thought, our internal relations, the old manners and methods and measures, no longer apply. None is exempt, not civil servants, teachers, lawyers, physicians, army officers, engineers, men of science, literature and the arts; least of all those animated by the pioneer spirit, whether they be pioneers of labor or of settlement, or in the realm of spirit itself."[36] The person of letters played a crucial role in Ben-Gurion's vision of Israel as a modern technological society

and was therefore expected by Ben-Gurion to combine his trade
with a pioneer spirit to aid the national effort. The scientist,
endowed with "messianic vision," was expected to explore the
secrets of nature so as to help overcome the country's natural
limitations; the philosopher was to reveal and promote the hidden sources of human strength needed to accomplish the impossible; the biblical scholar was to inspire the mission by revealing
its ancient ties; and the writer was to write the great epic of the
times. And although these demands remained within the sphere
of political and ideological rhetoric, the call had to be taken
seriously.

The challenge to the intellectuals did not lie, however, in the
demand to aid the national effort. Israel's intellectuals were *active*
participants in the nation-building process, whether scientists
taking part in large-scale technological projects under Ben-
Gurion's leadership or persons of letters joining in the formation
of symbols of national revival.[37] Intellectuals in Israel, like other
groups, were either pioneers or refugees, and the conditions
giving rise to the "ivory tower" status of intellectuals in many
Western countries had not yet crystallized.[38] In addition, the
political elite, whose origins were mainly in Eastern Europe, was
itself an "intelligentsia," very conscious of the link between action
and knowledge, which many of them had to acquire as autodi-
dacts. And although many politicians were ideologically opposed
to "knowledge for its own sake," there existed no serious sociological or intellectual barriers for the scientist, the philosopher, the
scholar, or the writer to become respected members of the charismatic center where a new reality had enthusiastically been
formed.[39]

The challenge to the intellectuals came from Ben-Gurion's
genuine belief that the leading role of the intellectual in the
material and spiritual transformation of the Jewish people required not blind obedience to the state but rather "obeying only
conscience and the vision in his heart, speaking his glorious message to the people at freedom's call."[40] In other words, pure and
applied science, as well as all forms of intellectual activity, were
expected by Ben-Gurion to confirm and inspire a definite social
message. Ben-Gurion's endless preoccupation with knowledge,
his thorough scrutiny of intellectual work and long debates with
persons of letters reflected a persistent effort to reveal and establish that tie. This forced the intellectuals to consider the nature

of knowledge as it combines with power in the fulfilment of national goals. Fundamental questions on the essence and function of intellectual activity had to be asked within a unique framework—one of cooperation with a statesman who was truly interested. Ben-Gurion's persistent challenge to intellectuals, accompanied by an ever greater complexity in the knowledge-power networks as the technological society developed, gradually forced the intellectuals to form a unified opposition against their patron. This became apparent in January 1961 when the intellectuals—never before active as a group—almost unanimously supported the public statement calling for dissociation of the leader from the destiny of the state.

It is significant that this political expression of group consciousness by the intellectuals did not occur in the late 1950s, when debates over knowledge and power were at their height. In those years, the intellectuals, though sometimes in opposition to Ben-Gurion, willingly accepted their nominal role in a charismatic center dominated politically and culturally by him. As one of them later admitted, Israel's intellectuals in the fifties "were outdone in their own 'metier' by a politician who, for this reason, could not just be ordinary."[41] It was only during The Affair, when Ben-Gurion for the first time in his political career was perceived to play an ordinary, partisan, non-charismatic role, when for the first time he no longer represented the *raison d'être* of the state, that the disagreement over the nature of knowledge and its relation to power had become a salient issue. The fading of Ben-Gurion's charisma in the early 1960s, and the rise of a powerful but faceless party apparatus to the central area of Israeli politics, gave substance to the scientists' worries about the political misuse of science and technology, the philosophers' fears regarding the overnight creation of new ideological orientations, the scholars' concern about selective uses of symbols, and the writers' fatigue with the constant burden of supplying norms. By a dialectical process, the contrasts between knowledge and power that had evolved during Ben-Gurion's extraordinary reign and that remained latent as long as the charismatic center was dominated by Ben-Gurion, now became sources of deep political conflict.

The intellectuals' preoccupation with charisma and the effect that the waning of Ben-Gurion's charisma had on the change of their behavior from cooperation to conflict is illustrated in the secret meeting held on March 28, 1961, between Ben-Gurion and six professors who led the struggle against him.[42] This was an unusual event, as the Prime Minister and his opponents engaged for three and a half hours in a serious attempt to define the principles at stake. The protocol of the meeting confirms repeatedly that it was not the association between Ben-Gurion and the state which worried the intellectuals, as their public statement claimed, but rather the loss of this association. Nathan Rotenstreich, the political philosopher, was explicit: "What happened to us is that your image had been distorted, this is the pain we are suffering, that the greatest asset we had among us, a man in whom all lines have met—this has collapsed." Rotenstreich, who became chief spokesman of the Lavon camp in The Affair, lamented the fact that Ben-Gurion no longer represented the "good order" in the state, its *raison d'être*," calling it an "unprecedented national disaster." "Rather than staying above all dispute," he complained, "you became a party to a dispute." When Ben-Gurion claimed he did not consider himself a historical figure, Jacob Talmon, the historian of ideas, disagreed. "You are a historical figure whether you like it or not." "People who think in such terms are abnormal," retorted the Prime Minister.

This exchange is particularly instructive if considered in a perspective provided by Talmon just six weeks earlier. In a newspaper article published in February 1961, Talmon related modern man's quest for an authoritative father figure to his lost sense of direction in the technological world after the events at Hiroshima.[43] As his own exchange with the Prime Minister indicates, Talmon and his associates clearly joined in modern man's quest for the father figure. In his article, Talmon admitted that the battle against Ben-Gurion resembled a child's uprising against his omnipotent father. In fact, it had been an uprising against the omnipotent father who has, for once, failed his child. This was clearly reflected in Talmon's own words. There were few leaders in the course of history, he claimed, whose historical vision had so often been proved right by the circumstances as had Ben-Gurion's. But the gods, he wrote, became jealous, and the statesman had finally made his one fatal error. Talmon considered this error to be his behavior in The Affair, which, for the first time, could not be considered as a defense of principles but the behavior of a politician entangled in a mere power struggle.

The dynamics of Ben-Gurion's relationship with the intellectuals can thus be summarized as follows. In the 1950s, the intel-

lectuals had willingly played a nominal role in a charismatic
center dominated by the towering figure of Ben-Gurion. Their
"nominal role" consisted of taking part in the institutional and
symbolic tasks of the nation-building effort while accepting the
statesman's authority in defining the parameters of the socio-
cultural dialogue and action. Ben-Gurion's unusual concern with
knowledge in its relation to power and the challenges he posed
to the intellectuals, however, gradually exacerbated fundamental
tensions—on the level of ideas—between knowledge and power.
With the fading of Ben-Gurion's charisma in the early 1960s these
tensions became politically salient, and deep conflict evolved.
This conflict marked the end of an era in the life of the Israeli
society. The nation-building era, characterized by a visionary,
messianic ideology carried by a legendary leader, had given way
to an era of more open, pluralistic social relations steered by a
pragmatic, albeit very powerful, political machine. The underlying tensions between knowledge and power, turning into political
conflict during The Affair, may be seen to have constituted a
major dimension in this transformation of Israeli society. Ben-
Gurion's dialogue with the intellectuals, which is the subject of
this study, both reflected and nourished the emerging model of
the open society.

Ben-Gurion's dialogue with the intellectuals is here described
in an attempt to reveal the underlying tensions between the
statesman and the four intellectual groups: scientists, philosophers, biblical scholars, and writers. All four groups had cooper-
ated with Ben-Gurion on a practical or symbolic level, were
intellectually challenged within the framework of cooperation,
and responded politically during The Affair. Although they varied
in the degree of their initial cooperation or in the intensity of
their response, all these groups showed a striking similarity in
their correspondence to the dynamics described above. This
leads me to propose, as a general hypothesis, that while intellectuals may be willing to play a nominal role in charismatic centers,
there seem to exist underlying intellectual tensions between
knowledge and power which constitute a societal force of great
potential for processes of social change. The political saliency
(and hence societal impact) of these tensions varies with the degree to which intellectuals perceive their patrons as endowed
with charisma. This perception is an important intervening

variable in the political behavior of intellectuals and their societal role.

Confirmation of this hypothesis requires, of course, a more comparative effort than is offered here, but it is safe to expect that many of the tensions between knowledge and power revealed in this study exceed their temporal and spatial setting. This is not because Ben-Gurion's interaction with the intellectuals constitutes a representative "case study" but actually because it does not. The unique features of the interaction, especially the personalities involved and their traditions of discourse, had made it touch upon fundamental questions in the life of the modern state. In one sense, however, the dialogue described in this study does constitute a "case study." Ben-Gurion, the leader of a developing society in the 1950s, preceded his times in his great concern with the combined role of knowledge and power in the fulfilment of national goals. As this concern becomes central in today's technological society and the role of "philosopher-king," defined by the effective utilization of combined knowledge-power systems, gets institutionalized all over the world,[44] the challenge to the intellectual by the philosopher-king, and the former's response to him, becomes a question of great general interest.

In the following chapters, Ben-Gurion's relationship with each of the four groups of intellectuals is discussed. The first chapter analyzes Ben-Gurion's theory of knowledge, which stresses the primacy of intuition over observation as the source of scientific and moral truth, and the intellectual and political implications of this position. A great admirer of Plato and Spinoza, Ben-Gurion believed that man, as an organic part of existence, which is both material and spiritual, has the gift of recognizing its deepest nature. He believed in the power of the mind to penetrate and explore the secrets of nature and human conscience and was often quite explicit about the lessons to be learned from such an exploration.

Ben-Gurion's theory of knowledge was articulated in the 1950s before audiences fascinated by the power of the mind, yet from a wholly different perspective. Israel's scientists, like their peers elsewhere, believed in experimental science and the new horizons it opens to mankind. The challenge they faced, and their response, is the major theme of this chapter.

The next chapter focuses on Ben-Gurion's debates with philosophers, notably Martin Buber, over the role of "vision" in the life of the state. Ben-Gurion repeatedly argued that the state of Israel was the creation of a "messianic vision" and hence the continued survival of the state depended on a persisting messianic faith. Ben-Gurion understood the importance of the messianic concept to social integration and assigned an important role in this regard to science, literature, and the arts.

At the same time, Israel's intellectuals grew restless with Ben-Gurion's talk about messianism which, they suspected, reinforced his own legendary role as a secular messiah. They were particularly uneasy during Ben-Gurion's long debates with philosophers in 1957 when he seemed to have substituted political messianism for the national ideology. In The Affair, intellectual restlessness turned into political fear for the democratic character of the state. The idiosyncratic nature of vision and the close association between vision and power worried the intellectuals. Reflecting a well-known historical trend, they began to demand adherence to clear principles of government instead.

The third chapter analyzes Ben-Gurion's biblical studies and his debates with scholars over such questions as how many Jews participated in the exodus from Egypt, when the Hebrew people first inhabited the land of Canaan, or how many kings Joshua actually overpowered. Unbelievable as it may seem today, these debates preoccupied a whole nation during Ben-Gurion's years in office and even led from time to time to parliamentary crises.

In those years, biblical scholars seemed to like the unprecedented attention focused on their intellectual endeavors. It was during The Affair that the implications of the selective choice of symbols were given serious consideration. The very emphasis on the Bible, or rather parts of it, served a specific ideology which played down 2,000 years of Jewish history in the Diaspora; the national preoccupation with such biblical heroes as Moses, Joshua, and David could indeed encourage the identification of individuals with the destiny of the state. This chapter describes the adoption by biblical scholars of the role of watchdog over the manipulation of symbols.

The fourth chapter reviews Ben-Gurion's long and complex relationship with the writers. Ben-Gurion believed that the gifted writer, as a true representative of the free human spirit, would naturally produce the great epic of the times. When the writer turned to social critique instead, something was amiss. This chapter shows how conflict developed, starting from March 1949, when the nation's leading writers assembled in Ben-Gurion's office to discuss the intellectual's contribution to the cultural formation of the state, and ending with the great public scandal over Ben-Gurion's statement in 1961 that he read no fine literature.

In the last chapter, a common denominator is proposed for all twelve debates described in this study. Ben-Gurion's model of leadership (the model of "philosopher-king") is elaborated, and his practices of knowledge acquisition and utilization are described. It is argued that the intellectuals by nature of their preoccupation with knowledge played a restraining role over the extension of knowledge implied by this leadership type. Their insistence upon the constraints of knowledge, it seems to me, provided a new set of social guidelines for Israeli society as it entered a second stage in its development.

The Scientists
Intuition vs. Observation

the dominant model of the relationship between science and government in scholarly literature has been one of exchange: "In Goethe's tragedy Faust sells his soul to the devil as the price of eternity; in technostructure the scientist yields to the will of power in order to be able to ply his trade."[1] This "exchange model" kept the state of theory in the field of science and government where political theory was at the time Goethe wrote *Faust*. Science and government were conceived as having independent and distinct goals. It was believed that at some Hobbesian moment (around World War II) the need for mutual dependence had been perceived and the trade-off agreed upon to last forever. In the exchange model, the scientist's goal is the advancement of knowledge and the state's goals are power, prestige, economic growth, etc. Since knowledge requires state funding, and the fulfilment of the state's goals requires scientific research, science and power ally in what resembles a business merger. Science tenders its services to power to become a partner in its decisions; power makes use of science and becomes a partner in its destiny.[2]

The exchange model, however, ignores three major characteristics of "technostructure" (the system of government by knowledge and power in the modern technological state): (1) the genuine interest science and power have in each other, (2) the

mutual learning process by which their goals are being determined, and (3) the underlying philosophical tension between
them. The exchange model recognizes the existence of tension
but reduces it to a state of alienation over a necessary yet immoral
trade-off between science and government. Salomon, for instance, in his study of *Science and Politics* expected scientific
research to be inevitably alienated by the mere fact that modern
science has ceased to be pure theory. The alienation of the scientist, Salomon wrote, "retains its own special significance and
form in the light of the idea of science to which it refers, that is
to say, the memory of a 'disinterested' science which does not
directly affect social practice and is not directly affected by it."[3]

The popularity of the notion of exchange stems from the fact
that most scholars derived their insights into the relationship
between science and government from the experience of developed societies, especially in the period shortly after World War
II. This is indeed when science and government became conscious of their structural dependence and where the trade-off was
conceived in terms of "paradise lost."[4] It was only natural that
scholars focusing on this experience would try to extrapolate from
it the general character and trend of the relationship between
science and government. Ben-Gurion's relationship with science
provides a different perspective. It reveals a relationship between science and government that can only partly be accounted
for by the exchange model yet seems to be more in accord with
the conditions of the emerging technological state. This relationship was characterized by the statesman's genuine concern with
science and its role in national development. This interest,
rooted in deep faith, posed a challenge to science that went far
beyond the need to make a choice over a trade-off. The problem
was how to preserve basic scientific notions *given* that collaboration; and, as the scientists began to tackle it, important conflicts
of principle between science and government had emerged.
These conflicts were not the outgrowth of societal or political
abuse of science but a reflection of the philosophical disagreement over the nature of science and its relation to power. Such
disagreement surfaces only in those instances—ignored by the
exchange model—in which science and power take each other
seriously and are forced to scrutinize their own goals and assumptions as a result of their interaction.

This chapter explores Ben-Gurion's relationship with the scientists by considering the ideas underlying it. The relationship described is consistent with the frame of reference elaborated earlier. Israel's scientists in the 1950s willingly played a secondary role in the "charismatic center" dominated by Ben-Gurion in both its practical and symbolic domains. Their association gave rise to impressive scientific-technological ventures, as well as to a "religion of science" which eventually posed a serious challenge to science. This challenge became politically salient only as Ben-Gurion's charisma began to fade, and he was replaced in the charismatic center by the collective leadership of his own party's political machine. In late 1961, following The Affair, new elections were held in Israel; and the Labor party, torn by the year's events, needed all the help it could get. By this time, the "war of inheritance" was practically over, but the party leadership emerging from The Affair—Eshkol, Sapir, and Golda Meir—was skilled enough in the games of politics to have Ben-Gurion head the party list in spite of his fall from power. (He ultimately resigned in 1963.) The party's campaign managers were equally skilled in exploiting Ben-Gurion's symbolic appeal, especially his association with advanced science and technology, as an asset in the election campaign. This reached its climax with the launching of a guided missile during the campaign, at which time the community of science began to understand the dangers involved in the strong association between science and the charismatic leader and the myth surrounding this association.

This event took place on July 5, 1961, when Jerusalem radio dramatically announced the successful launching of Israel's first self-made missile. For a moment, the country, preoccupied with The Affair and in the midst of a hard election campaign, rejoiced. People everywhere celebrated the scientific-technological achievement whose implications to national security were widely stressed. Prime Minister Ben-Gurion attributed it to the "Jewish genius,"[5] and opposition leader Menachem Begin offered a toast in honor of the scientists representing the "creative, inventive mind of the Hebrew people." But Begin, an experienced politician, also warned that it would be rash and shortsighted to attribute the national scientific achievement to the political party in power.[6]

Early next morning, Begin's worst fears came true. The morning papers carried a picture of the missile with the Prime Minister at its side, dressed in khaki uniform and surrounded by the leaders of the defense establishment. *Davar,* the newspaper voice of the ruling Mapai party, whose military correspondent had exclusive access to the launching site, stressed Ben-Gurion's ties to the project and hinted that leaders of other parties could hardly be attributed a similar achievement.[7] In the coming weeks, Mapai's campaign managers further capitalized on the event. Newspaper ads described the Prime Minister as "undefeatable," and his role in the missiles program was compared to his role as founder of the state.[8] This was in keeping with public sentiment. Letters arriving at the Prime Minister's office congratulated him for "his" project;[9] some writers had to be reminded that the launching of a missile is a complex technological project rather than a one-man operation.[10] Ben-Gurion's public image as closely associated with national science and technology became a political asset for a party elite gaining power but still lacking nation-wide legitimacy. It also became a source of political fury. Political leaders denounced the exploitation of science for partisan purposes,[11] and intellectuals charged that attributing national science to one individual indicates dictatorial tendencies.[12] However, Ben-Gurion's association with science and technology, which precipitated political unrest in 1961, had originated much earlier, with deep intellectual roots far beyond the manipulative power of politicians.[13]

Ben-Gurion's Concern with Science

born in 1886 in the small town of Plonsk in Russian-dominated Poland, David Ben-Gurion had little formal education. His primary education was in the traditional Jewish manner, learning the Bible, the Talmud, and books of prayer in small rabbinical schools. Tzarist rules restricting the number of Jewish students in Eastern Europe and the lack of financial means to study in Western Europe prevented the young man, intending to sail to Palestine as an engineer, from gaining high school or vocational education, and, like many incumbents of his generation, he was self-taught. In 1906, Ben-Gurion came to Palestine as a pioneer and in 1911 went to Constantinople to study law, but after the outbreak of World War I, he was expelled from the Ottoman Empire for his involvement in Zionist agitation and never pursued formal studies.

Ben-Gurion's biographers tend to divide his public life after his return to Palestine in 1918 into three phases: some fifteen years as leader of Histadrut, the federation of labor, fifteen years as head of the Jewish Agency, and fifteen years as Israel's first Prime Minister. In one biographical sketch it was shown how Ben-Gurion's reading and writing accompanied him in all these functions and formed the background and perspective for every period of his life. Ben-Gurion had a phenomenal memory and far-ranging interests. He spoke a dozen languages, read hundreds of books, and wrote several himself; these skills were always related to his public life. In his Histadrut period he read a great deal of socialist and revolutionary literature as well as books about mass psychology. In his Jewish Agency period he was greatly concerned with the history of the Jewish people and the prerequisites of a Jewish state, as well as with the philosophical foundations of any state. In the third period, as Prime Minister of Israel, he was deeply involved with science.[14]

Ben-Gurion's attitude toward science was characterized by great interest and affection, accompanied by deep regret for his own lack of scientific education. This was expressed in a sentence he wrote shortly before his death: "I am not skilled in science, and I think I am not skilled in anything, but I love science."[15] In spite of his fame and broad knowledge acquired as an autodidact, Ben-Gurion was often insecure about addressing scientific congresses. Before a speech at the Weizmann Institute, he had to be assured by scientists that "the speech is very nice and nothing has to be changed."[16] Ben-Gurion often expressed regret that he did not comprehend complex mathematical formulas in scientific reports,[17] and he hesitated to accept honorary titles requiring commitments he felt he could not fulfil "either for lack of time, or for lack of education."[18] When his daughter Renana became a microbiologist, Ben-Gurion was the proud father: "I received your article," he wrote his daughter, "and to my regret (or rather to my shame), I could not understand a word. When Mom asked to see the article, I told her I don't understand it and neither would she—but I gave it to her and she did not understand a thing. This is no indication whatsoever of its quality."[19] Having received an invitation to participate in an international conference of experts and world leaders on "global impacts of applied microbiology," he wrote to his daughter: "I don't know what contribution I can make. I know nothing about microbiology, I am not a man of science, and I don't know how to respond to this kind invitation. Waiting for advice. Dad."[20]

Ben-Gurion always expressed his interest in science, and the options it opens to mankind, with great affection. He was clearly a romantic when confronted by great scientific or technological achievements. In 1933, after one of his first flights by airplane, he wrote to his wife:

◆ ◆ ◆

I am certain the day will come when means of communication are invented that people will not have to travel at all. You will sit in a room, push a button, see a person located on the other side of the globe, and talk to him as if the two of you are seated in the same room. And maybe not on the other side of the globe but on Mars as well. This could happen long before we expect it, if no new world war breaks out in the meantime.[21]

◆ ◆ ◆

Thirty years later, Prime Minister Ben-Gurion was still making similar prophecies, although these would now often cause public scandals. One incident occurred when *Look* magazine, preparing its 1962 New Year's edition, asked Ben-Gurion for his image of the world half a century hence. Noting that "things that are desirable are not, it seems to me, unattainable," Ben-Gurion let his imagination run wild.

◆ ◆ ◆

The Cold War will be a thing of the past. Internal pressure of the constantly growing intelligentsia in Russia for more freedom and the pressure of the masses for raising their living standards may lead to a gradual democratization of the Soviet Union. On the other hand, the increasing influence of the workers and farmers, and the rising political importance of men of science, may transform the United States into a welfare state with a planned economy. Western and Eastern Europe will become a federation of autonomous states having a Socialist and democratic regime. With the exception of the USSR as a federated Eurasian state, all other continents will become united in a world alliance, at whose disposal will be an international police force. All armies will be abolished, and there will be no more wars. In Jerusalem, the

*United Nations (a truly United Nations) will build a Shrine of
Prophets to serve the federated union of all continents; this will
be the seat of the Supreme Court of Mankind, to settle all controversies among the federated continents, as prophesied by Isaiah.
Higher education will be the right of every person in the world.
A pill to prevent pregnancy will slow down the explosive natural
increase in China and India. And by 1987, the average life-span
of man will reach 100 years.*[22]

◆ ◆ ◆

In January 1962, an outraged Israeli public read these statements by its Prime Minister in *Look* magazine. Although
Ben-Gurion's "futurism" had obvious political functions, such as
stressing of the centrality of Jerusalem in the future world order,
his statements reflected a genuine belief in the potential of science. Ben-Gurion was truly fascinated by the power science and
technology granted the human race to overcome the constraints
of nature and to control its own destiny.[23] He was particularly
overwhelmed by the power of the atom.

◆ ◆ ◆

*It is now clear that the basic particle which the Greeks called the
atom is no longer the indivisible ultimate unit, but a complex
world, composed of a number of particles and positive and negative charges, temporary and permanent, which are on the borderline between matter and energy, and perhaps even on the
border of nothingness—if such a thing as "nothingness" exists—
and contains powerful latent forces, which can supply humanity
with limitless sources of creative energy, but also contain[s] the
potentiality of the destruction of mankind.*[24]

◆ ◆ ◆

While Ben-Gurion realized the destructive potential of science, he associated science mainly with positive values and was
equally fascinated by science and the scientist:

◆ ◆ ◆

*As a layman I do not know what is more marvellous; the wonder-
ful secrets of nature that conceal mighty forces, capable of building complex worlds, in these infinitesimal entities which the eye
of man cannot see and his imagination cannot even imagine,*

except in mathematical symbols whose meaning is incomprehensible, at least to people like myself—or the amazing powers latent in that divine organ called the human brain which—in spite of the shortcomings and the limitations of the human senses, penetrates to the infinite distances of the macrocosm, interspersed with billions of clusters of suns, whose tremendous size and enormous numbers our imagination cannot even grasp, and at the same time pierces the infinite recesses of the microcosm, which reach the very limits of nothingness both in time and space.[25]

◆ ◆ ◆

Ben-Gurion was only half joking when he questioned "whether the time has not come for the fulfillment of the aspirations of the greatest of Greek philosophers: that government should be taken out of the hands of politicians and handed over to the wise men or philosophers, who uncover the secrets of nature."[26] He believed in the applicability of norms involved in the conduct of inquiry to political action. Research, he believed, always brings about progress and achieves results, while the results of politics are often futile. "I am certain you will not follow the way of the vile politicians," he told a symposium on cancer research, "who, the more they discuss the reduction of armaments, the more armament is on the increase throughout the world."[27] Elsewhere he proposed "to establish harmonious cooperation between the students of nature and the rulers of nations, and to induce the statesmen to adopt the two distinctive characteristics of scientific research: truth and universality."[28]

He often stressed the nonpartisan nature of science. To him, the scientist was capable of really listening to the thoughts of another person by virtue of the fact that he was preoccupied with the search for truth.[29] In a symposium on life sciences he contended that biology provided the best guide for human relations since, as he interpreted it, "every cell of the organism is independent, yet always remains in the service of its associates."[30]

The political message Ben-Gurion derived from the scientific revolution was similar to that derived by leaders of other developing nations. A clue to his way of thinking (and theirs) lies in an address to scientists from third world countries. He discussed two revolutions occurring in the world at that time, a political revolution and a scientific one. The first consisted of the ending of the rule of one nation over another, the second consisted of "the marvellous achievements of science, the discovery of the secrets of the atom and the conquest of the elements of nature, for the sake of man's economic prosperity and spiritual advancement." Ben-Gurion suggested that if these two revolutions, which seem to occur independently, were combined, "the entire character of the human race can be transformed." He claimed that independence could be preserved only if third world leaders were willing to adopt modern science and technology. He observed with satisfaction that "more and more, the accomplishments of science are becoming the estate of all peoples in all parts of the world. This is perhaps the most universal spiritual triumph of our era, and no second asset is so shared by all the peoples in our time as is science."[31]

Ben-Gurion considered science a leading factor in the development of Israel, and he put his faith in pure and applied knowledge which he expected would remove the material and sociological obstacles to nation-building: "Our work in Israel is without parallel for difficulty, for internal and external hindrances. Our constructive work will fail unless we know to mobilize all the achievements of science to the aid of our economy, our education and our security."[32] The greater the obstacles, the more Ben-Gurion relied on the power of scientific and technological breakthroughs to overcome them.

In 1944, when he led a bitter struggle for independence and after a holocaust in which a third of the Jewish nation had been liquidated, Ben-Gurion declared that Zionism and science had a common source—the faith of the individual in his capability to liberate himself from the blind forces ruling him.[33] He often put his faith in Jewish scientists who would aid the Jewish state in those years. During the War of Independence, in one of its harshest moments, Ben-Gurion issued an order to try and find among the survivors of the holocaust in Eastern Europe scientists who could help the war effort. He was looking for scientists capable of "either increasing the capacity to kill many people, or on the contrary, curing people; both tasks are necessary."[34]

Ben-Gurion also played an important role in the formation of scientific institutions and the establishment of Israel's technological enterprises such as the nuclear research centers or the agency for the development of armaments.[35] He had a personal stake in questions of scientific and technological development and was frequently asked to intervene in conflicts over these matters.[36] This was all part of a conviction that Israel's fate lay in a long-range investment in science and technology. During his long walks in the desert in the 1950s, Ben-Gurion was said to be preoccupied with questions such as how the sun above his head and the rocks under his feet could be utilized as sources of energy. He would then assemble chemists, nuclear physicists and others to face challenges such as how uranium could be produced from stone. The Old Man, Israelis would relate, strikes the rock, and water comes out of it.[37]

Ben-Gurion's Philosophy of Science

                      Although Ben-Gurion was never a philosopher, it is possible to reconstruct a rather coherent set of principles from his fragmentary statements on science. One principle stands out: a strong belief in intuition—the unexplainable human gift for uncovering the secrets of nature. "To this day," Ben-Gurion said, "no one has unravelled the riddle of the genius of those divinely blessed personalities, who by their mighty intellect have shed light on the mysteries of nature or enriched the human treasury with majestic creations of art and literature; nor to this day has the secret been explained of the special greatness of those few exceptional peoples [who] left their imprint on human culture."[38]

As a socialist leader, Ben-Gurion often referred to the value of equality, but he admired the few persons in history who proved to possess extraordinary mental gifts:

♦ ♦ ♦

Equality between men, which lies at the foundation of our political and social consciousness, stands in no contradiction to our wonderment at the greatness of Descartes, Newton, da Vinci, Rembrandt, Beethoven and Einstein. Similarly, recognition of the equality of peoples cannot lessen our admiration for those few exceptional peoples which have played a uniquely fructifying role in the annals of humanity.[39]

♦ ♦ ♦

Attributing intuition to select collectivities, as well as to individuals, constituted no philosophical problem to Ben-Gurion, since his belief in intuition stemmed from an all-embracing monistic outlook.[40] The following paragraph of a speech given at Brandeis University is particularly illuminating in this regard.

♦ ♦ ♦

We do not accept the discredited theory that the world is composed of blind and crude matter, just as we do not accept the fallacious opinion that everything we see, feel and hear is only the disembodied creation of the imagination and spirit. All the great men of Israel, in days gone by and in our own times, whether through religious intuition or penetrating scientific comprehension, have always recognized the all-embracing unity of existence, the oneness of matter and mind. Man is part of a marvel of existence, single but with many manifestations, both material and spiritual, and man, as an organic part of this complex existence, which is both material and spiritual, both natural and divine, has the gift of seeing and observing, of understanding and recognizing the nature of the world.[41]

♦ ♦ ♦

These statements reveal a crude monism: the belief in the ability of the human mind stems from its identification with the universe it explores. This approach should be understood in its political context; this was the monism of a leader convincing his people and himself that there was a way to overcome natural hardships. In his address to the opening session of Israel's Academy of Sciences, he was explicit:

♦ ♦ ♦

History has been very hard on us. We were always a small nation, a small country; the people of Israel have almost never had an era of material and political greatness, nor can one be expected. However, we did possess spiritual gifts, although to a limited extent. Jews in ancient times did not pursue science and systematic thinking, but those capable of composing a book like the bible, can also excel today—and we know it—in the area of scientific thinking.[42]

♦ ♦ ♦

Ben-Gurion's monism allowed him to assume that spiritual gifts could make a difference in the material world. In fact, he rejected the duality between matter and spirit and believed in "the supremacy of the spirit that pervades matter and rules it."[43] This insistence upon the lack of duality between matter and spirit bore a promise for the transformation of material conditions, if the spiritual ones were kept. Ben-Gurion's "cosmology" could thus be described as normative and active. It was a theory of nature that implied a social and moral outlook, one which serves as a guide for human action. No wonder Ben-Gurion became a devoted disciple of Spinoza—Spinoza's philosophy, as he interpreted it, provided hope.[44] Ben-Gurion stressed its social and moral lessons, insisting that Spinoza never demanded blind adherence to the forces of nature but rather believed in the control of the human soul over them. Ben-Gurion shared Spinoza's belief in the power of reason to overcome external constraints and to achieve supreme happiness. To Spinoza, happiness consisted of the knowledge of oneself, the world, and God, three elements that were one. Ben-Gurion concurred, stressing that although the road to happiness is long and hard, it can be found.[45] He often reminded his various audiences that Spinoza concluded the *Ethics* by the words: "But all noble things are as difficult as they are rare." It may be mentioned that in 1953 Ben-Gurion called for the vindication of Spinoza, who had been boycotted by the rabbis of Amsterdam 297 years before.

The stress upon intuition as a source of knowledge was not by itself inconsistent with prevailing notions.[46] Ben-Gurion was proud to tell of his meeting with Einstein, in which the great scientist confirmed that intuition played a primary role in his scientific thinking. In an article in honor of Einstein's 75th birthday, Ben-Gurion could rely on distinguished sources to further his argument that "the wonderful and unique quality of Einstein's revolutionary findings has been their being derived not from laboratory experiments, but from the creative ability of the pure mind."[47] Ben-Gurion's terminology was not alien to contemporary scientists. He often claimed, for instance, that science stands beyond good and evil: "By its power we can explain the phenomena of Nature—and man is part of Nature, but science is incapable of telling man what path he should choose in life. . . . The tree of knowledge of good and evil does not blossom on the soil of science. Science strives to lay bare the secrets of Nature, but not to counsel man what he shall do."[48]

Yet, Ben-Gurion also felt that there was an organic link between science and ethics. Values, to him, were part of the same
"cosmos" to be explored by intuition.

◆ ◆ ◆

*I know [he admitted] that no laboratory, microscope or telescope
can reveal the wonderful material called "mercy." But mercy resides in the spirit of man, and Jewish thought always taught us
that the spirit of man, while not bound to be observed, measured
or scaled, is no less real and mighty than the matter we can sense.
. . . And it is significant that the Prophets of Israel have considered that moral values such as justice, mercy and truth are not
only human imperatives, but an integral part of the cosmos,
although the eye and other senses cannot perceive it.* [49]

◆ ◆ ◆

The role of science, Ben-Gurion claimed, is the revelation of
truth, but "truth" to him consisted of two meanings: setting an
objective standard for ideas and a moral standard for actions.
Science thus became meaningless unless scientific research was
combined with "the imperatives of the human conscience." [50]
Both intelligence and conscience exist, he declared, and only
through their integration will man derive the great and glorious
blessings that are hidden in each. The scientist "will not be dis-
charging the mission faithfully or be worthy of his task unless,
while yet augmenting the capacity of science, and enlarging the
bounds of pure knowledge, he makes every effort to foster the
moral values on which the relations between men and between
peoples must rest." [51] And he added, "The tree of knowledge of
good and evil must be planted in the soul of every man, and first
of all in the soul of men of science, so that their creative activity
may be a blessing to mankind." [52]

The content of these moral values was clear to Ben-Gurion:
"Only in faithfulness to the purposes of prophetic ethics is it
possible to direct the tremendous and fructifying power of science so that it may be a blessing to the people and humanity." [53]
And since prophetic ethics, to him, were manifested in specific
commitments, he demanded the scientist take upon himself a
practical commitment: "Morality itself . . . can be beneficial on
one condition alone; not if it is preached to others, not if it is
elegantly expounded, but if it is observed not just in theory but

in practice also, if it is attended by pioneering that fulfils."[54]
Israel's first President Chaim Weizmann—a Zionist leader and
scientist—served as a model: "I have always suspected, and still
do, that Dr. Weizmann's scientific work is not entirely disengaged
from his Zionist goals and activity. I trust the Zionist motive of
Dr. Weizmann did not discredit and did not harm the supreme
quality of his scientific work, and I know it was, and will be, a
great blessing to the Zionist endeavor."[55]

In Ben-Gurion's thinking, the scientist became a high priest
committed to the moral elevation of the human spirit, as well as
to more specific societal tasks. This was apparent in Ben-Gurion's
correspondence with Joseph Schaechter, an educator disap-
pointed by science and calling for a return "from science to
faith."[56] Ben-Gurion's response, expressed in a series of letters to
Schaechter, reveals what amounts to a "religion of science." He
wrote:

◆ ◆ ◆

Science cannot be discredited, abandoned or substituted by any-
thing else. Man cannot live without science, because science is
light, ever-increasing light, although as it lightens the darkness
of nature, man is confronted with even greater new secrets, but
science is ever-advancing, that is, man is advancing as a result
of science. . . . He who reveals a contradiction between science
and faith has to abandon faith.[57]

◆ ◆ ◆

The correspondence between Ben-Gurion and Schaechter reveals an interesting attempt by the statesman to redefine values
in light of the scientific revolution:

◆ ◆ ◆

I fail to understand your preaching of faith. Faith in what and
in whom? Certainly the world is not the creation of random,
blind forces (although I couldn't prove it), and there exists order
and regularity ("cosmos") in the world; perhaps even purpose
and direction. But all that is part of the intellectual wondering
of man, who is aware of his scant knowledge and its limited
scope.[58]

◆ ◆ ◆

Obviously, Ben-Gurion reduced faith to merely one aspect of the intellectual wondering of man, but science became no less than a supreme human activity to be cherished and honored by adults and youth. Even the style of his letters to Schaechter resembles that of the Holy Scriptures. He talked about science as a godly skill and considered it the gift that distinguishes man from beast. Realizing that science can have negative implications for the human race, he nevertheless called it a means by which human beings control, at least partially, the world around them.[59] Ben-Gurion not only substituted science for traditional faith, he turned it into a religion itself whose believers, like those of every religion, both carry a mission and are obliged by it. Here lay Ben-Gurion's challenge to the scientists.

Ben-Gurion's Challenge to the Scientists

The religion of science expounded by Ben-Gurion could not be ignored by the scientists at this time, nor could his philosophy of science be discarded. In order to realize the great challenge that Ben-Gurion's views posed to the scientists, one must consider the interaction between them in temporal perspective. This perspective was provided in Don K. Price's classic, *The Scientific Estate*, published in 1965.[60] Price noted the emerging relationship between science and government, arguing that scientists and administrators involved in the new relationship of politics and science must develop at least a tacit theory to guide them in dealing with it. Science, he wrote, would have to make some contribution to such a new theory about its proper relations to politics out of its own methods and its own approach. He expressed doubt, however, as to whether science could provide the intellectual basis for a new theory of politics unless scientists generally believed that their methods contained some promise of dealing comprehensively with major political issues (as the materialist dialectic proposed to deal with problems of history and politics as well as with problems of physics). Most American scientists, Price observed, seemed to think that this idea was either irrelevant to their interests or merely silly, in contrast to scientists in the nineteenth century to whom science was a completely adequate means of understanding reality.

According to Price, physicists began to lose that confidence of the nineteenth century as science took them beyond the solid and predictable matter that seemed to correspond to the ordinary man's notion of what was real. As the physicist "got inside" the atom, he entered a universe to which some of the older generation never became reconciled; to this generation of scientists, it seemed to contain phenomena that were for the first time perhaps unknowable and unmeasurable. Even in principle certain parts of inanimate matter seemed to disregard the classical laws of cause and effect. But the younger generation of physicists apparently became accustomed to this "new science" quite promptly. They did not even expect to think in terms of the mechanical models or the aesthetic analogies that had been the basis of their elders' scientific faith. If they could identify the things they could observe, and measure and predict their relationships, they were not interested in the kind of "reality" that was beyond their observation; and they were not sure that it made sense to assume that such a reality exists. Price admitted that science had achieved its great power by insisting on defining for itself the problems it proposed to solve and by refusing to take on problems merely because some outside authority considered them important. He added, however, that this power, and the precision of thought on which it depended, was purchased by a refusal to deal with many aspects of such problems.

Ben-Gurion did not allow Israel's scientists in the 1950s to ignore the metaphysical, normative, and political implications of their trade. Like Socrates, who annoyed the Sophists by constantly raising uncomfortable, seemingly irrelevant questions, the Prime Minister was relentless. He insisted that "even the man of science cannot help breaking out from time to time from his purely scientific research and stand face to face, in awe and wonder, with the transcendent problems of man and the universe."[61] Ben-Gurion often raised such transcendent problems when he addressed scientific conferences. Sometimes these observations were quite far-fetched, as when he told a conference on biological standardization that "as a layman I feel that I have no right to intervene in your deliberations, but even an ordinary mortal is aware that he is the outcome of marvellous biological forces."[62] But along with being far-fetched, they were always stimulating: "We cannot help asking whether it is indeed only blind, haphazard, mechanical forces that have produced this wonderful, if sometimes mischievous* creature called man, or whether there is design, purpose, intention—as part of the design, purpose and intention that pervade the entire cosmos, which, as its name implies, is a world governed by order, law and regularity—and perhaps by a supreme intelligence beyond the grasp of human reason."[63]

A comparison of Ben-Gurion, the modern statesman, to Socrates, the ancient skeptic, may be rash and superficial; but the analogy comes to mind in view of such events as the Prime Minister's official visit to the Weizmann Institute, where he kept a group of dignitaries impatiently waiting behind him while he discussed at length the limitations of cybernetics with scientists showing him a new computer. More importantly, he could not be ignored, since, like Socrates, he talked the language of contemporary intellectuals. Ben-Gurion fully understood that the universe studied by modern physics was different from that of classical physics. He realized the scientists were involved in a gigantic adventure and that quantum theory, molecular biology, etc., implied far-reaching changes in modern man's outlook. He persistently forced scientists to define these changes and extend their scientific notions to spheres they preferred to ignore. Since he himself had clear notions of the societal implications of modern science, and the subsequent political commitments demanded of scientists, the latter were forced to demonstrate how their scientific notions were consistent with *other* implications. The common defense for scientists—accusing the layman of superficiality or defining the questions as unscientific and hence beyond their concern—would not work. Although Ben-Gurion extended scientific notions beyond the acceptable limits of science, he was well-informed, and his intellectual curiosity was widely admired. Furthermore, while the debates Ben-Gurion engaged in were metaphysical, his adversaries in these debates were usually prominent scientists who worked closely with him, on the huge scientific and technological projects which Israel undertook under his leadership.

Ben-Gurion's main adversaries in debates over the nature of science and its relation to power—Aharon Katzir, the biologist,

---

*The words "if sometimes mischievous" were added by Ben-Gurion at a later date.

and Amos Deshalit, the physicist, were "insiders." Price defined
insiders as "eminent scientists who hold important positions in
the institutional structure by which government and science are
closely connected," and he expected them to accept the subordi-
nation of science to the value systems established by the nation's
tradition and interpreted by the authority of the government.[64]
But on the level of discussion described here, this became impossible. Prominent scientists were willing to extend the scope
of their concerns and often admitted they had to reconsider previously held notions as a result of their interaction with Ben-
Gurion.[65] Yet, the more precisely the issues were defined, the
more the scientists came to realize the inherent tensions between
science and government. Three intellectual conflicts then arose:
one over science and truth, one over science and values, and one
over science and societal self-control.

Science and Truth

the belief by Ben-Gurion in in-
tuition and its ability to reveal the "true" nature of the universe
was met with strong resistance by the scientific community. After
a series of discussions with the Prime Minister, Amos Deshalit, a
nuclear physicist at the Weizmann Institute and at one time a
member of Israel's Atomic Energy Commission, decided to write
an elaborate article in which he asserted the role of observation
in the study of modern physics, and the implications of this as-
sertion to the notion of truth.[66] While he did not ignore the role
of intuition in science, Deshalit stressed its major pitfalls: the
reliance on limited experience and the danger of wishful thinking. He wrote that most people, including scientists, tend to
ascribe to their experience the virtues of an "absolute truth," no
matter how superficial and fragmentary this experience may be.

♦ ♦ ♦

*The ideas resulting from such superficial experience are some-
times so deeply rooted in us, that we do not even give ourselves
any account of their existence and they form, so to speak, the
axiomatic background of our thinking. When the analysis of new
experimental evidence finally forces on us a reexamination of
such ideas, it is usually met with violent internal resistance.*

♦ ♦ ♦

Deshalit noted in particular man's resistance to new concepts that challenged his supreme role in the universe. The pre-Copernican concept of the universe was both egocentric and compatible with available information at the time. Thus, even after the planet was observed to be an unimportant corner of a medium-sized galaxy, man still maintained, though without being fully aware of it, a central position in his picture of the universe.

"Without questioning it," wrote Deshalit, "we asserted that the Universe at large could be described in the terminology, concepts and notions which *we* had acquired in our very limited daily experience. We extended the use of the intuitive concepts of 'length' and 'time intervals' also for the description of phenomena whose magnitude is very different from that of ordinary phenomena. There was no justification in doing so except for the natural tendency of taking so seriously the things we believe we 'know.'"

According to Deshalit, man was willing to abandon his perception of having a central position in the universe as a result of experimental evidence. For example, the concept of "simultaneity" forms one of the foundations of our daily thinking, and there is nothing in our daily experience that shatters our intuitive feeling of what "simultaneous" means. However, as was shown by Einstein, two events considered "simultaneous" by one observer will generally appear to be *consecutive* events to another if the second observer moves fast enough in relation to the first event. Deshalit admitted that although length, mass, energy, and other notions had the same fate as the notion of simultaneity, there was an attempt to continue describing the phenomena in terms of concepts properly modified, derived from daily experience. However, with the development of quantum mechanics, it became clear that our world of concepts, even if stretched and modified, was inadequate to describe all natural phenomena. Quantum theory, which describes atomic phenomena, necessitates the introduction of completely new concepts which cannot be obtained by a gradual change of existing ones.

Deshalit went on to explain the experimental origin of these new concepts, and the failure of intuition as such to generate them.

◆ ◆ ◆

We can perform experiments which, if described in terms of conventional concepts, must be interpreted by saying that a single

*electron passes through two distinct and widely separated holes
at one and the same time. Other experiments indicate, again if
we try to interpret them using conventional concepts, that light
behaves as a wave propagating in space and at the same time
produces effects which can only be attributed to bullet-like particles. From our daily experience we do not possess any picture
of what an "electron passing simultaneously through two holes"
may mean; neither is any vague mystical extrapolation of our
experience going to give us any idea of how this "simultaneous
passing through two holes" is going to affect the subsequent behavior of the electron. We are therefore forced to introduce completely new concepts. Their choice and properties are dictated
by experimental findings. Their usefulness and "truthfulness" are
determined by the extent to which they offer a unified description
of seemingly unrelated phenomena.*

♦ ♦ ♦

Ben-Gurion fully realized the meaning of Deshalit's critique.
Not only did the physicist consider intuition secondary to experimentation, he challenged Ben-Gurion's belief in intuition as
man's way of immediately grasping natural phenomena. Such
immediate grasp was limited, Deshalit claimed, by one's limited
environment and was an insufficient base for the study of nature.
Knowledge, for Deshalit, was no longer a means for revealing
the truth but rather a means for organizing ever-changing truths.
Ben-Gurion tried to hold on to his belief in man's capacity to
reveal the secrets of nature in a Spinozian sense. He declared he
preferred Einstein's "conservatism," that is, his use of conventional terms such as causality, even after the acceptance of quantum theory. Ben-Gurion often asserted that modern physics had
not "dismissed" matter but merely revealed the identity between
matter and energy. And while the duality between matter and
spirit had been abolished, the universe revealed by the physicist
was still dominated by the laws of nature.[67]

Now it was Deshalit who was relentless. He considered what
Ben-Gurion called the "laws of nature" as only conceptual means
by which predictions are made. In a letter to Ben-Gurion he
demonstrated how the laws of nature may be described as conceptual solutions to problems entailed by man's thinking about
the universe, rather than as rules derived from the "objective"
behavior of that universe.

♦ ♦ ♦

We define for ourselves a set of absolute truths, that is, statements based on a system of definitions and axioms, like "the black cat is black." We then try to attribute to every concept in the abstract system we constructed a certain property from the empirical world, and find, to our surprise, that our abstract system is usually too large. We have to limit the freedom of manipulation in the abstract system in order to adjust its concepts to the appropriate property from the empirical world. The rules by which we limit the freedom of manipulation in the abstract system are known as the laws of nature. Obviously, the more limited the abstract systems of those absolute truths, the smaller the number of the laws of nature and the more we identify the internal relationships between the various phenomena. Thus Einstein, for instance, has shown in his general theory of relativity that instead of describing natural phenomena in a regular Euclidian plane, and talking about two masses—an inertial mass and a gravitational mass—and then defining a law of nature saying that inertial mass always equals gravitational mass, the natural phenomena can be described in a curved space in which there naturally appears only one mass which serves as both inertial and gravitational. We imagine a bullet to be capable—a priori— of moving in every possible direction, but since it does not do so, we defined a law limiting the freedom we gave that bullet in our abstract system.[68]

♦ ♦ ♦

It is important to remember here the political functions of Ben-Gurion's convictions. He believed that if man is capable of grasping the objective rules of the universe, he is also capable of freeing himself from determinants imposed upon him by these rules. And if collectivities are capable of acquiring the gift of intuition, then the People of Israel, being deprived of "matter" but not of "mind," have hope. Ben-Gurion, leading a developing nation in the 1950s, was in great need of an orderly cosmos operating in the form of orderly routines and predictable laws. This not only reflected the desire of the weak for order in a contingent world but also the leader's need for reassurance that his nation has an "objective" place and function in a world order. The existence of "true" laws of nature was necessary for a leader believing his people had been deprived for two thousand years

of their natural place among the nations. Ben-Gurion turned to
science as an ultimate answer. It provided hope when all other
paths seemed unattainable. It proved to him the supremacy of
the human spirit, but in order to be of such value, science had to
be more than a language, more than a tool, more than a set of
questions. It had to be associated with ultimate truth. The scientists, however, objected. Deshalit and his generation of scientists shared Ben-Gurion's fascination with the power of the
human mind. They willingly participated in an effort to utilize
science for the defense of the country and its future. But science
to them meant everything it did not mean to the statesman; it
meant a never-ending process by which new hypotheses replace
old ones, a constant casting of doubts and examination of assumptions, a realization that no reality exists "out there":

◆ ◆ ◆

*Whatever the future development of physics is going to be, there
is one thing which its past history definitely teaches us: We ought
always to review and reexamine our ideas, concepts, and notions
in the light of accumulating experience. We should not be too
hasty in throwing away one point of view in order to accept
another; but if accumulated evidence is becoming manifestly con-
tradicting to our notions we should be courageous enough to
reevaluate them and change them to agree with observations.
Nothing should be taken as an "absolute truth" if there is new
evidence which contradicts it, for all our "absolute truths" result
from observation which is of necessity only fragmentary.*[69]

◆ ◆ ◆

Science and Values

the relationship between sci-
ence and values often concerned and puzzled Ben-Gurion.

◆ ◆ ◆

*In the evening we had dinner, as usual, at Renana's home. Amos
Deshalit and Aharon Katzir came—and Amos tried to prove that
theoretically there isn't any difference between machine and
man, and a machine can be designed which fully resembles man.
He did not admit the existence of knowledge—only of physical
processes, and denied any difference between a living individual*

and a perfect machine. I wonder whether two machines could exchange letters in matters of philosophy, morality or science. He admitted there is a difference between non-living and living creatures, but not an absolute one.[70]

♦ ♦ ♦

This discussion, referred to in Ben-Gurion's diary, continued to preoccupy the Prime Minister all that week. "I can't forget our conversation in Renana's apartment," he wrote to Deshalit on January 13,

♦ ♦ ♦

I am troubled by your stand as a physicist in matters of human reason and cognition. Does specialization in the science of physics really prevent one from recognizing the spiritual powers and reason of man? Do you believe that two machines could be designed to exchange letters on matters of art, philosophy and science, such as Spinoza's treatise, or that a machine could be invented which, while traveling all over the globe, would collect facts and deduce Darwin's theory from them? Don't you realize the entirely different nature of spiritual processes, which are, of course, related to physical processes in the human body, but differ completely from mere mechanical processes? Can you conceive of a machine which would compose the book of Job, or Plato's Symposium, *or Einstein's theory of relativity? The perfect machine would perhaps obey the will of its designer, but there is almost no limit to man's reason and intellectual ability.*[71]

♦ ♦ ♦

Such debates between scientists and laymen over the simulation of the human mind are usually of little importance. The rhetoric involved is enormous, and the low feasibility of such simulation makes the question of its possibility or desirability quite remote. The same debate, however, becomes more significant when conducted between the scientist and the statesman, since it concerns a major normative question, defined here by Goodall:

♦ ♦ ♦

We can regard the question "can machines think" as essentially empty. The relevant one, as a politician ought well to under-

*stand, is "who controls whom, and how, and for what is this
going to be done?"[72]*

♦ ♦ ♦

The question of control has, however, been operationalized by
Goodall too simply. He expected politicians to fear the actual loss
of political power presumably implied by automation. "Automation and data processing," wrote Goodall, "could very easily de-
prive the existing political blocks of their meaning, leaving power
in a kind of technical no man's land. . . . One can see perhaps
what this could mean. Government will no longer be able to
manage technical committees and will have to consider expert
assessments of various situations."[73] This approach suffers from a
stereotypical view of the politician. Rather than attributing to
him a general fear of the machine, the specific political ideas and
values affected by the notion of simulation and the types of political options such a notion opens or closes needs investigation. In
a study of the computer revolution in philosophy, Aaron Sloman
proposed the model for such an investigation, explaining the
basic features of intelligent machines and showing the dilemmas
they imply, for instance, that it is impossible to devise really
helpful mechanical servants without giving them desires, attitudes, and emotions.

♦ ♦ ♦

*[These machines] will sometimes have to feel the need for great
urgency when things are going wrong and something has to be
done about it. Some of them will need to have the ability to
develop their motives in the light of experience, if they are to
cope with changing situations (including changing personal relations) with real intelligence and wisdom. This raises the possibility of their acquiring aims and desires not foreseen by their
designers. Will people be prepared to take account of these
desires?[74]*

♦ ♦ ♦

Ben-Gurion's debates with Deshalit over the simulation of the
mind indeed wrestled with a basic question. Both sides extended
their philosophy of science to the sphere of values. The statesman, in line with his notion of intuition, implied that the creative
mind can derive absolute and eternal values from the laws of

nature. The scientist implied that values, like truth, are merely predictable (and hence artificially reproducible) human constructs derived from experience, with no objective (or "natural") ontological status.

The focus of this debate was set by Deshalit in his February 3 answer to Ben-Gurion's letter. Deshalit made a distinction among three functions of the brain—receiving, decoding, and encoding information—and he limited the debate to the decoding function. As far as receiving information, he saw no real difference between Darwin's explaining species from his travels around the world and a computer being fed the data on the size, weight, color, and other characteristics of a species. He dismissed the common argument regarding the lack of initiative by machines by claiming that the human initiative to travel and collect specific data is also the result of conditioning. The computer does not work on its own initiative, but neither does a person born and raised in a secluded dark room. And, since encoding is nothing but a process of communication, Deshalit focused on the similarities between the mind and the machine in fulfilling the decoding function, that is, the conversion of input into a different kind of output.

Deshalit argued that the similarity between the mind and the machine could be demonstrated by showing that every logical statement can be expressed in exact mathematical language.

♦ ♦ ♦

I do not mean, of course, that a computer would print, for instance, the statement: "A wise son makes a glad father, but a foolish man despises his mother," but that a machine could easily deduce the folk wisdom involved in that statement by other means, such as by finding a correlation between the parent's happiness and the children's wisdom. True, such folk wisdom sounds disgustingly dry, but this is only because the machine speaks its own language, not ours. And let's not forget that from the point of view of the truth of that statement, there is no difference in principle whether it is expressed in King Solomon's grandiloquent language or in the form of a dry numerical chart of numbers.[75]

♦ ♦ ♦

Deshalit's task was, of course, made easy once he argued that the source of knowledge (the "receiving" function) did not have to be taken into consideration. It is rather obvious that normative statements can be deduced from other normative statements; it is, after all, the source of these statements that determines their uniqueness and that raises the question of equivalence between man and machine. Deshalit did not, however, wholly ignore the question of the sources of knowledge. As shown above, he attributed ethical statements to cumulative experience, which provided the justification for considering them in algorithmic terms. In his later correspondence, it became even clearer that the debate was not over the feasibility of reducing logical statements into mathematical symbols but over the source of values. To Deshalit, observation was the only means to acquire any "truth," including the moral truth Ben-Gurion derived by "intuition."

But Ben-Gurion insisted upon the distinction between mind and machine. "I have friends, gifted scientists in the Weizmann Institute—physicists and chemists—who laugh at my view on this," he wrote to a psychologist. "The distinct mark of human thinking is the thinker's consciousness about it, and since man knows he thinks, he is the master of his thought and its creator." He objected to the behaviorists' attempts in the 1950s to reduce human behavior to algorithmic dimensions: "Let the behaviorists ignore as much as they wish the individual's consciousness, and observe merely his motions and reactions—but they cannot escape recognizing their own consciousness."[76] Two years after his conversation with Deshalit, he found a quotation in Niels Bohr's *Atomic Physics and Human Knowledge* which he deemed appropriate to send to the physicist: "The existence of life itself should be considered both as regards its definition and observation, as a basic postulate of biology, not susceptible of further analysis, in the same way as the existence of the quantum of action . . . forms the elementary basis of atomic physics . . . such a viewpoint . . . condemns as irrelevant any comparison of living organisms with machines."[77]

Deshalit responded to this at length on July 3, 1959. He first explained that Professor Bohr revised the argument, derived from Bohr's complementary principle, that the explanation of life requires wholly new concepts. Deshalit noted recent developments in molecular biology that blurred the distinction between living and nonliving phenomena. He noted, for instance, the attempts to "teach" electronic machines to distinguish between geometrical forms by storing relevant but partial information in their memory and then reinforcing desirable answers. "Let's not forget," he wrote to the socialist Prime Minister, "under what hard conditions the machine has to operate. . . . Let's try and imagine what would happen to a child who forgets every morning all the information he was fed the day before." He insisted, however, that a physical system consisting of millions and millions of memory units and whose various centers are interdependent, could, in principle, create new ideas by the intrapolation and extrapolation of former ideas, and possibly by mutations of former ideas.

Deshalit had now reached the core of the debate. Being aware of Ben-Gurion's fascination with the objective harmony of nature, he cast doubts upon that harmony and left no ambiguity over the ethical implications of his approach. "If I may," he wrote,

• • •

I shall add a remark about the order and harmony we witness in nature and the feelings of wonder with which they fill our hearts. I believe that under slightly greater scrutiny we might realize that we are not enchanted by the fact that nature is what it is. After all, what are order and harmony if not those things to which we are conditioned since childhood? The eye and ear react, as is well known, to waves—the one to electric waves and the other to acoustic waves. While the ear distinguishes between different wave lengths even when they are interwoven, the eye observes only an average effect of the waves. Thus, for example, the ear hears two sounds played simultaneously as two sounds, while the eye sees two colors placed on one another as a new color. If one day these characteristics were changed, the Ninth Symphony would sound to our new ears as a tasteless and boring mixture of strange sounds, while the greatest landscapes would disintegrate into strange and uninteresting sets of separate colors. Our fascination with sounds and colors is thus the result of certain habits and is affected to a great extent by the "education" we are constantly exposed to from our environment. When I realize sometimes how many times a day I repeat in my little boy's ears what is just and unjust in the world, I am not surprised that people (at least some of them . . .) later distinguish between good and evil; I only wonder why they do it so poorly. I am sure that a machine would have learned such matters much faster and more efficiently. It was, I believe, Helmholtz who said that if a

*worker in his artisan shop had approached him with as incom-
plete a tool as the human eye he would have fired him. I am
afraid that in the not so distant future someone will say the same
about the human brain.*[78]

◆ ◆ ◆

Ben-Gurion responded immediately: "Nature's order and harmony are not the outgrowth of habit but of reason and cognition.
Had there not existed such order, there would have been no
habit, or human being, just a commotion and we would not have
even known it." And he added: "The machine is incapable of
wondering. It does not ask questions. The (relative) greatness of
man is his ability to ask questions, and sometimes also answering
them—while no machine in the world would ever try and explain
by itself that there is no difference between itself and Amos
Deshalit's brain."[79]

The statesman was indeed fighting for control, but it was not
the control of politician over machine but rather the control of
the human mind over its environment. He attempted to derive
both intelligence and conscience from the universal laws of nature, and he attributed absolute validity to both. If modern physics did not yield support to this position, the ancient prophets
certainly did:

◆ ◆ ◆

*Our Prophets demanded justice in the life of man and envisaged
justice in the cosmos. Isaiah, one of the greatest of the Prophets,
said: "Drop down, ye heavens, from above, and let the skies pour
down righteousness; let the earth open, and let them bring forth
salvation, and let righteousness spring up together." And when
the Psalmist seeks in one short verse to catalogue supreme values,
he says: "Mercy and truth are met together; righteousness and
peace have kissed each other." And he adds: "Truth shall spring
out of the earth; and righteousness shall look down from heaven."
In the words of our Prophets, the moral content is inherent not
only in man but in the whole of nature. And I say that only by
the guidance of Prophetic ethics can we direct the tremendous
power of science along fruitful paths, so that it becomes a blessing to mankind. Science unguided by moral values can lead to
catastrophe.*[80]

◆ ◆ ◆

Herein lies the solution to an apparent contradiction between Ben-Gurion's belief in free science as a lever for human perfection and his call for moral values to guide the scientist in his work. To him, science and values were not separate entities but two aspects of the same "cosmos" to be revealed by the human mind. The call for integration between intelligence and conscience stemmed from a belief that neither is possible without the other. The scientist who wishes to flourish and make a contribution must be part of a normative and political structure. Science in isolation is not only dangerous but above all fruitless. In one letter he wrote:

♦ ♦ ♦

Science, but not science alone, will have an ever greater role in the formation of the state and its might. The nature of the state will also be determined by social and moral values. This does not undermine the importance of science, but rather adds a mighty force to it which, when combined with science, will elevate the state, and possibly also contribute to science itself.[81]

♦ ♦ ♦

Ben-Gurion admitted that the problem of integration between science and ethics preoccupied him "not only outside office hours but as part of my general concerns as prime minister."[82] This was apparent, for instance, when he angered Jewish leaders in the Diaspora by declaring that the intellectual contribution of the Jews—as a community—was made only in those periods in which they lived in their own homeland. In the Diaspora, he felt, the people's spiritual lives, like their material lives, were impoverished; and the Jews lived in a spiritual, as well as a political and economic, ghetto. "This was not because our creative power had entropied . . . but because we had been torn from the source of our people's vitality, their independent homeland."[83] To Ben-Gurion, intellectual activity was meaningless if performed outside a specific normative context, and the scientist, therefore, had to be endowed with a specific set of norms and commitments. Deshalit, however, could not accept the existence of a fixed set of norms that ought to guide science, since he did not consider norms to be derived from laws of nature. To him, normative "truth," like any other truth, was derived from human experience and could, therefore, vary and change. Deshalit, the insider, was willing to accept the statesman's value system in the choice of certain research subjects or in their utilization. He could not accept the status of these values as natural laws or their integral role in the process of inquiry.

Science and Societal Self-Control

In his study *Autonomous Technology*, Langdon Winner explained the statesman's fascination with technology by the fortuitous combination of the certainty and control involved in technology. Many historical forms of statecraft and almost all conceptions of utopia, Winner noted, rest on an implicitly technological model. When conditions in the political world seem uncertain, unmanageable, or otherwise undesirable, technique and artifice offer an attractive solution. However, Winner had to acknowledge, as does almost every social theorist, technology's paradoxical role. It may help solve the problems that society encounters, but at the same time, each addition to the technological aggregate contributes to the process of helpless drift in society. Science and technology, believed to enable man to control his life, often result, instead, in man's disorientation.[84]

The question of science, technology, and societal self-control became a major source of tension between Ben-Gurion and the scientists. Insiders and outsiders alike questioned the technological society and feared the loss of control that it implies. The same scientists who put science and technology in the service of national development expressed doubts about the ability of the nation to guide the technological revolution. As scientists in a new nation, they realized the importance of science and technology, but as world scientists, they were members of a growing community of intellectuals fearing its implications. The atomic bomb sparked important moral questions to be considered in an age of science and technology. It also signaled the difficult problems that lie ahead: how to assure the capacity of leaders to make decisions in a complex new world and how to avoid the abuse of technology (and power) when citizens are unable to comprehend the issues and to apply democratic controls.[85]

In 1958, Aharon Katzir, a prominent biologist and close associate of the Prime Minister, delivered an important lecture on
the scientific revolution.[86] He stressed the stability in the past of
values such as freedom, equality, fraternity, and human dignity
and claimed that at the turn of this century, stability had been
lost. The nineteenth century had already witnessed the proletar-
ianization of the masses and the loss of individualism, but in the
twentieth century, the crisis gained new proportions. Science
had undermined man's value and position in the world.

Katzir pointed to the problem of a society based on the
achievements of science, a society whose whole future depends
on scientific research left in the hands of elites. The individual in
society is not acquainted with science, and neither is its leadership. Modern society, Katzir argued, undergoes crises due to the
distance between a leadership unaware of the potential power in
its hands and the scientist who is detached from the power he
himself created. As a result, today's societies suffer from fears
resembling those of primitive man; gigantic forces created by
science are threatening humanity, and nobody knows how to
control them. Modern societies face a great challenge, Katzir
said, to liberate man, through education, from the primitive fears
created by the rule of science, to familiarize the modern child—
and political leader—with science, and hence enable society in
the long run to be in control of its own destiny.

The significance of these words lies in the role of the speaker.
Katzir was a representative of the "new science," a scientist involved in the utilization of research for national development and
a member of every important committee on the subject. His
perception that science results in a loss of control was therefore
significant, as was his view that the loss of control stems from
scientific specialization. Two years after this lecture, Katzir was
elected first vice-president of the Israeli Academy of Sciences.
On this occasion he was explicit about the effects of specialization. He noted that the world's best researchers and thinkers felt
science had become a "tower of Babel" with a roof already touching the sky, with builders who have lost the ability to communi-
cate with each other. Katzir defined the task of the Academy as
creating a unified language in order to restore the self-control of
science.[87]

Katzir's argument was supported by two philosophers, Martin
Buber, the president-elect of the Academy, and Hugo Bergman,

who expressed great concern over specialization in science. Specialization causes science to run amok toward its own destruction, Bergman said, and added that in spite of his background in physics, he was unable to understand a word of a young physicist's recent doctoral presentation.

At this point, David Ben-Gurion, who was present in the first meeting of the Academy of Sciences as part of his ceremonial duties as Prime Minister, asked for permission to comment. His whole soul, he said, resisted the pessimistic notion that science leads to destruction, that it runs amok, and that this is a necessary course. Ben-Gurion got into a long and unstructured speech discussing the blessings of scientific specialization. The picture that emerges from the speech is most interesting. To the scientists, specialization meant loss of communication and hence of control. They seemed to generalize from their own feelings to the level of society. Specialization, they contended, leads to an inability of science to comprehend itself, and of society to comprehend science. Ben-Gurion, from the statesman's point of view, saw it quite differently. To him, specialization was a *condition* of scientific development. The societal contribution of science did not depend on the comprehension of science by every scientist but on the overall utilization of science in society.

Specialization, Ben-Gurion claimed, expands collective knowledge. The various details cannot be known by any one person, but as they accumulate, the spirit of man as a whole becomes richer. If a twenty-year-old girl, who is fifty years younger than Professor Bergman, knows more than he does, that is proof that physics has made progress in those fifty years. This is a positive sign, he said. "If I had learned physics in my childhood, reached 70 years of age and failed to understand my granddaughter's physics, I would have rejoiced, since I would have seen it as a sign of the unending elevation of the human spirit."

Ben-Gurion criticized those who lamented and feared the increasing role of the scientist in society. He claimed he did not fear the power of science, since, after all, man's capacity to understand the world is limited. Furthermore, politicians lead societies to disaster, scientists do not. Oppenheimer and Einstein could not be blamed for the misuse of the atomic bomb by politicians. Einstein endowed humanity with a great gift; Oppenheimer enriched the spirit of man.

Three days after this speech, Hugo Bergman wrote the Prime

Minister a letter in which he tried to clarify his views on the disaster involved in scientific development. He agreed that scientific work cannot be conducted without specialization but expressed great concern over such specialization. Researchers even in closely related fields do not talk a common language. Who, then, would coordinate their work toward harmony?[88]

This question illuminated the source of the disagreement. To Ben-Gurion, there was no doubt that the politician was in charge of this synthesis. Bergman, a scholar belonging to a passing generation, was searching for a unified language and world view to be developed by world scientists in order to determine a desired path for humanity. Ben-Gurion belonged to a generation claiming a new relationship between science and politics, and both the scholar and Prime Minister knew it. Said Bergman:

◆ ◆ ◆

Just one generation ago the natural sciences had one world view, or at least the chance to have one. Today, there is no common world view, nor is there a desire to develop one. The sciences form practical hypotheses which allow for new experiments and new facts, without taking these hypotheses seriously. Today they are accepted, tomorrow they are rejected; everything is judged merely by its practical utility. We pile up mountains of data, but lack those people with an overall synthetic approach to build a world view out of these data.

◆ ◆ ◆

The aging professor went on to describe the lost paradise he knew long ago as a young scholar:

◆ ◆ ◆

Once upon a time, the teacher, the priest or the rabbi in every village or small town was a carrier of humanity's values and a symbol to the people. Today, the scientist is nothing but a technician. This is the danger I tried to point out. The technician no longer has an awareness of values. He is a slave, and his knowledge is enslaved by the master—be he a politician as you said, or a rich man paying for the scientist's services, and utilizing them for his own needs. Science has lost its glory, and this is a loss not only to science, but to humanity as a whole.[89]

◆ ◆ ◆

In his answer to Bergman, Ben-Gurion apologized for the harshness with which he had treated the professor during the meeting of the Academy. He noted that to the extent of his familiarity with writings by prominent scientists, there seemed to exist a willingness to crystalize a common world view. He then wrote that he could not accept the definition of the specializing scientist as a technician. The specialized study of the atom involves as much wisdom as the wisdom of the renaissance man who was familiar with all the sciences of his times. Scientific research and the teaching of values, he added, are two different activities, but both are necessary to man and humanity.[90]

"You claim, and justifiably so, that 'scientific research and the teaching of values are two different activities, but both are necessary to man and humanity.'The question worrying me is: whose function is it to teach those values to our youngsters?"[91] replied Bergman. It is not surprising that Bergman's question remained unanswered.

Katzir and Bergman, representing two different scientific "cultures," shared a common fear, in a sense, the fear of the primitive man mentioned in Katzir's 1958 lecture. They were both aware of the power granted to science, in contrast to the impotence of the individual scientist specializing in a tiny bit of knowledge. This idea was once vividly expressed by Abba Eban:

♦ ♦ ♦

The great conquerors—Alexander, Caesar, Napoleon, the dynasties and rulers of all times—have profoundly influenced the lives of some generations. But the total effect of all their influence shrinks to small dimensions when compared to the entire transformation of human habits and mentality produced by the long line of men of thought and science—men individually powerless, but ultimately the rulers of human destiny.[92]

♦ ♦ ♦

Ben-Gurion did not share this fear. Society could not lose control because its capacity for self-control was only partly dependent upon the state of its scientific and technological development. Nor could science run amok, because the scientist, for Ben-Gurion, was to be endowed with the stable, universal values by which society guides itself. While social scientists were writing long essays on "the new priesthood" and its dangers,[93] the statesman foresaw a status quo between science and society. At the foundation of this was the notion of politics. Ben-Gurion questioned neither the authority nor the ability of political leaders to interpret norms and determine the path of society. Science remained the source of human perfection, since he could not even imagine it as an independent estate. While scientists were worrying about the new power in their hands, Ben-Gurion simply refused to grant it to them.

Ben-Gurion and Scientific Expertise

His admiration for science and his close association with persons of science were no indication of Ben-Gurion's willingness to accept their advice. He never denied the importance of the expert, but he believed that expertise must be imbued with the normative spirit that would allow it to make a contribution. Ben-Gurion was always critical of scientific expertise that derived its insights from professional knowledge but lacked the perspective and values of those it intended to serve.

Therefore, Ben-Gurion, the lover of science, ultimately had to distinguish between "true science" and "false science." He held one useful guideline for separating the two: the "true" scientist is he who tells you what can be done, the "false" scientist is he who tells you what cannot be done. In 1944, he said:

♦ ♦ ♦

If a scientist came and claimed that Jews could be settled on a certain piece of land, his claim should be accepted. From the point of view of science, if he is a scientist, he says it on the basis of experience, and science is the collective experience of man; if he says it on the basis of experience that people have already done it here and there, I take his word for it. But if an expert came and claimed in the name of science: "in the Jezreel Valley you should not plant grapefruits," "in the Negev desert you cannot settle people," or that it is impossible to bring a million Jews to Israel, you should tell him "no, this is no science, you are not talking in the name of science," because when he tells us such things, the meaning of his words is that he does not know, or that he does not know yet that it can be done.[94]

♦ ♦ ♦

Ben-Gurion often suggested that his refusal to listen to the experts when he made his historic decisions, such as the decision to proclaim the state's independence, was not because he objected to science but because he realized the objections by the experts were "unscientific." Ben-Gurion was particularly troubled by the experts who in 1948 anticipated that Israel would lose the War of Independence. It may have been his way of reassuring himself when he declared:

♦ ♦ ♦

If experts, scientists, tell us that the weak cannot beat the strong, and that this is a lesson from nature and history, we cannot accept the verdict, not because we object to science, but because in matters of survival the senses and the mind of the individual sharpen, and we begin to scrutinize these concepts of weak and strong, and we ask under what conditions the strong could really overpower the weak . . . and this whole business of weak and strong is not so simple because there is no absolute weak and strong in science. Science knows that these are relative terms, and science ought to investigate where lies the vulnerability of the strong and the strength of the weak.[95]

♦ ♦ ♦

As Prime Minister, Ben-Gurion had to establish far more sophisticated guidelines to distinguish between types of expertise that were acceptable to him and types that were not.[96] According to these guidelines, derived from his rather explicit philosophy of science, the scientific expert was expected to tell the "truth," that is, to propose a set of deterministic relations between cause and effect. Uncertain or probabilistic knowledge was scrutinized by the statesman to determine the element of truth. And since such knowledge does not incorporate the criteria by which to determine "absolutely true" from "absolutely false," external criteria had to be employed, such as the statesman's own belief system.

Ben-Gurion's concern with certainty in the face of probabilistic information was demonstrated in his correspondence with Edward Poznanski, a logician who served for many years as academic secretary of the Hebrew University. Their correspondence began on November 7, 1962. That day, Ben-Gurion was preoccupied with important issues: the democratic victory in the

Congressional elections in the U.S., a Saudi warning against Egypt, another Chinese expedition into Indian territory, Syrian fire on an Israeli tractor, the coming U.N. debate over the Palestinian refugees, and, of course, various problems within the party. Yet on the same day, Ben-Gurion found the time to write the following letter:[97]

◆ ◆ ◆

Jerusalem, Nov. 7, 1962

Dear Mr. E. Poznanski:

I have read your article "Bernays, Carnap, Fraenkel" in I'Yun, Volume 13, no. 2. On page 88 you praise Carl Hempel's study of "inductive incompatibilities," and you emphasize the problem, raised by Hempel, regarding two syllogisms "each of which seems completely sound, while the conclusions are incompatible."

1. Petersen is a Swede.
Less than 2 per cent of the Swedes are Roman Catholics.
So Petersen is almost certainly not a Roman Catholic.

2. Petersen made a pilgrimage to Lourdes.
Less that 2 per cent of those making a pilgrimage to Lourdes are not Roman Catholics.

So, almost certainly, Petersen is a Roman Catholic.

According to Hempel the two syllogisms are incompatible.

I have not read Hempel's article but if the whole article is on the level of this example, than I am afraid he does not know what he is talking about, because there is no incompatibility between the two conclusions. The first inference is true, and so is the second, and there is no incompatibility here.

In the first syllogism it is not said: 'therefore certainly Petersen is not a Roman Catholic' but rather 'almost certainly Petersen is not a Roman Catholic.' The expression 'almost certainly' allows for the possibility that Petersen is a Roman Catholic, which can be inferred from the assumption that 'less than 2 per cent of the Swedes are Roman Catholics.' In Sweden there are about 7½ million inhabitants, and less than 2 per cent is about

149,000 Catholics, and Petersen is perhaps one of them. Hence his pilgrimage to Lourdes as a Roman Catholic is in no contradiction to the first syllogism.

The same applies to the second syllogism. It says 'almost certainly Petersen is a Roman Catholic,' which means that he may not be a Roman Catholic, and it does not contradict syllogism 1.

The addition of the word "almost" in both syllogisms allows for the possibility that Petersen is not a member of the majority but of the minority.

I am almost certain that you, too, realize that there is a logically significant difference between "certain" and "almost certain" and it is hard to imagine that Hempel does not realize that difference. And if his whole article is based on such "incompatibilities" it makes no sense.

Sincerely
D. Ben-Gurion

◆ ◆ ◆

On November 16, the academic secretary thanked the Prime Minister for taking the time to read his article, enclosed Hempel's article, informed the Prime Minister that Hempel was a great authority on inductive logic, and did not forget to mention that he was also a friend of Israel and had visited the country as a guest of the Hebrew University in 1960. As far as substance is concerned, Poznanski's letter made little sense, since, as he realized a month later, wherever he put down the word "Roman Catholic," his typist put down the word "Swede." By the time Poznanski finally realized the mistake, he had already received a polite but somewhat perplexed letter from Ben-Gurion claiming that he failed to comprehend the logical discourse and its resemblance to Hempel's argument. He therefore had to read Hempel's article in the original and was still unconvinced there was an incompatibility between the two syllogisms.[98]

On December 14, Poznanski apologized for the mess, mentioned (twice) his willingness to discuss the problem in person with the Prime Minister, and invited Ben-Gurion to a lecture on "Three kinds of alienation: Is modern man a stranger?" in a symposium to be held on December 26 for a philosophical society of which he was member. This time, however, his substantive points were of interest. He wrote:

• • •

We argue over an inductive syllogism, a statistical syllogism, and not over a deductive one. This means that we do not expect an answer which is 100% certain, but an answer determining the degree of certainty, the degree of probability. We are not interested only in the distinction between "certain" and "uncertain," but in the question to what extent could we rely on the conclusion. No inductive syllogism can assure us that things are not different from what the syllogism implies. Even the event which has the smallest probability to occur, might occur. Let's take as an example the throwing of a die. Statistics teaches us that the probability of throwing a "6" five consecutive times is very low, the chance is 1 to 7576, that is, it is almost certain *we shall not succeed in throwing a "6" five times, yet it could happen.*

The question, thus, is not the "certainty" vs. "uncertainty" of the conclusion, but, rather, the probability of the conclusion. And now let's return to our examples. The first syllogism tells me that 'almost certainly' Petersen is not a Roman Catholic. The second syllogism tells me that 'almost certainly' Petersen is a Roman Catholic. We (Hempel and I) argue there is an incompatibility here, while you argue there is not, since both syllogisms are compatible with the fact that Petersen is a Roman Catholic.

Well, first of all, two incompatible statements could be compatible with a third statement, and this fact does not eliminate the initial incompatibility between them. This is so obvious that no examples are needed.

But secondly, according to the first syllogism the probability that Petersen is a Roman Catholic is very low, *smaller than 2%. According to the second syllogism the probability that Petersen is a Roman Catholic is* very high, *higher than 98%. Thus, both syllogisms together bring me to the conclusion, that the probability of a certain statement is less than 2% and it is also higher than 98%. Isn't there an incompatibility here?*[99]

• • •

Poznanski went on to explain the source of inductive incompatibilities—that the postulate of total evidence is not fulfilled. Each syllogism is based on limited information only, the first on Petersen's nationality, the second on his visit to Lourdes. Due to the lack of total evidence, one is forced to sort out those data that enable him to reach a conclusion. Poznanski admitted that although in the above example this poses no great difficulty, since Petersen's nationality seems clearly more relevant than his visit to Lourdes, the difficulty may often be so great as to allow statistics to prove everything.

On December 20, Ben-Gurion replied.

◆ ◆ ◆

I hope you would not consider it mere stubbornness if I told you that I cannot move from my position that both Hempel and you are wrong. Exactly because this is an inductive syllogism there is no logical contradiction between the first and second syllogisms . . . "almost certain" is different from "certain" because the expression "almost certain" explicitly assumes it may not be so.

◆ ◆ ◆

Ben-Gurion elaborated at length on this argument, claiming that Petersen's pilgrimage to Lourdes could have taken place whether he was a protestant or a Roman Catholic, and his religion cannot be predicted from his pilgrimage, although most pilgrims are Roman Catholics, etc. And he concluded:

◆ ◆ ◆

I do not accept the paradoxical statement that statistics allows us to prove everything. As long as the statistician is careful, and phrases his conclusion as it is phrased in Hempel's example, and yours, the statistical conclusion as such is true. It does state explicitly that the number of Roman Catholics among the Swedes is less than 2%, which is to say that there are Roman Catholic Swedes. It also does say that Protestants make pilgrimages to Lourdes, even if they make up only 2% of all pilgrims.[100]

◆ ◆ ◆

This is an important clue to the understanding of the choice process by which Ben-Gurion absorbed information. Science, to him, was a perfect means to approach the ultimate causes and deterministic rules of nature. Even probability theory, although an imperfect tool in this regard, was a stage on the way toward an immediate meeting between mind and reality. Intuition was thus used to distinguish between true and false, relevant and

irrelevant, temporary and eternal, and so forth. Ben-Gurion did
not necessarily expect the statesman to determine truth and relevance. He did, however, expect the scientist to be endowed
with the right state of mind and operate within the right normative context to allow him to make these choices. This is why he
was not particularly concerned with those pitfalls of scientific
expertise usually mentioned as barriers to communication between the expert and the statesman.[101] Imperfect use of statistics, conflicting expertise, confusion between facts and values
and similar deficiencies did not worry him since he scrutinized
each study in terms of one criterion only—its contribution to the
truth.

Ben-Gurion's choice process in the face of expertise may be
demonstrated by reference to his responses to studies by social
scientists. In 1963, Hans Kreitler, a psychologist, submitted to
him a study on young Israelis' attitudes toward ideals. Among the
findings he discovered that young Israelis showed a greater willingness to pursue national ideals than universal ones, a low correlation between the salience of an ideal and their willingness to
pursue it, a strong correlation between the willingness to pursue
an ideal and the recognition of available means but also a lack of
familiarity with such means. Thirty-six and one-half percent responded to the question of their familiarity with such means by
claiming "helplessness." There were three interesting interpretations of this study. Kreitler himself considered the correlation
between the willingness to act and the recognition of means of
action as the most important finding. It implied to him that the
stress upon ideals by educators is less relevant than their pointing
out available means.[102] The press discerned from the study that
politicians were wrong in stressing ideals rather than the ways to
fulfill them.[103] And the Prime Minister reacted to the study by
stressing its importance for two reasons: first, because of the very
willingness of youth to act in order to pursue desired goals, and
second, because 50% of the respondents mentioned the education of the underprivileged as salient to them.[104]

Another example concerns Moshe Czudnowski's study of the
political socialization of eighteen-year-old Israelis. Czudnowski,
a political scientist, investigated whether, and to what extent,
this age group agreed to the establishment of a dictatorial regime
in Israel. In this study, 57.95% of those living in towns in Israel
agreed to some form of dictatorship. In other types of settlements

the figures were slightly lower. There was little variance among ethnic groups and some variance, although unobvious, among educational levels and various other affiliations. The study seemed quite convincing; the sample was large and stratified, and the methodology carefully explained and restricted.[105]

Ben-Gurion responded immediately to the study results sent to him. He expressed great surprise and concern and noted that the results were "almost unbelievable." "Is really such a high percentage of youth striving for dictatorship? and why?" he asked Czudnowski. Ben-Gurion said he required more information about the rationales given by the respondents. "Do they know what dictatorship is?"[106]

Czudnowski handled his response carefully. He stressed that one should not derive simple generalizations from any sample, and he reminded Ben-Gurion that the respondents were eighteen-year-olds, who search for simplistic solutions to problems. About 10% of the respondents, he estimated, did not know what a dictatorship was, but he preferred not to speculate beyond the data.[107] He did enclose additional information indicating that lack of political knowledge might be related to the desire for dictatorship, and in publishing his initial findings, he therefore claimed that the educational system had failed.

Ben-Gurion responded again. He accepted Czudnowski's belief that the educational system had failed and that a lot remained to be done. He claimed, however, that he knew young people, too, and that the sample just could not be considered representative. Ben-Gurion therefore tried a survey of his own. "Last Friday night," he wrote to Czudnowski,

♦ ♦ ♦

we had a meeting of the members of our Kibbutz. About 50 people were present. They were asked if they support dictatorship and some answered negatively. I asked again—can I announce in the name of the Kibbutz members that they object to dictatorship—and they all raised their hands and even called out loud: yes, we object.[108]

♦ ♦ ♦

Another interesting encounter with political science occurred in 1959 when a political scientist, Benjamin Akzin, proposed to establish a committee of experts to look "thoroughly and impartially" into the question of the electoral system in Israel.[109] Ben-Gurion's demand for a change in Israel's electoral system, a proportional representation system which he had long considered unresponsive and a source of political instability, became a major campaign issue before the parliamentary elections of 1959. In the months before the elections, a group of intellectuals who were close to the Prime Minister organized to support Ben-Gurion's demand. Akzin's letter came at this time. He noted that the decision over the electoral system would ultimately be made in Parliament but that a committee of experts should first look into the matter in depth and with objectivity. The findings and recommendations of this committee, Akzin wrote, would guarantee that the solutions proposed in Parliament would be free of political interests and superficiality.

Ben-Gurion's response was not surprising:

◆ ◆ ◆

Sdeh Boker October 17, 1959

Dear Professor Akzin,

I acknowledge receipt of your letter of Oct. 7, 1959, which I received only yesterday, regarding a committee to study the electoral system. This is a strange proposal coming from a political science professor. As a scientific expert, you are certainly familiar with that question; it is only strange you do not publish and explain your position on scientific grounds. From your articles in the daily press I get the impression that you object to regional elections, and you are no doubt entitled to your opinion. I am only puzzled as to why you do not express your opinion clearly enough.

I don't have any claim to political expertise, although I studied political studies as a law student, and I skim from time to time through the political literature, although I obviously do not consider myself a political scientist, if such a science exists.

But as a citizen of this state who observes its life and needs, I have a definite opinion that the existing system is a cancer in the nation's body. It weakens the political responsibility of the small parties which flourish in this system, and weakens national unity. . . . The proponents and opponents of the existing system

will not need "objective experts," and like every political ques-
tion, this one will also be decided by the majority, and there is
no use and no need for a research committee, in my humble
opinion.

Sincerely,

David Ben-Gurion

◆ ◆ ◆

Akzin responded on October 25 in a long and detailed letter
that began with a thorough exposition of the scientific nature of
political science from Aristotle to the present. He noted that the
analogy between the proportional representation system and cancer was highly exaggerated and then explained why the regional
system, despite its successful adoption in Britain, the United
States, and other countries, might not be easily adopted by every
polity. He expressed doubt as to whether those in charge seriously regarded the merits of the different electoral systems and
the conditions in which they were applied. He repeated his proposal that prior to any parliamentary discussion the idea should
be investigated by a committee of experts of the type he himself
had headed in the past. "Even if the objectivity of experts is only
relative," wrote Akzin, "the problem should not be left entirely
to the representatives of political parties whose objectivity, as
well as knowledge of the material, is incomparably smaller."

Ben-Gurion responded on November 19. He thanked Akzin
for his detailed and enlightening letter and admitted his own lack
of expertise on the question of the scientific nature of political
science. The question of the electoral system, however, was not
a scientific one, he claimed. Explaining again his position on the
subject, Ben-Gurion wrote:

◆ ◆ ◆

With all due respect, there is no basis for assuming that the
scientist understands the needs of the state better than the non-
scientist. The state is an unusually complex creature, and only a
scientist with the mind of an encyclopedia who is an expert on all
sciences, and is familiar with all their details and has an all-
knowing cosmic brain could be an expert on matters of state. The
democracies are therefore right in not leaving the management
of security and military affairs in the hands of generals, but

rather utilizing the generals' professional expertise, because the conduct of war is more than just a military profession. And the affairs of state are even more complex than matters of war, and I see no use for an experts' committee.

◆ ◆ ◆

And he added: "I bow my head to the scientist, and I consider the development of science as one of our major national tasks, but the affairs of the state should be left to the statesmen and to the representatives of the people."

The Philosophers
Vision vs. Principle

in July 1957, Professor Jacob Talmon, Israel's foremost historian of ideas, held a lecture on utopianism and politics at the English Conservative Party's summer school in Oxford. Talmon argued that since the time of the French Revolution, people have tended to equate politics with utopianism. Yet the two are, in essence, quite different. Politics is concerned with the careful manipulation of the concrete data of experience, by reference to the logic and to the limitations inherent in any given historical situation; utopianism postulates a definite goal or preordained finale to history, for the attainment of which you need to recast and remold all aspects of life and society in accordance with some very explicit principle. Talmon also expressed his feeling that a curse was besetting utopianism; while it had its birth in the noblest impulses of man, it was doomed to be perverted into an instrument of power and hypocrisy, for the two deep-seated urges of man, the love of freedom and the yearning for salvation, cannot both be fulfilled at the same time.[1]

These statements provide a useful frame of reference for our understanding of the relations that developed between Ben-Gurion and the philosophers. The temptation must be resisted, however, to attribute the two ideal types—politics and utopianism—to any of them. Philosophers have indeed often been associated with utopianism. Lewis Feuer, for instance, referred to "an impressive tradition of philosophical utopias, from Plato to Bellany and Wells, which illumine the unconscious strivings of intellectuals toward scientists' rule."[2] But such references to the unconscious motives of sociological groups are self-fulfilling; the utopian leader becomes a philosopher by definition and the non-utopian philosopher is ignored. It seems more useful to investigate the sets of ideas implied by "politics" and "utopianism" as they are manifested in empirical political behavior. Utopianism could be expected to evolve as a result of the combination of intellectuals and power: "If the reign of dogma required an intellectual elite to expound it, indeed to impose it on the unenlightened," wrote Talmon in his explication of Saint-Simonist thinking, "living faith needs priests of special emotional depth."[3] Nothing symbolizes this collaboration better than a short letter of June 3, 1960, in which Talmon, the critic of utopian messianism, offered to become the biographer of David Ben-Gurion, the "political messiah."[4]

This chapter tells the story of political messianism in Israel in the 1950s. It stresses the intellectual origins of this idea as well as the intellectual tensions it aroused. The latter lay at the core of the campaign against Ben-Gurion during The Affair, which was largely led by philosophers. It is significant that these tensions also became politically salient only when the "messiah" no longer played his charismatic role.

Political Messianism and Its Critics

The Ben-Gurion era in Israel was characterized by an extensive debate over the meaning of the establishment of the state. The debate was nourished by the unique position of the state of Israel as the manifestation of Jewish nationalism while only a minority of the Jewish people lived in Israel. This unique position was the major cause for the national preoccupation by Israeli elites in the 1950s with such questions as the extent to which the state of Israel resembled other states or had a broader commitment to the Diaspora (the Jewish communities outside Israel), what its relationship with the Diaspora should be, what national problems the state had solved, what new problems were created by its formation, and so forth.[5]

These questions were debated at great length by politicians and intellectuals, keeping bystanders, including the majority of Israeli youth, rather perplexed. As one observer reported from the "First World Ideological Conference" held in Jerusalem in 1957, "The notion of a group of deep thinkers gathered in Jerusalem to meditate on fundamentals has its obvious elements of humour."[6] But the ideological conference, famous for Ben-Gurion's declaration, "I am not a Zionist," was an important event in Israel's intellectual history. There, Ben-Gurion was very explicit about his political philosophy, as were his critics. In essence, his philosophy reflected the attempt by modern national leaders to find a compromise between the two competing forces that posed a challenge to nationalism: religion and secularization. Ben-Gurion began his speech by dismissing the centrality of religion as an integrating force in modern Jewish nationalism, claiming that Jewish nationalism had always been nourished by nonreligious sources. Trends of secularization could thus not have a significant effect in weakening the three major components of Jewish nationalism: the people's link to the homeland, the Hebrew language, and, above all, the messianic vision of redemption. Ben-Gurion conceived all three components in secular terms and claimed that they were always present in the life of the nation, whether or not Jews lived in their own homeland.[7]

What then was the meaning of "messianic vision" to Ben-Gurion? As Avraham Avi-hai has correctly noted, in order to understand its meaning, the concept must be stripped of its personification of a physical Messiah, a concept which both Judaism and Christianity shared at one time. It refers instead to an era in which the redemption of mankind will be preceded by the redemption of the Jewish people, restored to their own land.[8] Ben-Gurion believed that this messianic vision of a restored Israel was one of the three elements which kept Jewish nationalism alive in the Diaspora and accounted for the Jews' immigration to Israel in what had been, for him, the beginning of the process of their redemption. But, as Ben-Gurion liked to remind his listeners, he did not have in mind the biblical notion of "The Coming of the Messiah," which implies a passive attitude toward redemption. The vision that he described implied an active commitment to the restoration of Jewish national life on its own soil, as well as to "the establishment there of a model society which will become a 'light unto the nations.' Through it will come universal redemption, the reign of righteousness and human brotherhood and the elimination of wickedness."[9]

The link between national and universal redemption was an important element in Ben-Gurion's political thought. He stressed the growing interdependence between nations and claimed that in the modern world even the strongest nation could no longer survive in isolation. No nation could expect to live in peace unless global peace was assured. "As long as there are wars in the world, there will be wars against us," he said, "and it is easier to liquidate us than others. Hence, it is necessary for us not to have wars in the world!"[10] These global thoughts were supported by the biblical notion: "For out of Zion shall go forth the law and the word of the Lord from Jerusalem," which Ben-Gurion often quoted. He also liked to describe the model society to be formed in Israel by using the term "chosen people," while giving the term an active rather than passive connotation: "I am convinced that Jews were the 'choosing people' rather than the 'chosen.' "[11] In other words, the model society he foresaw depended on no other force than the people's commitments and actions. He stressed that the ideal sought by the prophets was not a "model state" or a desired governmental framework but a perfect society. While to Plato the political ideal was the superior regime, maintained by the authority and wisdom of the philosopher-king, the prophets' ideal of goodness, justice, and mercy would be realized not through the rule of the superior man but through social revolution in all spheres of life by which the people would become "chosen." This was more than mere rhetoric. Ben-Gurion believed that if Israel would not exploit its moral and intellectual ability to the utmost and thereby become a "light unto the nations," its survival and welfare, as well as its international status, could not be assured. His messianic concepts had a clear ideological function. These concepts, familiar to all factions of the population, were used to mobilize the nation toward the formation of a social order that Ben-Gurion considered a precondition of national survival. The ideological function of the conception of messianism is apparent in Ben-Gurion's words in a meeting at his office:

◆ ◆ ◆

I say the Messiah hasn't come yet, and I am not waiting for him to come. The moment the Messiah will come He will be no Mes-

*siah anymore. When you will be able to find a Messiah's address
in the phone directory, He will stop being a Messiah. The greatness of Messiah is that his address is unknown and it is impossible
to reach him, and it is unknown what vehicle he uses, if he uses
a vehicle at all, or whether he rides a donkey or flies on eagles'
wings. But a Messiah is necessary—in order for him not to
come.*[12]

◆ ◆ ◆

The Messiah was merely a symbol to Ben-Gurion, but the
"perfect society" was not. It had a concrete meaning discussed
under the general label of "pioneering," a label incorporating a
specific set of commitments. Traditionally, "pioneering" was associated with a commitment to settle in agricultural settlements
which, in the early days of the return to Palestine, were considered to be the base of the social transformation of the Jewish
people. Ben-Gurion extended the term to include a commitment
to the tasks of the modern state, especially defense and scientific-
technological development. The tasks of the modern state thus
became values of social transformation, which itself was associated with messianic redemption: "Although there are many shadows in our life today, among them heavy shadows, there is good
reason to believe we may become a chosen people. And it is
already possible to observe three forces operating in the State of
Israel which clearly point to the moral and intellectual strength
hidden in us: the agricultural settlers, Israel's defense forces and
the scientists, researchers, writers, and artists."[13] Here was the
essence of political messianism. Worldly, daily, secular activities
had been endowed with a utopian mission, and the tasks of nation-building became associated with the fulfilment of messianic
visions: "Israel is the creation of the Messianic faith, but it is still
in its beginnings. Time has not yet come for us to rest and enjoy
our gains. And we need this faith to continue our struggles."[14]
Ben-Gurion considered the establishment of the state "the most
majestic deed in the life of the Jewish nation since the conquests
of Joshua Bin-Nun."[15] At the same time, he warned that the state
was still far from the fulfilment of the vision.

The ideology of political messianism in Israel in the 1950s must
be considered within the context of political development. Although this ideology had clear political functions—presenting the
Jewish state as the beginning of a renaissance of the Jewish people and recruiting support for the activities falling within this

process[16]—and although it served obvious electoral functions, such as convincing new immigrants of the messiah's residing in the ruling Mapai party,[17] it was, above all, an ideology of nation-building. Like other third world leaders, Ben-Gurion was searching for a symbolic frame of reference for the tasks of nation-building, and political messianism provided him with this. In his article "Words and Values," he expressed the search by third world leaders in the 1950s for an updated set of symbols:

◆ ◆ ◆

Our generation has almost nothing to learn either from Socialism and the Socialist classics of the 19th century or from the early theorists of Zionism fifty, sixty or a hundred years ago. . . . The Socialist thinkers of the 19th century exposed the faults of the social system of their time. The problem of our generation, however, is not to demonstrate the need for reforms or revolutions, but to bring them about and to know how to do it.[18]

◆ ◆ ◆

Israel has rarely been regarded by scholars as a developing country, which leads to some misinterpretations about the Ben-Gurion era. While expressing himself through unique terminology, Ben-Gurion's message was similar to that of other nation-builders:

◆ ◆ ◆

It is the task of our generation to build a new society, which will be able to make use of all the improvements and the know-how of American industrial economy, while remaining free from all the contradictions and social defects inherent in the capitalist order of that rich and highly developed country. . . . Moreover, we must establish and maintain a workers' society which shall be immune to all the malignant evils inherent in a totalitarian regime which is based on the enslavement of man to a tyrant or a group of tyrants.[19]

◆ ◆ ◆

Ben-Gurion considered the awakening of the third world as proof that the Marxist interpretation of a class struggle was outdated in a world motivated by nationalism. At the same time, his observation of national revival in Israel revealed that most immigrants coming to Israel lacked any national ideological background. Zionism, the ideology calling for the Jews' return to Zion, had its roots in European nationalism, and to the Jews from the Moslem countries, the verse, "And may our eyes behold Thy return to Zion in mercy," meant more than all the Zionist literature generally unfamiliar to the great majority. Ben-Gurion applied the same observation to the generation born and raised in Israel. "The generation that lives in Israel was born in the homeland; they are its builders and the sons of an independent people. The problems which occupied the minds of the thinkers and founding fathers of the Zionist Movement no longer exist so far as they are concerned."[20] Ben-Gurion realized that a new vision was necessary: "Where there is no vision, the people perish. Our literature has not yet plumbed the depths of the significance of the Messianic vision in the history of the Jewish people, from ancient times till our own day."[21]

So Ben-Gurion's political messianism attempted to relate the actual deeds of statehood to broad universal meanings, which were derived from these deeds. It was an ideology nourished by, and tailored for, a society engaged in nation-building, in the most practical sense. It was an ideology attributing a symbolic meaning to the most pragmatic acts of the state. Ben-Gurion went as far as to attribute a messianic meaning to the Sinai War of 1956. "To the thousands of our soldiers," he wrote, "this was no mere battle. The halo of Sinai and all the deep and mystical experiences associated with that name for thousands of years glowed over our soldiers' heads as if their parents were present at the Mount Sinai event."[22] And when daily, secular actions could not by themselves serve as symbols, Ben-Gurion turned to the Old Testament, where he found the perfect society that he hoped he was creating:

◆ ◆ ◆

The tales of the Patriarchs four thousand years ago; the travels, deeds and life of Abraham; Israel's wanderings after the Exodus from Egypt; the wars of Joshua Bin-Nun and the Judges who followed him; the life and acts of Saul, David, and Solomon; the achievements of Uzziah, King of Judah, and Jeroboam II, King of Israel—are nearer and more topical, more instructive and full of life, for the generation that was born, grows up and lives in Israel, than all the speeches and debates at the Basle Congresses.

The human, Jewish, social, and national values which we believe
in, and which alone gave our Movement its moral and conquer-
ing force, were formulated and enunciated by Israel's prophets
with more fire and vigor, with a more profound and convincing
faith, than anyone has done ever since.[23]

◆ ◆ ◆

It is only recently, however, that scholars have begun to treat
Ben-Gurion's messianism as an ideology. Harold Fisch in his book
on the Zionist revolution wrote that Ben-Gurion's biblical ideals
gave him a messianic sense of purpose, resembling in some way
that of the early American settlers in New England. For them,
too, biblical inspiration was a source of dynamic energy, legitimizing an unflinching use of political power for exalted ends.[24]
Dan Segre in his recent study stressed the existentialist nature of
Ben-Gurion's messianism, its reflection of pragmatic reality. He
contended that for Ben-Gurion the establishment of a Jewish
state was the beginning of the renaissance of the Jewish people.
Freedom, climate, hard physical labor in the land of their fathers,
service in a national army, science—all of these would eventually
revive Jewish civilization. "Spartacus and Moses," Segre wrote,
"that was Ben-Gurion's utopia for Israel."[25] While Fisch and
Segre realized the ideological function of messianism, they both
criticized it for its lack of genuine biblical inspiration, a comment
which seems irrelevant considering the ideological function of
the concept. Fisch claimed that Ben-Gurion's inspiration was
"messianic, prophetic, and yet in some subtle way it is also non-
prophetic. . . . There was . . . no sense of personal dependence,
no fear and trembling, no existential anxiety, no true Biblical
humility."[26] Segre argued that "the idea of existentialist Messianic
redemption put forward by Ben-Gurion was too passionate,
crude and open to alien influences to offer a framework for selective acculturation and promotion of the new Israeli elite."[27]

In the 1950s, intellectuals were less concerned with the lack of
"Biblical humility" than with the historic distortion involved in
the stress upon messianism. "We must look at the historical facts
as they are," wrote Nathan Rotenstreich, the political philosopher, in response to Ben-Gurion's "Words and Values." He
claimed that the messianic consciousness was not the chief factor
in the awakening of the modern Jewish revival, neither in the
systems of thought of individuals nor in the collective movements

and trends. "We are inclined to give ourselves a good deal of
license in our own explanation of the Messianic idea in Zionist
concepts or those pertaining to the establishment of the State of
Israel."[28] Rotenstreich claimed that the great impetus to the Jewish revival in recent generations was a realistic, rather than messianic, consciousness. "Even if we make the evaluation of our
present period by Messianic criteria we shall still only be able to
see it at the most as a dialectic summation of changes that in
themselves were not Messianic. Thus, the historiosophical conception which ties our position to a Messianic consciousness
evinces signs of subjectivity and wishful thinking."[29] Rotenstreich
illustrated the futility of this concept in serving as a historical
base for nationalism: "It is very doubtful if the contemporary
Israeli youth looks upon our position as a Messianic one, and that
not just because one sees the tangible spiritual and moral problems in it, but because of the inclination to make a distinction
between a real social position and an ideal Messianic one."[30] The
political philosopher warned that no revival movement could
overlook the recent past no matter how much it seeks to take
hold of the distant past, and he added: "There is room to fear that
if we rely on the distant past alone to nourish us, it will not do so
and we shall be left deprived of a past no matter how much we
want the attachment to it."[31]

Ben-Gurion's response to Rotenstreich's comments came in a
letter dated January 9, 1957:

◆ ◆ ◆

*You are mistaken in your belief that there are no sudden leaps in
history; indeed there are. In the establishment of the Jewish State
there was a leap over a gap of centuries; in the War of Independence we drew close to the days of Joshua Bin-Nun, and the story
of Joshua became closer and more comprehensible to the youth
than all the speeches at the Zionist Congresses. "The recent past,"
to our deep regret, no longer exists—for the Jewry of "the recent
past" has been destroyed. I am afraid you do not realize the full
significance of this appalling event in our history.*[32]

◆ ◆ ◆

In that same letter, Ben-Gurion made the statement that became a source of controversy in the Jewish world for years to
come: "The distant past is closer to us than the recent past of the

last two thousand years and not only that of the sixty years in which the term 'Zionism' has been in existence."

On January 11, the philosopher responded to the leader:

♦ ♦ ♦

Now with reference to the matter of sudden leaps in history. I agree with you entirely that such do exist, and in our history too, and that the fact of the existence of the State of Israel is the product of one such leap forward. I would go further and venture the thought that if you had not possessed this concept of historical leaps forward you would not have been the builder of the State. But we have to distinguish very clearly between domains. Such a leap is possible in matters which appertain to a position or attitude; it is much more difficult in matters relating to character, sources of spiritual nourishment, consciousness. . . . There is a difference between revival or resurrection and a leap. True it is that we are renewing our background of biblical reality here since this is a reality related to this country. But, as in every revival its complementation must happen in a place and a historic time in which we actually are.

♦ ♦ ♦

Ben-Gurion refused to consider the formation of the state in a materialistic-historic perspective. In a letter written on January 13, he noted that he was not a disciple of German idealism and did not believe in vision alone as affecting history without the intervention of political, economic, and social conditions. He admitted that conditions present at the end of the nineteenth century and beginning of the twentieth century played a role in encouraging Jewish immigration to Palestine. He insisted, however, that these conditions merely *activated* messianic consciousness. Furthermore, Ben-Gurion did not accept the claim that messianic consciousness was not a significant element in modern Jewish revival. Materialistic conditions had contributed to the political revival of Jews and to the immigration from Eastern Europe to North America or Argentina, but immigration to Israel could not have come without messianic vision.

Two months later, Ben-Gurion remembered that he still owed Rotenstreich an answer regarding the ideological futility of the concept of messianism, and on March 28, he replied: "You expressed a fear that the distant past would not nourish us. Of course not. But that distant past, which became less distant—together with the state's and the world's future will nourish us and this is where messianic vision is necessary." At this point, Rotenstreich became far more explicit about Ben-Gurion's ideological use of concepts, and on April 3, he responded: "Your perception of the link between us and the messianic idea, and of the messianic nature of our times, makes you divide Jewish history into everything preceding our period and everything beginning with it. How can we attribute any real meaning to our period as the fulfillment of messianic vision other than as a metaphor? What is happening today is the passage from one historic stage to another, a passage by leaps. But I do not think it is a passage from an historic stage to a metahistoric stage." Ben-Gurion answered on April 29: "I do not understand the meaning of these words at all. I do not grasp what 'metahistoric stage' means." Just as he refused to distinguish between "matter" and "mind," Ben-Gurion presented his conception of messianism as social-cultural and moral rather than metaphysical. To him, the messianic idea did not signify the end of history but was identical with the historical process itself. The state had thus been promoted to become a means by which historical redemption was achieved, but this made the state more than a means. The very existence of the state became equivalent to such values as freedom, independence, and creativity. State activities, such as the absorption of immigrants, economic development, and security, became an expression of humanity at its best. The association between a political entity and universal values had totalitarian connotations, and Ben-Gurion was aware of it; but he discarded this point, putting his faith in his own nontotalitarian tendencies, and in those of the ancient prophets. He claimed that the prophetic preaching of justice and mercy, peace and truth could not be associated with totalitarian regimes or even with totalitarian aims. Events occurring in his own lifetime also involved only mankind's highest values. "The fears of Professor Talmon and his students or friends that a messianic faith leads to despotism and dictatorship," he wrote, "are the result of a misleading and incorrect understanding of history. The French Revolution was a blessing to humanity. And without the messianic faith, the last three generations of our people would not have done what they did."[33]

Although many intellectuals had not shared Ben-Gurion's his-

torical interpretations on the blessings of the messianic faith
(Prof. Talmon's famous works on the totalitarian nature of political
messianism were written and widely acknowledged in Israel in
the 1950s), this hardly showed in their actual behavior before
The Affair. It is hard to tell whether this was caused, as Talmon's
student and associate Shlomo Avinery had claimed in his 1966
"Nemesis of Messianism," by the intellectuals' fascination with
Ben-Gurion and his preoccupation with their own "métier."[34] It
is possible to tell, however, that Avinery himself, like many other
intellectuals, participated in the ongoing national festival in the
1950s in which a symbolic meaning was attributed to every possible pragmatic event associated with the state. For instance, in
1957, as Israel began to pursue relations with the new state of
Ghana, Avinery, then a high school teacher, wrote Ben-Gurion a
letter in which he demonstrated that "Ghana" had already been
mentioned in historic Hebrew sources.[35] For years, the scholarly
community supported "biblical contests," huge media events so-
cializing a whole generation into a consideration of the pragmatic
(and often gray) present in terms of the biblical past. And one
must add to the list the convergence of politics and archeology in
those years, the hallowed air surrounding the Dead Sea Scrolls,
the public rituals on the Mount Massada, etc. Although some
observers had noted the "bizarre, and sometimes strangely pagan, air"[36] surrounding the promotion of political messianism in
Israel, the intellectuals showed an enthusiasm for participating
in it and relatively little awareness for its long-range implications.
This holds true even for critics of the messianic style. While
Rotenstreich understood the implications of political messianism,
and Talmon devoted his life to the study of these implications,
they both failed to realize their own role in the promotion of that
ideology. Rotenstreich failed to realize the political significance
of his own debate with the Prime Minister. The great debate—
held entirely within the frame of reference and terminology set
by Ben-Gurion—contributed as much as anything to the spread
of the messianic interpretation of the state and its recent history.
In an interview, Rotenstreich reported he was surprised to find
his correspondence with the Prime Minister in the press. Considering the centrality of the conception of messianism in Ben-
Gurion's thought and action, he should hardly have been surprised. Later, Rotenstreich himself published the correspondence in a semi-professional journal. Talmon's request to write

the "political messiah's" biography was understandable, considering Talmon's own preoccupation with the history of political messianism. The request was prompt and ethical but also miscalculated, if indeed Talmon believed his own statement that "the vision of the oneness of history and of universal concord at the end of days must always somehow degenerate, when embodied in a Church militant, into a pattern of Machiavellian ruse and infinite casuistry."[37]

Martin Buber and Political Messianism

The ideology of political messianism in Israel in the 1950s had its roots not only in ancient biblical thought but also in modern theological and intellectual works—especially those by Martin Buber. It is difficult, even "heretical," to try to link Buber's messianism with any form of political ideology, for Buber was the greatest critic of messianism in its political version. "We cannot prepare the messianic world," he wrote, "we can only prepare for it. There is no legitimately messianic, no legitimately messianically-intended politics."[38] Furthermore, it is often claimed that Buber had little impact on Israeli thought, at least far less than his impact world wide. Yet as contradictory as it seems, political messianism could not have flourished were it not for the depth and meaning Buber's philosophy gave to messianic thinking. This is perhaps the reason why no other relationship—on both a theoretical and practical level—was as complex as the relationship between Buber and Ben-Gurion.

In order to explain Buber's conception of messianism, it is useful to begin with his article on "Biblical Leadership."[39] Here Buber elaborated on what he called the negative features of that leadership, beyond both nature and history. To the men who wrote the Bible, nature, as well as history, are of God, but then the biblical events go beyond these. For instance, in the Bible, it is the weak and the humble who are chosen for leadership. In nature, however, it is the strong, those who can force their cause through, who are able, and therefore chosen, to perform the historical deeds. World history is the history of such successes; the Bible knows nothing of this notion of success. When it announces a successful deed, it is duty-bound to announce in complete detail the failure involved in the success. The existence in the shadow, in the quiver, is the final word of the leaders in the biblical world.

Buber's biblical leaders—the patriarch, Moses, the judge, the king, and the prophet—are not sketches of characters but descriptions of persons in real situations. According to Buber, the Bible is not concerned with the differences between persons but with the differences between the situations in which the appointed person stands his test or fails. Biblical history, in Buber's thought, is "a dialogue in which man, in which the people, is spoken to and fails to answer, yet where the people in the midst of its failure continually rises up and tries to answer. It is the history of God's disappointments, but this history of disappointments constitutes a way, a way that leads from disappointment to disappointment and beyond all disappointments; it is the way of the people, the way of man, yes, the way of God through mankind."[40]

Buber claimed that when the Bible tries to look beyond these five manifestations of leadership to one that no longer stands amidst failure, when the idea of the messianic leader is conceived, it means nothing else by it than that "at last the answer shall be given: from out of mankind itself the word shall come . . . the word that answers God's word."[41] The messianic belief is a belief "in the real leader, in the setting right of the dialogue, in God's disappointment being at an end."[42] Buber made it clear that the biblical question of leadership is concerned with something greater than moral perfection. "The biblical leaders are the foreshadowing of the dialogical man, of the man who commits his whole being to God's dialogue with the world, and who stands firm throughout the dialogue."[43]

Buber's concept of biblical leadership means, therefore, everything political leadership does not. Biblical leadership always means a process of being led, of being lifted out of the community, and of a widening gulf between leader and community. According to Buber, the ever-greater failure of the leader, the ever-greater incompatibility with history in the common sense, means, from the biblical standpoint, the gradual overcoming of history:

• • •

The real way, from the Creation to the Kingdom, is trod not on the surface of success but in the depths of failure. The real work,

from the biblical point of view, is the late-recorded, the unre-
corded, the anonymous work. . . . The way leads through the
work that history does not write down, and that history cannot
write down, work that is not ascribed to him who did it, but
which possibly at some time in a distant generation will emerge
as having been done. . . . And when the biblical writer turns his
eyes toward the final, Messianic overcoming of history, he sees
how the outer history becomes engulfed, or rather how both the
outer history and the inner history fuse.[44]

◆ ◆ ◆

This interpretation set the tone for a concept of "Zion" as something greater than a patch of land in the Near East or a Jewish
state on this patch. As Buber said, "Zion implies a memory, a
demand, a mission. Zion is the foundation stone, the bedrock
and basis of the Messianic edifice of humanity." At the same time,
Zionism in its actual manifestations—country, language, political
independence, etc.—implied the opposite: "It is nothing more
than one of the vulgar forms of nationalism in our day, one which
recognizes no authority other than an imaginary national
interest."[45]

Buber did accept Ben-Gurion's emphasis on messianic vision
as a cornerstone of Judaism. But to Buber, this vision implied a
concrete commitment to the Kingdom of God: "Quasi-Zionism,
which strives to have a country only, has attained its purpose.
But the true Zionism, the love of Zion, the desire to establish
something like 'the city of a great king' (Psalms 48/3), of 'the king'
(Isaiah 6/5) is a living and enduring thing."[46] To Buber, the messianic ideal implied a concrete commitment to a dimension of life
that is truly historical, that is, ahistorical in the common sense of
the term. Ben-Gurion represented the leader engulfed in the
common—one may say vulgar—historical dimension. His ideas
and visions, under this system of thought, were nothing but
"witchcraft." Here is Buber's critique of Ben-Gurion at the ideological conference in 1957:

◆ ◆ ◆

Ben-Gurion rightly sees in the Messianic vision the second cor-
nerstone of living Judaism. But this . . . is in need of more
concreteness. It is not enough to set "the redemption of Israel"
side by side with "the redemption of the human race." The Mes-

sianic message is unique in the demand God makes upon the nations of men to realize His kingdom and in this way to take part in the redemption of the world. The message is applied especially to Israel and demands of it that it make an exemplary beginning in the actual work of realization, that it be a nation which establishes justice and truth in its institutions and activities. Therefore, Isaiah not only calls upon the Gentiles to stream to Mount Zion and there to receive the second Torah, the universal one, he supplements this by his summons to the House of Jacob to walk before them in the light of the Lord. Israel's monotheism differs from that of other nations in that the people, from this point of view, ought to live all their life in the service of the King, so is the message of redemption distinguished in that it calls upon the people to begin and pursue its active part. There are no mere ideas and visions here. There are demands of great actuality, upon whose fulfillment depends the destiny of the nation. These demands are not addressed only to those generations in which they were made, but to all generations, and to our generation in particular.

Behind everything that Ben-Gurion has said on that point there lies, it seems to me, the will to make the political factor supreme. He is one of the proponents of that kind of secularization which cultivated its "thoughts" and "visions" so diligently that it keeps men from hearing the voice of the living God. This secularization takes the form of an exaggerated politization. This politization of life here strikes at the very spirit itself. The spirit, with all its thoughts and visions, descends and becomes a function of politics. This phenomenon, which is supreme at the whole world at present, has very old roots. Even some kings in Israel are said to have gone so far as to employ false prophets whose prophesying was wholly a function of state policy.[47]

♦ ♦ ♦

Ben-Gurion's answer to Buber's critique in the ideological conference reflected the complexities involved. While stressing the common elements in their two approaches, Ben-Gurion only made clear once again the deep gap between them. He expressed pride that his concept of messianism as a cornerstone of Judaism and of the association between national and universal redemption were in line with Buber's thinking. He felt, however, that attributing to it a "politization" of redemption was wrong. "It is true that in my opinion, and I am sure this is shared by Professor Buber, there can be no redemption as long as a nation lives on foreign soil and depends on the goodwill of others, and that national revival in the homeland is one of the bases of the redemption of the Jews, but, like him, I think it is only one of the bases, and not complete redemption. There is no complete redemption without an ingathering of the exiles, without a society based on freedom, justice, equality and fraternity, and without redemption of the whole of the human race." Ben-Gurion claimed that he did not comprehend the meaning of the coming of the Kingdom of God and would not dare to argue over heavenly matters. But the messianic idea, in the sense of the striving for universal redemption, lives in the hearts of large numbers of youth, workers, and intellectuals in Israel, even if not all of them label their vision messianic, as did Professor Buber and himself. Ben-Gurion concluded by accepting Buber's claim that vision alone cannot bring about redemption. Actual commitments and actions are needed—like the nation-building tasks at hand.[48]

The meeting between Martin Buber and David Ben-Gurion in the ideological conference was far more than a meeting between "utopianism" and "politics." Buber considered both of these as false relationships between the spirit and everyday life. He objected equally to spurious idealism "toward which we may lift our gaze without incurring any obligation to recover from the exigencies of earth," and spurious realism, "which regards the spirit as only a function of life and transforms its unconditionality into a number of conditional characters: psychological, sociological, and others."[49] Ben-Gurion's messianism, on the other hand, represented the combination of both utopianism and politics. It had its intellectual roots in the search for meaning "beyond" historical action but rejected the duality between history and an ahistorical condition. To Ben-Gurion, ahistorical vision became associated with the historic moment; politics received messianic meaning.

The philosopher and the statesman were both devoted Zionists, both conceiving of the Zionist movement as an aspect of Jewish messianism. But while to the philosopher Zionism implied a commitment to the life of dialogue between man and God (and man and man), to the statesman it had a social-political meaning. Both men conceived of present reality as the beginning of redemption, in a universal context; but to Buber, redemption lay in the yielding of earthly life (through its true self-fulfilment) to a meeting between earth and heaven, life and spirit, while to Ben-Gurion it lay in the application of heavenly ideals to the tasks on earth.

In his article "Buber or Ben-Gurion?"[50] Ernst Simon tried to prove that Buber and Ben-Gurion, who shared the honor of being the most famous Jews of the mid-twentieth century, could not exist in the same spiritual climate. While Simon's thesis is supposedly based on an analysis of ideas, it remains on the level of political issues and stresses political disagreements as well as differences in rhetorical style. The political disagreements between Buber and Ben-Gurion and their Gogmagog clash during The Affair should not, however, overshadow the mutual interest the philosopher and the statesman had for each other and their mutual role, unobvious as it may have been to both of them, in the development of political thought in Israel. Simon claims that there could not have been true respect between the philosopher and the statesman since there was no mutual willingness to learn something real from each other's values; the common ground of their ways of life was too narrow to provide a basis for it. Yet ideas have a strange tendency to affect, and be affected, in spite of differences—even great differences—in life-styles and attitudes. As a matter of fact, both men admired each other for the characteristics they had in common. Buber admired Ben-Gurion's attempt to attribute meaning to realistic deeds. Ben-Gurion admired Buber for his earthly concerns. They both had a role in each other's thought, which made their political clashes particularly hard and emotional. Ben-Gurion had been extremely hurt and shocked by Buber's signing of the public statement of 1961, although their political struggles dated back to the 1940s. No other intellectual stood in such firm opposition to Ben-Gurion before The Affair as had Buber, and no other intellectual posed such a challenge to his most basic decisions and actions.[51] This was because both men combined comprehensive world views with very realistic concerns—a combination which characterized all their correspondence. For instance, on Buber's 85th birthday, Ben-Gurion sent the philosopher the greetings of an "admirer and opponent."[52] Buber's response demanded that Ben-Gurion parole Aharon Cohen, an intellectual convicted for security charges in the late 1950s.[53]

The Tensions over Political Messianism

although the philosophers large-
ly participated in the promotion of political messianism in the
1950s, deep intellectual tensions over this notion gradually
evolved. Three of these tensions will be discussed: those over
ideals and force, over state and society, and over messianic vision
and policy making.

Ideals and Force

in April 1950, Ben-Gurion gave
a talk before the military high command. In his speech, published later as an article called "Uniqueness and Destiny," Ben-
Gurion established a link between the military, as one of the
major forces of nation-building, and the fulfilment of universal
values.[54] There is no soul without a body, he declared, and no
universal human destiny without existence as a nation. And since
Ben-Gurion's idea of existence as a nation included a physically,
intellectually, and morally strong army, the military, an instrument of force often considered to breed stupidity, careerism,
idleness, arrogance, etc., became a carrier of the eternal values
of the ancient prophets. This was one of the strongest expressions
of political messianism—attributing a universal meaning to an
earthly institution like the army and demanding that it adhere by
a messianic mission. This demand required very real policy decisions regarding the army, which Ben-Gurion did not hesitate to
make in his role as Minister of Defense:

◆ ◆ ◆

*It is incumbent upon the army to implant within the youth under
its influence—from the youth brigade and upward—the basic
values of cleanliness—physical and moral, a knowledge of the
language and the country, physical and mental dexterity, love of
the homeland and fraternal loyalty, bravery and creative initiative, discipline and order, fitness to work and a pioneering
drive—these in addition to the military qualities which are
needed for security in the most narrow sense.*[55]

◆ ◆ ◆

Under Ben-Gurion's leadership the army took on many civil activities in line with these notions. Facing the unprecedented problem of absorbing immigrants from 70 exiles, Ben-Gurion hoped that young immigrants would integrate into the society through a knowledge of the language and the country obtained through service in the army. In 1950, the military seemed one of the only institutions in which a "melting pot" could be effective within a reasonable time. Ben-Gurion, therefore, expanded the scope of army activities to include educational tasks, settlement of the land, and various social service activities.

Some intellectuals, however, could not accept this association between an instrument of force and universal values. Significantly, those who objected did not do so on the grounds of the moralism which characterizes modern political thought whenever it considers the question of force. In one of the most important intellectual pamphlets written in Israel, Yeshayahu Leibowitz, a philosopher and scientist, provided a strong critique of political messianism on different grounds. Leibowitz's statements are particularly interesting since they were written in response to a specific event—an overzealous reprisal by an Israel army unit in which 50 Arab civilians in the village of Kibbya were killed.[56]

Without referring to them explicitly, Leibowitz addressed his criticism both to Buber and Ben-Gurion. First, he objected to the condemnation of violence on the grounds of a moralism that does not entail responsibility. He considered use of violence as part of the hard test a nation faces once it is liberated. It is easy, he claimed, to object to violence in situations in which the means of violence are not available. But when a nation gains independence and wishes to live in a real historical dimension rather than in a metahistorical or metaphysical one, it accepts war as an undesirable, yet inevitable, phenomenon. Leibowitz argued that it is possible to justify the killings at Kibbya before world opinion; it is even possible to justify them in terms of certain moral principles that can be reduced to a rational calculation. "There undoubtedly exists a justification for that deed, but let us not attempt to find it," wrote Leibowitz, demanding that the burden of these killings be shared by all Israelis. He claimed that despite all the right and justified calculations, there exists a moral postulate, which is not bound to any calculation and which carries a curse over all calculation. This, he wrote, is demonstrated in the biblical story of Jacob's sons who were morally justified for a massacre they committed but were cursed by the Lord for all generations that followed.

Leibowitz made it clear that his use of a biblical example had nothing to do with a special biblical morality. It was merely to illustrate, he wrote, that that act itself is forbidden. All his life, Leibowitz, a religious man, objected to the derivation of moral values, especially national moral values, from the Bible. He never accepted the existence of a moral code unique for any nation, including the Jewish one. Ethics, he claimed, is a human secular category. In Judaism, the only ethics is that implied by the demand to fulfill the Godly commandments. Any ethical interpretation of these commandments stands beyond religion and is open to many different interpretations. Leibowitz was particularly harsh on justification of acts of statehood on the grounds of "religious ethics," calling it in later years "a prostitution of the Jewish religion in the interest of national cannibalism and lust for power."[57] But nowhere was Leibowitz's critique as penetrating as in the words he used after the Kibbya incident:

♦ ♦ ♦

This was a consequence of the application of the religious category of sacredness *to social, national and political matters—a use widely made in our education and mass media. Concepts of sacredness—that is, concepts regarding the absolute* beyond all categories of human thinking and evaluation—*are applied to the earthly sphere. From a religious point of view* only God is sacred, and only his imperative is absolute, while all *the values of man and all his duties and roles are secular and lack absolute meaning. Homeland, state, nation—these are supreme duties and roles, which sometimes even demand hard commitment, but they never become sacred, that is, they never stand the test, and critique, of anything above themselves. In sacred matters—maybe only in sacred matters—man can operate* without any restraint. *We are uprooting the category of sacredness from its ground and applying it to matters for which it was not destined, with all the danger implied by this distorted use.*[58]

♦ ♦ ♦

Leibowitz, an unusually outspoken person, always used equally harsh language when he addressed politicians or his fellow intellectuals. (Stalin, he said, had to send intellectuals to the camps to keep them silent. Here, all that is needed is for the leader to warn that a writer or other humanist would not be invited for lunch.) Leibowitz never got along with Ben-Gurion even long before The Affair. The Prime Minister accused him of hating the Bible, while he accused the Prime Minister of hating "empirical Judaism" and scorned Ben-Gurion's preoccupation with the Bible as "Sabbaticism." They regarded each other as complex personalities (both being right of course) and suspected each other's motives. The statesman accused the philosopher of insisting upon the separation of church and state in order to have an independent church which would persistently challenge the state. The philosopher accused the statesman of keeping religion a "mistress of the secular government" and defined the state of Israel under Ben-Gurion "a secular brat known in public as religious." He objected, he said, both as a believer and humanist.

The objection from the humanist's point of view is of particular importance. To Leibowitz it was not the use of force that was problematic but its legitimation as part of a universal system of ethics. Such a concept of force overlooks those imperatives which forbid the use of force, or certain degrees of it, under *any* circumstances. The philosopher's objection went beyond the fear that universal or messianic values would be abused to justify particularistic action. He was no less concerned, he wrote, when the same ethical system that justifies force is the one that restrains it. Leibowitz objected to any application of an absolute code to human morality, which is by nature pragmatic, relative, and changing. Not only is it not in line with principles of the Jewish religion, it is dangerous, because the more genuine the belief in universal values as guides and restraints, the wider the margin of error in their application.

Ben-Gurion was an activist in foreign affairs, but he never glorified war. Warfare to him was never an end in itself, and he truly rejected any philosophy of that kind. But this only made the intellectual tension more profound. "It was the Prophets of Israel," Ben-Gurion declared to the intellectuals' dismay, "who called upon nations not to 'lift up sword against nation,' nor 'to learn war anymore,' but to 'beat their swords into ploughshares, and their spears into pruninghooks.' They taught that it was man's mission to labour creatively and live at peace with his fellows. But they also taught the importance of defense and military preparedness when threatened by hostile forces."[59] Ben-Gurion was proud of building an army which he could easily describe as the fulfilment of prophetic demands. But this was exactly the problem, as Leibowitz realized in the 1950s and others a decade later. The army did indeed play a formidable role in welding together the different immigrant groups, in breaking down clan and community barriers, in establishing flourishing agricultural settlements, and it did generally keep out of politics. But this blurred the distinction between ideals and force, as it had to if the army were to be blessed with a messianic mission. In The Affair, the intellectuals would doubt that link, and the messianic rhetoric regarding the military would not seem right, especially once this instrument of force would no longer be under the tight control of Ben-Gurion. For instance, under Ben-Gurion's leadership such slogans as "the good ones to the air force" were commonly used as part of the recruitment efforts of the army. In the 1960s the philosophers would awaken to the messianic overtones involved in those slogans. "The good ones," Rotenstreich would then declare, "to do good; the pilots to the air force."[60]

State and Society

One of the important implications of political messianism concerns the primacy of the state over society. In the messianic conception, the state becomes both a means and an end. The state is an end in itself because its very existence has a historical, even metahistorical, meaning. But it is also a means to the end of national and universal redemption.[61] The state, therefore, serves both the pragmatist and the utopian. As an end in itself it engages in the pragmatic tasks of maintaining security and social order, collecting taxes, distributing and redistributing resources, and so forth. As a means to an end it engages in the preparation of man for his utopian role; it brings out the "hidden forces" which supposedly make such a role possible and lifts society toward a higher (or "perfect") stage of development. The combination of pragmatic politics and utopian vision, as well as the need to carry out the tasks of nation-building quickly and efficiently, give rise to an ideology of "statism," attributing to the state those functions and values traditionally associated with the social infra-structure.

"Statism" has always been an issue in Israeli politics due to the voluntary nature of Israel's pre-state society. Israeli politics in the 1950s were dominated by debates over Ben-Gurion's abolition of the pre-state paramilitary organizations and his efforts to integrate the various educational systems in the country which were controlled by partisan factions into a national educational system. Intellectuals took relatively little part in those debates and generally sided with Ben-Gurion in his efforts to build an integrated state. The question is why they hooked up the issue of statism during The Affair and why Lavon became a symbol of those spontaneous forces in society suppressed by the state and its ruler. The origins of this political stand can be traced to the philosophers' objection to the role of the state in the ideology of political messianism—an objection becoming increasingly more salient with the growing functions assumed by the modern bureaucratic state. In 1959, Rotenstreich had made his objection explicit, warning that the utopian motive in modern developing societies and the endowment of the national government with the halo of utopia could result in the total identification of social creativity with the bureaucratic institutions of government. In a lecture before Labor party activists, Rotenstreich argued that social life should not be conceived as existing only within the framework of the state. The state is merely an abstract entity requiring social approval and legitimacy and cannot be conceived separately from the social processes composing and legitimizing it. The state is nothing but the sum of these processes, and its decisions are not made in a vacuum; they are expressions of human decisions in the social sphere.

Rotenstreich presented this state of affairs as not only desirable but necessary. He claimed that a state lacking the element of social debate loses its vitality. Furthermore, as man's dependence on the state bureaucracy increases, the state is faced with the unprecedented need to reallocate some of its power. The modern state must limit the power granted it by the many functions it fulfils in order to maintain its ability to function at all. Nonpolitical social activity must thus be encouraged in order to avoid degeneration. Rotenstreich concluded that if indeed the historic function of government is the formation of a new society, such a society must be formed not by messianic theory but by daily social activity.[62]

The philosophers' belief in social association and human spontaneity as existing, or having to exist, beyond the sphere of government received its fullest expression in the philosophy of Martin Buber. A nation, Buber contended, is a community to the degree that it is a community of communities. If the family, for instance, does not flourish, neither does the nation-state, which becomes nothing more than "a machine stoked with the bodies of generations of men."[63] In the many interviews Buber gave on current issues, he criticized one major phenomenon: the politization of social life. He called for a rebirth of the commune and defined the state as the mere territorial concentration of a nation intended to serve "true development—in body and soul."[64] He objected to the politization of social life in modern Israel, although he realized it was a universal phenomenon:

◆ ◆ ◆

Society's assimilation in the State was accelerated by the fact that, as a result of modern industrial development and its ordered chaos, involving the struggle of all against all for access to raw materials and for a larger share of the world market, there grew up, in place of the old struggles between States, struggles between whole societies. The individual society, feeling itself threatened not only by its neighbors' lust for aggression but also by things in general, knew no way of salvation save in complete submission to the principle of a centralized power; and in the democratic forms of society no less than in its totalitarian forms, it made this its guiding principle.[65]

◆ ◆ ◆

But Buber's main contribution lay in evaluating the state by considering it in the broader societal and human context, while disallowing for an idealization of that context beyond the meeting of man and man. Questioned in an interview about how the messianic ideal of the prophets could be realized under contemporary conditions, he had this answer:

◆ ◆ ◆

The men of politics think that all they need strive for is the good of the State at this hour, as they see it. Nor do they consider this to be at cross-purposes with morality. On the contrary, if someone should come and say their conduct is immoral they will unceremoniously shut him up. They will say it is the very essence of

morality, because their means and ends serve the life of the na-
tion. As if group selfishness is any more moral than individual
selfishness. In contrast to them you find the men of morality, who
quote general principles of right and wrong based on the given
situation—without asking each day what can be done under the
conditions of that day—and without harm to the nation's life. For
such a scrutiny requires the interaction of things—a conscience
that is not readily deceived and a trustworthy view of reality.[66]

◆ ◆ ◆

This statement is of great importance, defining three ethical
positions derived from competing approaches to the relationship
between state and society. The first position associates social ethics with the interest of the state. The second applies it indiscrim-
inately to the conduct of the state. The third recognizes the
tension between the two, as well as the need for reconciliation
between social choice and political reality. The temptation to use
this typology for a classification of ethical positions in the Ben-
Gurion era must be avoided. As will now be demonstrated, the
typology helps explain a major ethical conflict of this era in terms
of differing attitudes toward state-society relations, but Ben-
Gurion and the philosophers did not simply find themselves in
different cells of the typology. Reality was far more complex.

The hardest political issue ever debated in Israel concerned
relations with Germany. Should Israel accept reparations from
Germany? Should diplomatic relations between the two countries be instituted? Should arms deals with Germany be signed?
Should the Nazi executioner Adolf Eichmann be tried by Israeli
courts? These questions required some of the hardest choices any
state ever faced. Political institutions conducting the affairs of a
sovereign state were forced to touch upon matters involving the
essence of social life. And these considerations went far beyond
the need of the government to cope with societal sentiment.
Israel in the 1950s was, in essence, a community of refugees
who had just escaped the horrors of the holocaust and whose
whole *raison d'être* consisted of the human imperative to memorize the holocaust for all generations to come. The historic answer to the holocaust, and the avoidance of future holocausts, lay
in the building of a Jewish society and state. The state was now
to conduct *normal* relations with Germany, and both societies
were to engage in transactions that in the minds of Israelis were
largely conceived as deals with Satan.

The debates over this issue brought to the fore the three ethical positions discussed above. The first suggested that the survival of the state, being an end in itself, justified a pact even with "Satan." This notion was expressed simply and boldly by a young Kibbutz member during one of the controversies over the purchase of arms from Germany. To him, any policy intended to assure the existence and security of the state was moral. He did not ignore the question of morality but wrote that he envied those who knew how to relate it to political life. He justified the weapons purchases on the grounds of the survival of the state. When there is no choice, he wrote in a small Kibbutz publication, weapons should be purchased even from Satan.[67]

However, many objected to this position on the grounds that there exist societal imperatives beyond the scope of state interests. One writer questioned whether there remained any ethical principle unsubordinated to political calculations. He claimed that not only must ends be considered in ethical terms, but means as well. He who justifies all means for the sake of a just end loses the ability to choose not only between moral and immoral means but between useful and unuseful ones. Since such a choice is crucial, it should be made by one criterion only—social ethics. The choice whether or not to purchase arms from Germany must be made by considering such factors as the concept society has of its desired way of life, its concept of the meaning of human and national dignity, and its overall position in matters of conscience.[68]

Ben-Gurion's justification for his policy of reconciliation with Germany is significant in that it did not follow either of these two positions. Loyal to his way of thinking, he could not accept a sheer utilitarian approach; nor did he accept, as statesman, the primacy of the social imperative. For him, political messianism provided a solution, expressed in a series of letters he exchanged with Yariv Ben-Aharon, the young Kibbutz member. This young man happened to be the son of a prominent Labor leader who sent Ben-Gurion his son's essay from what amounted to a combination of fatherly pride and political reasoning. Ben-Gurion's response was unexpected:

♦ ♦ ♦

I was shocked by your essay, and shocked by the immoral attitude expressed in the essay, although it is hard for me to assume you do not consider ethics at all, only practical utility. . . .

You supposedly discard morality for the sake of utility. I am not ready to accept this wrong and dangerous approach. And I assume you don't believe either that the end justifies all means. There are moral values and they are obligatory! *I object to your approach in the name of ethics, and I am willing to admit—in the name of Prophetic ethics. And the essence of Prophetic ethics in the area we deal with here, and in your essay, has been defined in two short verses by Jeremiah the Prophet:*

"In those days they shall no longer say: 'The fathers have eaten sour grapes, and the children's teeth are set on edge.' But every one shall die for his own sin, each man who eats sour grapes, his teeth shall be set on edge." (Jeremiah, 31: 29–30)[69]

Several days later, Ben-Gurion received the following response:

A statesman may believe in prophetic ethics, devote himself to its study, use it as a compass directing his way, and at the same time admit that it is impossible in this world of ours to consider every political act as its fulfillment. . . . Prophetic ethics would benefit if it were disengaged from contemporary political questions concerning our need to receive robbed Jewish property from Germany.[70]

◆ ◆ ◆

Yariv Ben-Aharon added that even the Hasmonean Kingdom, which restored Jewish political independence after 400 years of Hellenistic rule, had not considered itself a prophetic movement since Jewish tradition contends that prophecy and miracles have not been renewed since the destruction of the temple. Hinting at a possible analogy to modern times, Ben-Aharon elaborated on the Hasmonean belief that prophets no longer existed—a belief held by them in spite of the military victories of the times and the gaining of political independence.

Ben-Gurion's response outlined at length his German policy, but he had this to say in defense of political messianism:

◆ ◆ ◆

I do not feel, as you do, that prophecy has ceased. I can hear the voice of the prophet also in later writings, as late as Spinoza, and Einstein, and Marx. I agree with you there are no miracles performed in our times—and I don't believe there ever were miracles. But prophecy has not ceased. Prophecy is the voice of human conscience—and this has not been silenced and will not be silent.[71]

♦ ♦ ♦

In light of this exchange it is understandable that the two contenders for a conciliatory policy toward Germany—Buber and Ben-Gurion—were also great adversaries over the German problem. Both the philosopher and the statesman found themselves in a tragic dilemma: having to cope with a phenomenon that did not fall into any conceivable pattern of human behavior. To Buber, the Nazi executioners just had no place in the dimension of human existence. "They have detached themselves from the human realm so immensely into the sphere of monstrous inhumanity inaccessible to my power of imagination that not even hatred could rise in me."[72] To the extent that hope could be derived for future generations, Buber singled out those Germans who opposed the crimes. The satanic element in man, he warned, must not hamper man in achieving his goals for the future. The future lay in a dialogue between man and man and between nation and nation.

Ben-Gurion's German policy, as he often declared, was no less derived from deep, emotional sources. He also searched for conciliation between a social sentiment about the past and a rational policy for the future. At the same time, the lessons he learned from the past, and his goals for the future, were different from those of Buber: to make all effort, on the national level, to avoid future holocausts and become a strong sovereign state with equal status within the family of nations. Ben-Gurion, like Buber, refused to place all Germans into one satanic category. It is impossible to get weapons from Satan, he declared. He insisted, instead, on a definition of relations with Germany as one of friendship and trust, claiming there existed a "new Germany." But the statesman's notion of friendship did not resemble that of the philosopher; in the field of politics, friendship and national interest are inseparable.

It is now possible to grasp the significance of the famous meeting between Buber and Ben-Gurion in March 1962 in which the philosopher demanded that Adolf Eichmann, who was on trial in Israel, should not be executed. Buber objected to the trial in

Israel from the beginning, suggesting that since Eichmann's crimes were crimes against the human race as a whole, he should be tried before an international tribunal. He was opposed to the penalty, since no penalties exist for such crimes. To Ben-Gurion, however, the fate of humanity and that of the Jewish people were not separable. Both the societal imperative and the imperative of universal justice thus demanded, to him, a trial and a penalty by the courts of the sovereign state.

Vision and Policymaking

An implication of political messianism that caused much debate between Ben-Gurion and the intellectuals in the early 1960s concerned the role of vision in policymaking. In the context of policymaking, vision may be defined as a set of goals exceeding the obvious parameters of systems of resources. This is what Ben-Gurion referred to when he called for the need to use messianic vision as a guide to policymaking. If the state is the creation of messianic faith, then the continued survival of the state depends on persisting messianic vision. There was a strong realistic element involved in that demand. Ben-Gurion believed that the whole endeavor in the state of Israel would fail if only "normal" social, economic, and political conditions were relied upon. He also understood that policies beyond the normal path involve a cost that can only be borne in a specific state of mind. The intellectuals were assigned an important role in both regards: exploring extraordinary alternatives and creating the state of mind necessary for their pursuit.[73] The challenge worried them mainly because of the arbitrary nature of vision. Messianic vision translated into action cannot keep up with established sets of principles; calculations of economic costs must be ignored, and many other constraints overlooked. Utopianism opens the door to very earthly modes of behavior such as "doism"—the tendency to pursue desired policy while disregarding systemic consequences (which principles are intended to guard.) Great projects are undertaken both as monuments of nation-building and as the fulfilment of a historical mission. If the drying of swamps, land reclamation, or the housing of immigrants has messianic meaning, then no other considerations should stand in the way. This entails a specific policymaking process, one based on "big" decisions, great determination, centralization, and gross improvisation when things go wrong. Planners, economists, and other representatives of rational decision-making become a hindrance to the tasks at hand. They are often neutralized by the representatives of messianic faith. The man of vision and the man of principle can hardly coexist in the policy-making system. Both have a claim to the "long-range" but the first considers its benefits while the second its costs. Their relationship becomes even more complex due to the difficulty in every specific situation in deciding who is right and who is wrong, or what path to follow when both are right.

That difficulty came to light in a meeting between Ben-Gurion and eleven men of letters assembled in Aharon Katzir's home on July 4, 1961.[74] Ben-Gurion opened the meeting (recorded by a stenographer) by stating, "[the meeting] has nothing to do with politics." The subject of the discussion, Ben-Gurion announced, was purely prosaic: "Can we become a chosen people? Can we become a light unto the nations? Is the redemption of the people of Israel possible?" Having outlined the "prosaic" agenda, Ben-Gurion described at length the major goals for the country and the conditions under which they might be fulfilled. National goals such as security, education, population of the land, absorption of immigrants, and economic independence, he argued, have no solid economic and sociological ground. The pursuit of these goals on the basis of routine policy procedures is thus impossible. Furthermore, the demand for such procedures may prevent the recruitment of the unobvious resources needed. The intellectuals' claim that the messianic era is over, Ben-Gurion added, endangers the nation-building effort, which depends on their willingness to combine scientific and literary work with a messianic vision.

In their reply, the intellectuals acknowledged the important function of visionary statements to the setting of societal tasks and to the recruitment of support for their accomplishment. They strongly objected, however, to their use as standards of performance. It is necessary at times to give up messianic vision, they argued, in order to clarify discrepancies between desired goals and existing reality. Ephraim Urbach, a famous Talmudic scholar, referred to the Prime Minister's frequent mention of the messianic vision with which the ancient prophets were blessed and reminded him that there are fewer paragraphs in the book of Isaiah dealing with messianism than with social critique. Under existing conditions in the state of Israel, he said, the proportion between vision and critique should follow the example set by Isaiah. Even Jeremiah, who had strong messianic beliefs, took a very realistic nonmessianic position when Jerusalem faced destruction.

A leading economist, Don Patinkin, was mainly concerned with the negative correlation between vision and efficiency. Vision permits the overlooking of considerations of resources. With messianic vision as a guide, important goals are considered, but their systemic implications are not. Population of the desert is important but so is education, and the trade-off has to be calculated. Had anyone ever considered how many schools had not been built as a result of the national water carrier, he asked. And if a decision is made to avoid cost considerations in the light of a policy's expected benefit, it should still be asked whether this particular policy justifies such a costly decision. Furthermore, messianic vision prevents an operationalization of goals. Should the desert be inhabited by 50,000, 100,000, or 200,000 people? What are the implications of any of these alternative models to agriculture in other regions of the land, to industry, to the overall quality of life? Hinting at a possible division of labor, he claimed that while the man of vision may not pay attention to questions of resources, the economist must.

Ben-Gurion's reply included a surprise. To him, population of the desert went far beyond the obvious goals mentioned. The desert, if inhabited, would serve as Israel's strategic gate to the awakening third world in Asia and Africa—a goal the distinguished economist did not even consider. Vision, Ben-Gurion argued, consists of the observation of conditions that are nonexisting at the moment but which might exist. Everything the experts have told us not to do for lack of resources, he added, we have done, and successfully so. Ben-Gurion admitted that the experts trying to prevent him from supposedly irrational acts had adhered to their professional duty. If one considers all scientific data and nothing else, he claimed, the position of the experts is justified. But science rarely goes out of its way, while the individual qua individual does. Man, Ben-Gurion argued, is capable of vision.

Ben-Gurion stressed the departmentalized nature of systematic knowledge which prevents the intellectuals from sensing reality as a whole. The setting of national goals, however, required an overall picture. For instance, the Israeli economy, Ben-Gurion argued, will not flourish as long as it is oriented merely toward the European market. The Europeans can satisfy their needs by themselves, while the millions of people in Asia and Africa cannot. Reaching new markets of this kind is a goal derived neither from calculations by the economist, nor from the word of God, but from man's intuition—from his ability to consider the whole scope of things and their future course. How Jews can reach the people of Asia, Ben-Gurion concluded, and why the population of the desert is relevant to this task, is not written in books, it has nothing to do with economics, or with sociology, philosophy, biology, or physics. There exists no such science.

Ben-Gurion's point was well taken. Most social thinkers rarely evaluate societal performance by comparing it to extraordinary goals of the kind he proposed in the meeting. The division of labor, according to which the statesman supposedly determines the goals and the person of knowledge the means, is strictly adhered to.[75] It was the unholy alliance between behavioral positivism and political inactivism that Ben-Gurion hoped to avoid.[76] He understood, in principle, the importance of the intellectual's participation in the policymaking process. The perfect society required intellectuals to point the way. Messianic (and socialist) thought always acknowledged the need to expose internal faults and make efforts to mend them. The intellectual, as teacher, was expected to have vision in order to teach it to future generations.

It must be noted, however, that vision had a very specific meaning to Ben-Gurion: the goals were predetermined. Nowhere did he consider institutionalizing the intellectual's participation in the determination or evaluation of goals. The intellectual was not to concern himself merely with means; however, the goals to be achieved were not really open to debate. This was never obvious in Ben-Gurion's references to the intellectual in Israel, who was expected to operate within the right state of mind, but it can be detected in his references to intellectuals in general. For instance, in response to a letter his daughter sent him from France, in which she noted the intellectuals' objection to de Gaulle, Ben-Gurion simply associated those intellectuals with communism. He labeled them "doctrinaires," acquiring their patterns of thought from Moscow and incapable of observing reality as it is.[77] He could not accept their critical role as a contribution to society. The intellectual was expected to

carry a vision and disseminate it, but not to determine its content. This may have been a convenient status quo for both the
statesman and the intellectual in the 1950s, but it became a
source of political dispute during The Affair. This can be demonstrated with regard to the debate between Ben-Gurion and Ernst
Simon, a philosopher of education.

In February 1963, Ben-Gurion appeared before Parliament in
his role as Prime Minister and Minister of Defense to respond to
a proposal to abolish military rule over Israel's Arab population.
As usual, Ben-Gurion's parliamentary appearance included a long
controversial speech in which every political opponent since time
immemorial received his due share of comment. This time, Ben-
Gurion reserved special words for a group of intellectuals who
had just signed a public statement calling for the abolishment of
military rule.

◆ ◆ ◆

*The day before yesterday I read in one of the newspapers of a
public statement by professors, doctors and other dignitaries
against military rule. I know some of the signatories of this statement and I admire them as intellectuals and great scholars. But
I must say to my regret that this statement has not raised their
reputation in my eyes. . . . I cannot find any intellectual or
ethical justification for the assumption behind it, that the opinions of professors Buber, Avimelech, Urbach and others in matters of security have any special weight, greater than that of
every other citizen of the state, as if they understand better
the external and internal security needs of Israel than the inhabitants of Tel Katzir and Degania, or the officers of the
airforce and armored forces or other scientists and professors
who refused to sign the statement. . . . If I shall need an expert
opinion in matters of Talmudic commentary I shall gladly refer
to Professor Urbach, in Godly matters to Professor Buber and in
matters of wheeling and dealing and economics to Professor Patinkin. But I do not recognize the supreme expertise of these
distinguished professors in matters of security or in matters of
political ethics.*[78]

◆ ◆ ◆

Simon's response in a newspaper article expressed wonder over
whether Ben-Gurion's insistence upon specialization implied that

matters of security were his speciality as Minister of Defense and matters of political ethics were his speciality as Prime Minister. Simon mentioned Ben-Gurion's declared opposition to intellectuals speaking in one voice, and his interest in active participation by the intellectual in the formation of the social character of the state—two views which contradicted his claim that intellectuals have no special say in matters of politics. "Isn't politics one of the elements forming the social character of the state?" asked Simon. If Ben-Gurion feels, as he always claims, that teaching and education are interrelated, then teachers have not only a right, but a duty, to express their opinions. Simon added that while politicians qua politicians are sometimes required to lie, scientists qua scientists are associated with the quest of the truth, and, hence, deserve to be heard.

Simon acknowledged that Buber's speciality might be labeled "Godly matters" but reminded the readers that Buber's philosophy did not distinguish between religion and ethics. If Buber or his students were to find out that an ethical imperative had been overlooked, he queried, doesn't their opinion carry special authority? Simon noted that while Buber objected to the notion of the philosopher-king, Ben-Gurion accepted it. To Ben-Gurion, like Plato, philosophers are the real experts on matters of statehood, and statesmen are the real philosophers. Thus, wrote Simon, while Ben-Gurion goes to greater extremes than Buber in the authority he grants the intellectuals in principle, he plays down every attempt on their behalf to voice their opinion on crucial matters.[79]

Ben-Gurion's response, which appeared two days later in the same newspaper,[80] is very interesting, since while he acknowledged again the national, historic mission of the educator, he stressed that teachers should refrain from partisan conceptions. In other words, the teacher, "from kindergarten counsellor to university professor" should disseminate national and universal values, which supposedly exist beyond any partisan conception. This sheds light on Ben-Gurion's thinking. Political messianism implied the existence of knowledge and values of an objective status, beyond partisan interpretations. Once national action is considered in light of universal ethics, then the mainstream interpretation of national life carries eternal value, while all other interpretations (such as those by Buber's group) become partisan. Ben-Gurion did not see any contradiction between his demand that the intellectual should become more active in the formation of the social character of the state and his refusal to grant the intellectual a greater say in matters of politics. Activity, to him, implied a specific set of commitments and values, not a dialogue of "partisan" nature. Ben-Gurion's perception of the true intellectual as a mainstream thinker became even more apparent when he claimed, in response to Simon, that he did not accept Simon's distinction between the politician and the scientist in matters of truth. The scientist has no monopoly over the quest of truth, Ben-Gurion claimed, with great justification. He did not elaborate, however, on who does.

In 1963, this point could not pass unnoticed. *Min Hayessod*, the publication of Ben-Gurion's opponents during The Affair, had this reaction to his debate with Simon:

◆ ◆ ◆

One person in the country has a monopoly over everything: over truth and righteousness, justice and morality, over the kingdom of the spirit and over democracy. Not only does he have a monopoly, he is the one and only in charge of determining what is truth, who can talk in the name of truth, what is intellect and who is entitled to be called an intellectual.[81]

◆ ◆ ◆

Another reaction to the debate came from Shmuel Sambursky, a philosopher of science who was close to Simon's political circles while remaining an admirer of Ben-Gurion. In a letter to the Prime Minister he tried to justify the scientist's special role in politics. Scientists have learned the lesson of scientific specialization—he who specializes for many years in one field, such as national security, may attribute to security questions a greater role than they deserve. Thus, the scientist's request to restore the right proportions stems not from his greater wisdom but from his academic experience and approach, that is, the perception of things from a certain distance.[82]

Ben-Gurion's answer to this letter indicates how strongly he conceived policymaking within the framework of political messianism. He accepted every point made by Sambursky. He asserted the right of the scientist to voice his opinion, allowed his own fallibility on questions of security, and recognized that a person specializing in matters of national defense may attribute too much weight to security. But to the extent to which he can judge himself, Ben-Gurion wrote, he specializes not in defense but in the future of the nation. To Ben-Gurion there was no distinction between the pragmatic and the utopian, the short-range and the long-range, the particular and the universal. Political messianism was strongly linked to philosophical monism. Preoccupation with national defense, he believed, was not in contradiction to a comprehensive outlook; emphasis on the security question was part of a far greater vision. "To some extent [security] is the most crucial problem but—this is at any rate what I feel—it does not conceal from my eyes and blur in my consciousness the importance of other problems and needs, because I experience every day, not just all the problems of the state, but the main problems of the whole of the Jewish people."[83]

The Biblical Scholars
Symbols vs. Facts

Pedestrians who happened to pass by Tel Aviv's Press Center on the afternoon of May 12, 1960, witnessed an unusual event. Local and foreign journalists, military and civilian officials, writers, artists, members of the Prime Minister's family, and many other dignitaries were arriving at the Center holding small pocket Bibles in their hands. The press conference that took place inside made headlines the next morning:

Ben-Gurion Gives His Version of Tale of Exodus from Egypt
Jerusalem Post Reporter
Tel Aviv.—The prime minister turned bible scholar yesterday to preach his theory to the press that the biblical version of the exodus referred to only a comparative handful of Hebrews, and that the great majority of the Children of Israel never went to Egypt.

Mr. Ben-Gurion declared before a press gathering at Beit Sokolow that no more than 600 persons wandered through the desert with Moses. . . .[1]

Ben-Gurion's theory on the exodus from Egypt was only one of the many unconventional biblical theories he expounded during his years in office. His well-publicized biblical studies were a masterpiece of symbolic politics, which is the subject of this chapter. First, a description of Ben-Gurion's lecture in the news conference is given in order to highlight the political functions of the Bible during this era. Then, the chapter analyzes the challenge put forth to biblical scholars. These scholars, especially members of The Israeli Society for Biblical Research, played a major role in the enhancement of Ben-Gurion's political symbol system. The challenge, it is argued, was only seriously contemplated with the routine use of biblical symbols and their incorporation into the common language of politicians and bureaucrats in the early 1960s.

The Lecture of 1960

In his essay on "The Mask of Politics," Maurice Cranston stressed the politician's preoccupation with symbols. "First of all," he wrote, "politicians talk! If politics is an art, it is one of the performing arts, and not one of the creative ones."[2] The political speaker, he added, is not simply a citizen who stands up spontaneously and speaks his mind. His function is to persuade his audience to accept, or agree to, or approve of a certain policy.

Although my analysis stresses the ideological and political functions of Ben-Gurion's speech, it should be noted that in the case of Ben-Gurion's biblical studies, the "mask of politics" is not easy to lift. Ben-Gurion's lecture had policy functions, but not obvious ones; and he did use political slogans, yet rather sophisticated ones.[3] While slogans are composed of "one word, one meaning,"[4] Ben-Gurion's studies were an impressive intellectual effort. It should also be noted that although Ben-Gurion attributed special significance to the Bible, his approach to it was secular, as a historian and perhaps as a politician but not as a believer, in any strictly religious sense.

Ben-Gurion began his lecture[5] by claiming that a person need not be a believer, or be bound by the written tradition, in order to appreciate the exodus from Egypt as an undeniable historical fact. An event that has been etched so deeply into the consciousness of a nation and whose reverberations are heard in almost all the books of the Prophets and in several of the books of the Writings, is without doubt a historical event. Citing various references to the event, Ben-Gurion declared that one need not blindly accept all traditional assertions linked to the event. A thorough study of the books of the Bible and the Prophets might encourage conclusions different from those commonly accepted. He admitted that he had doubts regarding traditional interpretations of the exodus, which stemmed from an explicit ideological perspective.

◆ ◆ ◆

The rebirth of Israel and the War of Independence placed the bible before me in a new light. After I delved into it, considering the facts of the War of Independence and the settlement of Israel in our day, questions were raised within me to which biblical commentators in Israel throughout the generations had not paid sufficient attention, because to them the concepts nation, tribes, conquest, war, geography, Israel, settlement, and mother tongue were abstract concepts.[6]

◆ ◆ ◆

This perspective led Ben-Gurion to propose an interesting thesis suggesting that the Hebrews had always lived in the land, and only one of its families went to Egypt.[7] Now Ben-Gurion ventured to prove that the third generation of those who went to Egypt, numbering only 600 people rather than 600,000 as traditionally believed, left Egypt and returned to their land after wandering in the desert, during which time Moses refined the ancient faith of the Hebrews in one God. The event of the exodus from Egypt, he claimed, attained its historical importance thanks to Moses and the role he played in shaping the image of those who left Egypt, but the tribes of Israel remained in the land throughout the years.

Ben-Gurion supported his claim with complex evidence consisting of detailed genealogical analyses and biblical arithmetic. He began by a count of the members of Jacob's household who came to Egypt—a total of 70 persons. He then mentioned the contradictions in the Bible regarding the number of years the Hebrews stayed in Egypt and the number of Israelites counted in the desert. Although these contradictions were never resolved by scholars, Ben-Gurion argued, it should be possible to calculate the number of those who left Egypt by the number of generations born there after Jacob. By tracing the names of those who left Egypt to the families who came to Egypt, Ben-Gurion tried to prove that only two generations were born there. As to the Bible's mention of 600,000 who participated in the exodus, Ben-Gurion had an answer. Going through a long list of biblical references in which the Hebrew word for "thousand" (*Elef*) is mentioned, he maintained that it could actually mean "family" in all these cases. He argued that in some instances, the double meaning of the word already had caused corruptions and exaggerations of the text.

Having demonstrated that only two generations were born in Egypt, Ben-Gurion went on to estimate how many children could have been born in two generations to the 70 couples who went there. He based his estimate on the number of people of the Levi family whose ages and names of parents and grandparents are given. The Levi grandchildren totaled 25, or 50 including their wives. Considering the birthrate of the sons of Levi as average, and ascribing the same average number of grandchildren to all the 12 sons of Jacob, Ben-Gurion arrived at approximately 600 people (including wives) who left Egypt. This, he claimed, was consistent with many previously unexplained events such as the Israelites' wanderings in the desert (a greater number could not have survived in the Sinai desert for an extended period of time), their entering the land, and their eating from the produce of the land immediately after arriving there. To Ben-Gurion, this group had returned to their countrymen, who had always lived in the land along with several of the Canaanite nations.

This lecture reflected the nation-builder's need to relate the present to the past. Ben-Gurion's fascination with events taking place during his lifetime led him to search for their ancient source, and his biblical studies were an outgrowth of his curiosity over the true meaning of these events. This led him to subject biblical events to what he considered a logical test. He also felt that a contemporary perspective could enrich biblical studies, which to him lacked the right perspective before the establishment of the state. In a speech before a Jewish studies conference in 1957, Ben-Gurion was explicit about the need to "rewrite history," that is, consider historical processes from a contemporary perspective. Jewish studies, he told the scholars, require a "reevaluation in the light of the revolutionary occurrences of the last ten years." While the past undoubtedly sheds light on the present, he declared, the present can help explain the past.[8]

Intellectual curiosity is not a common variable in discussions
of political leadership, but Ben-Gurion's biblical studies definitely involved such curiosity. It seems that the same qualities of
mind that allowed him to make unconventional decisions also
made him question established biblical truths. In 1959, when he
came out with his thesis on the antiquity of the Hebrews, he
rightly presented himself as a "student who is learning, not as a
scholar; as a simple student when it comes to the antiquity of the
monotheistic belief."[9] His common sense did not allow him to
accept some established scholarly conventions, and his political
role enabled him to turn his doubts into political symbolism. But
above all, it was Ben-Gurion's curiosity that raised some very
perplexing questions:

• • •

*I ask: How did the nation sustain itself from the time it crossed
the Jordan until the end of the conquest? Who supplied food to
this vast people over a period of many years when they were
engaged in war with all the people surrounding them? . . . It is
known that a pastoral people needs a greater land area than an
agricultural nation. Where did the herds of the Israelites pasture
during the entire period of the conquest? . . . Above all, the
question arises: Is it possible that the people of Israel, possessed
of a national character so manifestly different from all the nations around it, could have been established as a people in a
foreign land while in a state of enslavement?*[10]

• • •

It is quite common for nation-builders to stress the uniqueness
of their nations, or to establish links between the people and
their common heritage, that is, the language, land, tradition, and
so forth.[11] But there was more here. Ben-Gurion's doubts were
consistent with his world view that the origins of Jewish culture
can be found in "normal," historical surroundings rather than in
the Mount Sinai event. The antiquity of Israel in its land was to
him the only explanation of how the Jewish nation could have
survived and flourished during and after the enslavement in
Egypt. This belief had obvious current connotations:

• • •

*We have witnessed in our day how a Jewish community of
5,000,000 arose in the United States, and behold, not even 50*

years have passed, and they have not preserved the language
which they brought with them from overseas, and have almost
all switched to the use of the English language.[12]

◆ ◆ ◆

Ben-Gurion could not accept the existence of historical processes attributed either to abstract revelations or to sheer inertia. As shown in previous chapters, his thinking was monistic and messianic; ideas and deeds were interwoven. This led him to ask questions which even he labeled strange and insolent: "What motivated the people in Egypt to go to the land of Canaan? There is no doubt that the authors of the bible believed in the promise which God made to Abraham, Isaac and Jacob, and later to Moses and Joshua. But if we want to understand the matter naturally, we must ask ourselves: 'What in particular motivated those who left Egypt to go to the land of Canaan?' "[13] In spite of his skepticism regarding sociological laws, Ben-Gurion preferred a sociological answer to one that stressed divine miracles, and by this he helped transform the Bible from a sacred to a secular symbol. No wonder biblical studies, from a historical and archaeological point of view, flourished during the Ben-Gurion era. Considered from a secular point of view, the Bible provided many images with which the new nation could identify.[14]

This was one area in which Ben-Gurion clearly dominated the "charismatic center." Not only did he play a personal role in the promotion of activities, such as international bible contests or bible study groups (one of which met in his private home on a biweekly basis), he also determined, to a great extent, the subject matter to be discussed. A question such as what motivated the Hebrews to go to the land of Canaan portrayed the return to Canaan as a major biblical event to be studied and debated. Military officers turned amateur archaeologists, and journalists engaged in the writing of long essays on questions such as how many kings Joshua actually overpowered. Prophetic statements were incorporated into the political language, often as a substitute for genuine public ethics. Ben-Gurion himself used biblical quotations in every speech. These quotations not only decorated his speeches but often served as sources of political insight. For instance, he had an unusual understanding of the constraints, as well as the possibilities, of the small state in international politics. He himself traced this understanding to his preoccupation with Israel's independence during the periods of the first and second temples. Ben-Gurion had an impressive capacity for deriving insights from biblical strategic thinking while carefully analyzing the differences between past and present conditions.[15] Political intrigues described in the Bible, such as King David's betrayal of his loyal military commander, always made Ben-Gurion think of the causes and analyze the consequences.[16]

It should also be remembered that the new state of Israel lacked a tradition of statesmanship, and the Bible served Ben-Gurion as a source of inspiration. His style as statesman was clearly affected by a biblical style; the visionary sermons, the prophetic rage, the tolerance of torch parades and other "bible-like" ceremonies in spite of his own modest life-style, and so forth. In one instance, the inspirational role of the Bible was particularly apparent. In 1950, a columnist was critical of an over-elaborate political ceremony orchestrated by the Labor party, with the help of professional producers and directors, labeling it an attempt to imitate the Mount Sinai event. Ben-Gurion responded that although he was not present, he was sure the original Mount Sinai event was also orchestrated by professional directors and producers, for it involved no less theatrical and musical effects:

◆ ◆ ◆

. . . *thunders and lightnings, and a thick cloud upon the mount, and the voice of the trumpet exceedingly loud. And they stood at the mount. And the smoke thereof ascended as the smoke of a furnace. The voice of the trumpet waxed louder and louder. And torches, which you object to so much, were, of course, also present. It is explicitly said: "and, all the people saw the thunderings and the lightnings, and the noise of the trumpet, and the mountain smoking: and when the people saw it, they removed, and stood afar off."*[17]

◆ ◆ ◆

Ben-Gurion deliberately presented the Mount Sinai story in modern terms. It allowed him to further his argument that current events were no less majestic. Each generation, he claimed, talks with sacred respect about events of the past. However, those who were present at Mount Sinai were probably not too impressed by the Tablets of Covenant brought to them by Moses.

The implication was that the great events associated with the redemption of Israel in Ben-Gurion's lifetime would be attributed a similar significance in the future, even if they were belittled or misunderstood at the time. In this sense, Ben-Gurion clearly identified with Moses, who had a vision that his contemporaries refused to see. Writing this letter during the economic hardships of the early 1950s, Ben-Gurion mentioned that Moses' contemporaries also complained about their leader, "who lifts himself up above the congregation of the Lord, who maketh himself altogether a prince over them, who leads the people in the desert without water, and without ice, and without meat, and does not provide them with the onions, and the garlic, and the squash and the watermelons they ate in Egypt."[18] And although this is hard to prove, Ben-Gurion's uncompromising behavior during The Affair may have also been affected by the biblical image of Moses who remained alone with his "truth" while the people danced around the golden calf: "And it came to pass, as soon as he came nigh unto the camp, that he saw the calf, and the dancing: and Moses' anger waxed hot, and he cast the tablets out of his hands, and brake them beneath the mount."

The Challenge to the Scholars

In the 1950s, the community of biblical scholars played a significant role in the national preoccupation with the Bible and the subsequent dissemination of selected political symbols. This was particularly true regarding The Israeli Association for Biblical Research, which enjoyed a golden age during Ben-Gurion's leadership. Scholars interviewed for this study remembered with nostalgia the flourishing study groups, especially the biweekly sessions in the Prime Minister's home in which Ben-Gurion in person would arrange the chairs for his guests. They noted Ben-Gurion's private meetings with biblical scholars in which he insisted, out of respect, that he stand up while they sit, and the care he took of the winners, often poor, of biblical contests sponsored by the Association, during which contestants would memorize hundreds of biblical verses by heart. Some scholars, however, were critical. Professor Urbach, the Talmudic scholar, labeled the study group in the Prime Minister's home "a court," and he refused to join, although he himself conducted a Talmudic study group in his own home, which received

no less publicity. Professor Leibowitz warned that superficial
preoccupation with the Bible would "politicize" Judaism, but his
warnings went unheeded. The press, for one, loved the national
preoccupation with the Bible, especially its ceremonial dimension. Reporting on the study groups in the Prime Minister's
home, journalists would often describe the house as "filled with
great light" and the evening as "an evening of spiritual inspiration."[19] Newspapers would print pictures of the Prime Minister,
the country's president, and other dignitaries and scholars sitting
around a table comparing biblical texts. The subjects discussed
on these occasions reveal the dominance of Ben-Gurion's preferences. In 1959, for example, all sessions were devoted to the
book of Joshua—one of Ben-Gurion's favorites—and the lectures
by foremost scholars concerned such topics as the conquest of
Canaan, the military aspects of the conquest, and the settlement
of the tribes in the country.

This cooperation between knowledge and power was rarely
criticized, probably due to the perception of the Bible as an
overall national asset. There seemed to be nothing unusual about
a picture of the country's prime minister, or president, or chief of
staff engaged in a study of Joshua's conquests. Ben-Gurion's
preoccupation with the Bible seemed natural even to political
opponents, who engaged in its study themselves. There was an
element of pride involved in the fact that persons of power paid
so much tribute to intellectual matters. In a comment on Ben-
Gurion's press conference of 1960, a newspaper wrote, "We tried
to recall when it had happened that the prime minister of any
country, big or small, would take a few hours' leave to appear
before a large crowd of journalists and dignitaries to present not
a political statement of importance, but a chapter in the history
of his nation, the product of research and deep thought."[20] The
biblical scholars were proud to engage in a relationship with the
Prime Minister that exceeded partisan lines. In fact, in November 1959, when it seemed as if Ben-Gurion would not invite the
National-Religious party to join his coalition cabinet, three foremost members of The Israeli Association for Biblical Research
offered to do "whatever will be required" in order to help restore
the peace.[21]

As The Affair progressed, however, scholars became more conscious of the symbolic uses of the Bible. It was always clear, of
course, that the very emphasis on the Bible, or rather parts of it,

served an ideology that played down 2,000 years of Jewish history in the Diaspora. It must have been clear that the national preoccupation with biblical heroes such as Joshua and King David could encourage the identification of certain individuals or roles (such as the military) with the destiny of the state. But as long as Ben-Gurion dominated the scene, it did not seem to be a political issue. His ideology was taken for the national consensus, his party for the nation-building force, and he himself for the personification of a desired national image. Biblical scholars, like other intellectuals, willingly, perhaps even eagerly, joined in the promotion of the messianic ideal of the state. Ben-Gurion's political dominance, and that of his symbol system, did not cause worry, due to his adherence to democratic and parliamentary practices. But all this changed when Ben-Gurion's status as a national figure began to lessen. The same symbolism sounds different when articulated by politicians in pursuit of partisan goals; biblical quotations sound vulgar coming from state bureaucrats, and prophetic ethics become dangerous when the property of party bosses. The "routinization" of Ben-Gurion's charisma involved a process whereby the leader's terminology prevailed long after the policies for which it stood disappeared or changed. During The Affair it became clear that national unity was largely an ideal, not a reality. Any attempt to promote symbols of national unity, especially biblical symbols, was from now on to be considered with suspicion by political rivals and viewed as a distortion by intellectuals.

The feeling of many intellectuals who witnessed the transfusion of Ben-Gurion's symbol system into the state bureaucracy was expressed in a comment which referred to Ben-Gurion's famous objection to the use of the article "the" in the Hebrew language: "According to my estimate—which is non-scientific of course—there are in Israel at least 100,000 people; government officials, as well as secretaries of parties, labor unions and cooperatives who, out of admiration for the prime minister, tend to imitate him, not in fundamental matters (this would be hard indeed) but in idiosyncrasies. . . . When the prime minister excludes from his speeches and articles the article 'the,' his stubbornness may raise a smile—after all this same stubbornness contributed to the establishment of the State of Israel. But when you receive a letter signed by a bureaucrat who has not even cared to study elementary Hebrew, and who considers it his duty to exclude the 'the,' very pedantically, the smile on your face wanes."[22]

Ben-Gurion's biblical studies could be taken seriously if only for their unconventional approach. But it was hard to take seriously the biblical and archaeological "revelations" subsequently made by dozens of amateurs. Consider the following letter to Ben-Gurion by a bureaucrat in support of the Prime Minister's thesis on the exodus. He noted that in a public administration course at the university, the lecturer discussed the administrative proposals by Jethro, Moses' father-in-law, to provide, out of all the people, able men to be rulers of hundreds, rulers of fifties, and rulers of tens. Jethro said to Moses, "Every great matter they shall bring unto thee, but every small matter they shall judge: so shall it be easier for thyself and they shall bear the burden with thee." Were there 600,000 people, it would have meant that Moses had personal contact with 600 rulers of thousands, which is impractical from the point of view of the "span of control."[23]

Even if the scholars preferred to ignore the problems inherent in Ben-Gurion's biblical studies, they could not ignore them once these studies became a subject of political dispute, as they did following the news conference of 1960. At this point, rival political parties—especially the Orthodox ones—no longer tolerated Ben-Gurion's symbolic use of the Bible. On May 18, 1960, following his lecture on the exodus from Egypt, the matter was brought up in Parliament.[24] Rabbi Levin, head of a religious opposition party, raised a no-confidence motion on the grounds that Ben-Gurion's lecture involved heresy. To the believer, he explained, the Torah was given by God, and Ben-Gurion's free-floating interpretation was in contradiction to religious belief. Spokesmen for other parties were also critical of the Prime Minister's talk before journalists, military officers, and others on a subject which offended the believers. The lecture was defined by a secular opposition member as an expression of the motive, common to all dictators, to rewrite history. The no-confidence motion was defeated by a great majority, but the fact that it took place was significant. It was not new for Ben-Gurion to get involved in controversies with the Orthodox parties, and he had run into political trouble before over such questions as "Who is a Jew?" and his call for the vindication of Spinoza.[25] But now The

Affair had begun, and everybody, including the scholars, was to take sides.

The scholarly critique which followed Ben-Gurion's lecture of 1960 reveals three intellectual tensions between the statesman and the biblical scholars. The first concerns the rules of historiography; the second, the limits of speculation; and the third, the norms of scholarly behavior.

The Rules of Historiography

toward the end of World War II, the Social Science Research Council voiced its concern over the abuse of history in practical affairs.[26] In a report by the council's committee on historiography, Charles Beard complained that while history is treated as having little or no relation to the conduct of practical affairs, it is constantly used to validate policies and dogmas. "Either historians have failed in giving precision, limitations, and social significance to their work," he wrote, "or, by their writings, have lent countenance to the idea that almost any pressing public question can be indefeasibly answered by citations or illustrations selected from historical writings."[27] The report proposed a set of basic premises to guide historical research. These premises stressed the need to adhere to the rules of historiography, defined as a critical approach to the sources and development of history. Every written history, the report said, particularly that covering any considerable area of time and space, is a selection of facts made by some person or persons and is ordered or organized under the influence of some scheme of reference, interest, or emphasis—consciously or not—in the thoughts of the author or authors. Written or spoken history is best understood not only by analyzing its structure and documentation but also by studying possible attitudes arising from the life and circumstances of the author.

This historiographical imperative—that the intellectual context and attitudinal background of historical materials ought to be exposed—was confirmed by most modern historians[28] and was applied to biblical research as well. Even the biblical scholar, to whom the Bible represents "a document of the true history of the world,"[29] relates his investigation of biblical facts to one or more world views represented in the Bible. The message by the authors of the Bible, as perceived by the scholar, constitutes a context against which the facts are being evaluated. The biblical scholars' criticism of Ben-Gurion concerned, above all, his lack of consideration of either a historiographical context or the overall biblical point of view. His approach was found deficient in its neglect of whether any of his conclusions were consistent not only with facts but also with biblical premises and notions.

Yehuda Elitzur, a member of The Israeli Association for Biblical Research, called Ben-Gurion's approach "solid and moderate" but questioned its ability to explain a biblical story. In an essay written in response to the Prime Minister's press conference,[30] Elitzur stated the scant relevance of arithmetical, statistical, or linguistic analyses to the problem at hand. The question, he claimed, is not whether the Hebrew word for "thousand" may or may not mean "family," but what the author of the biblical story believed. The assumption that only 600 participated in the exodus is inconsistent not only with facts that the Prime Minister had not considered but with basic conceptions and with the "historical consciousness" of the Bible. Elitzur illustrated what scholars consider basic conceptions by quoting from the book of Exodus: "And the children of Israel were fruitful, and increased abundantly, and multiplied, and waxed exceeding mighty; and the land was filled with them." This, he explained, represents "biblical evidence" and provides true insight into the idea the biblical author had in mind.

Elitzur's essay demonstrated how the scholar's perception of the biblical world view is derived not from subjective judgment but from the historical and historiographical context of the biblical text. One of Ben-Gurion's speculations had been that the number of Hebrews who lived in Canaan during the time of the exile to Egypt may have been about 400,000 descendants of Abraham's 318 servants who, as told in 18 Genesis, were circumcised with him. Elitzur acknowledged the courageous attempt to try and investigate their fate, a question which preoccupied ancient scholars too, but showed, by citing historical and archaeological evidence, that similar groups existed throughout the ancient world, had the status of slaves, and never survived as a coherent group. It would, therefore, be hard to imagine Abraham's servants as an ancient prophetic sect that maintained a monotheistic faith. Elitzur also stressed the need to acknowledge the special character of biblical historiography. For instance,

Ben-Gurion counted in the Bible only three Egyptian kings during the exile and concluded, therefore, that the period could not have been long. Yet the Bible has its own rules of writing history which ought to be considered. It never counts the names of kings in chronological order but mentions them whenever important events, from the biblical point of view, require their presence. Often, the biblical story discards long periods in which no important events, from its point of view, had occurred. The scholar must reconstruct the chronological, and logical, order not by counting years (which are often given as symbols, not as real numbers), but by studying historical processes and trends. For example, the expression "but the more they afflicted them, the more they multiplied and grew" hints at a significant trend, while the mention of 400 or 430 years of exile does not. The beginning of a biblical tale with the expression: "And it came to pass in the process of time, that the king of Egypt died. . . ." also indicates a concept of a long time span.

The Limits of Speculation

In his fascinating study of "remembered, recovered and invented history" in the Middle East, Bernard Lewis stated that the essential and distinctive feature of scholarly research is, or should be, that it is not directed to predetermined results. The historian does not set out to prove a thesis, or select material to establish some point, but follows the evidence to where it leads. Lewis admitted that no human being is free from human failings, among them loyalties and prejudices which may color his perception and presentation of history. But the essence of the critical, scholarly historian is that he is aware of this fact, and instead of indulging his prejudices, he seeks to identify and correct them.[31]

This is the essence of another level of criticism of Ben-Gurion's lecture. Commentators present at the news conference were struck by the correlation between Ben-Gurion's biblical revelations and his political views. It goes without saying, one of them wrote, that if indeed a large population lived in Canaan all the time, then the Israelites' right to the land has been stronger than if it were based only on God's promise to Abraham.[32] Another commentator stated that once a scientific theory articulated by a statesman is perfectly consistent with his other views, something is suspicious.[33] But the most important critique came from Israel Eldad, a scholar known for his strong right-wing views.[34] Eldad's critique is enlightening since his own political standpoint made him aware of those thin lines the scholar should never cross.

Eldad proposed a distinction between three approaches to the Bible. The first approach is that of the believer. He believes in the biblical story as it is presented, with no doubt and no role for investigation. The creation of the world, the miracles, the fact that the Torah was given by God on Mount Sinai, etc., are all givens, not to be tested by human thinking or scientific experimentation. The second approach is that of the scientist. To him, nothing told in the biblical source is above doubt. This regards not only supernatural events but ordinary ones as well. The scientist compares sources, analyzes texts, accepts some, discards others, etc. The third approach is that of the interpreter. He studies the Bible not for its own sake but as a means to derive a contemporary, or universal, lesson. Thus, the interpreter chooses from the Bible whatever is convenient for him, views it through his own perspective, and considers matters the Bible did not deal with, while being explicit about it. All three approaches, wrote Eldad, are legitimate as long as they are not mixed up with each other.

Eldad was particularly critical of the scientific aspects of Ben-Gurion's lecture. He praised the Prime Minister's insistence upon the biblical text as a basis of his study and noted Ben-Gurion's humble approach, indicated by his recognition that his conclusions were only hypotheses. But he strongly attacked the lack of a consistent methodology. Science requires a method and a set of principles to guide the scholar's investigation. No such method was apparent in Ben-Gurion's study. First was the idea, then came the (impressive) search for evidence to support it. Such an approach, Eldad wrote, is arbitrary; it leads one to ignore a whole series of facts, without explaining their presence in the Bible and without justifying their absence in one's theory. Such selectiveness is appropriate if it is part of an explicit interpretation but not as part of a scientific inquiry.

Scholars have long been aware of the need to distinguish between hypothesis-testing and speculation.[35] The scholar formulating a hypothesis faces the danger of getting carried away and selecting those facts which confirm his hypothesis, while ignoring others. In the past, philosophers of history took sides on this question, some claiming history to be an objective compilation of facts, and others stressing the primacy of the scholar's interpretation.[36] Today's scholar generally agrees with Carr that "history is a continuous interaction between the historian and his facts, an unending dialogue between the present and the past."[37] The historian's hypotheses are, or should be, regarded as provisional, and the good scholar is expected to give facts rejecting his hypothesis the same attention as he gives those supporting it. This is where the statesman's approach differed. Ben-Gurion recognized contradictions in existing interpretations and legitimately proposed an interpretation of his own. He did not, however, conduct a serious search for possible loopholes in his approach. Ben-Gurion was correct when he argued, in a letter to one citizen, that every interpretation can be wrong, and every person must therefore choose the most logical interpretation to him.[38] What Ben-Gurion did not seem to realize was that the scholar's main work (and commitment) begins after an interpretation is chosen, which is why history is usually written by full-time researchers rather than by busy politicians. True, no professional group has, or should have, a monopoly over scholarly research. Ben-Gurion's biblical studies reveal the contribution a statesman can make by providing a fresh perspective in a field in which such new perspectives are often needed. Furthermore, Ben-Gurion's debates with scholars reveal that their methodology was often not carried out any more carefully than his. As Charles Beard claimed, it may be the scholar's own failure to give precision and limitation to his work that opens the door for the politician to step in. But the scholar, in contrast to the politician, is expected to check and recheck his findings, to question his own assumptions as thoroughly as he scrutinizes those of others, and, above all, to cast doubt even if the truth seems to have been found.

The Norms of Inquiry

Following Ben-Gurion's news conference, a journalist remarked that no scientific projects other than those directly influencing the fate of humanity, such as the Salk vaccine or the space program, had ever received such immediate world publicity as did Ben-Gurion's speculations.[39] Scholars drawing conclusions from their studies do not commonly assemble their country's civilian and military leadership for a lecture, and historians rarely give news conferences. This may stem from a lack of access to such media, but there may also be good reasons why they choose to refrain from overt publicity. In the long tradition of scholarly research, norms of inquiry were established as a result of the feeling that these norms were crucial to a free, creative system of inquiry. Professional associations often deemed it necessary to specify codes of behavior for their members who come into contact with the public. Consider the principles set by the American Psychological Association regarding public statements: "Modesty, scientific caution, and due regard for the limits of present knowledge" are expected of the scholar addressing the public. He is obliged to report fairly and accurately. "Exaggerations, sensationalism, superficiality and other kinds of misrepresentation are to be avoided."[40]

The meaning of these terms, however, was never defined by scholarly communities. It is recognized that today's exaggeration may become tomorrow's accepted view or that what one scholar considers as due regard for the limits of knowledge, another views as simply conservatism. In the world of letters, as in any other human endeavor, the borderline between right and wrong is context bound and authority bound. Sensationalism is rewarded when the time seems ripe for a discovery, and misrepresentation by celebrity scholars is often tolerated. But there also seems to exist a sense of self-preservation. Once sensational discoveries become a daily occurrence, once superficiality flourishes, scholars understandably begin to fear for the survival of their enterprise. Recognizing the fragility of human knowledge, the scholar knows that there are no shortcuts to the "truth," although these may be expected by the public. If knowledge is to advance, every bit of it must face scrutiny and critique. The public statement creates a constituency for knowledge, which makes it hard to subject it to scrutiny. Conclusions presented to the press before they are scrutinized by peers may stay around long after they are refuted. This is particularly true in the humanities and social sciences, where rewards from the public flow easily and quickly while refutations by colleagues are delayed. The famous scholar delivering to the public the grand declarations it is waiting for, or satisfying politicians in search of legitimizing symbols, may have a damaging effect on the body of knowledge he represents if only because his less famous colleagues may try to imitate him. As found in various studies, public exposure has significant effects on the mode and essence of scientific research, sometimes for the better, but often for the worse.[41]

Sensationalism by men of letters was not uncommon in Israel in the 1950s. Eldad reminded his readers of the publicity surrounding the recovery of the Dead Sea Scrolls by archaeologists, but he also noted a difference between these findings and Ben-Gurion's statements. The archaeological excavations revealed material findings while Ben-Gurion's news conference involved mere hypotheses. Hypotheses ought to be discussed thoroughly and investigated rather than presented to the masses, especially when such presentation is made by the country's Prime Minister.

Eldad and many others who raised this objection pointed at an important difference between the statesman and the scholar. To the statesman engaged in symbolic politics, the medium may be as important as the message. To the scholar, any but the most appropriate forum to express his message may lead to its distortion. The scholar works alone, is nourished by peer review, and is confined, by the nature of his material, to a specialized language shared by a relatively small audience. The statesman speaks to large crowds, and to the extent to which he is engaged in scholarly work, must simplify, compromise, and above all indicate a great degree of confidence. Biblical scholars did not object to Ben-Gurion's involvement in their trade; on the contrary, they seemed to revel in the attention focused on it. But they objected to his nonadherence to the rules of inquiry; in a press conference, Ben-Gurion naturally sounded more confident than he would have in smaller study groups. He was speaking to an audience that was unable to listen with the necessary skepticism and who took his authority for granted. This was obviously detrimental to the evaluation of the knowledge at its face value. Whether or not the statesman's intentions were positive, the scholars felt, knowledge should always remain autonomous.

ד

The Writers
Epic vs. Critique

$\mathbf{f}$or the modern writer, George Panichas wrote, politics in all its forms, as a theory, as a commitment and as action, has become a matter of consciousness and of conscience. Aesthetic considerations are invariably colored by sociopolitical demands. In effect, both in his art and his actions, the writer has—whether reluctantly or otherwise—ventured into the public realm.[1] Panichas, like other scholars of the "literature of commitment,"[2] describes the modern writer's commitment to social and political life optimistically: "We have come to identify him with concern, candor, courage. To him, we have turned for help that we seem unable to get from the traditional sources of state and school and church. Often, too, we have heeded the voice of the writer when other voices have been silenced or corrupted."[3]

The 35 writers who in March 1949 assembled in the Prime Minister's office to discuss "the incorporation of writers and intellectuals into the formation of national character in the State of Israel" hardly fell into this ideal category. Nor did their political behavior resemble what Benda described as "the tendency to action, the thirst for immediate results, the exclusive preoccupation with the desired end, the scorn for argument, the excess, the hatred, the fixed ideas."[4] There was simply no correlation between the master works produced by individual members of

this group and its performance as a group. The writers' elite
(including the young elite) spoke the same language and expressed the same values as any other group of dignitaries. Despite the extraordinary nature of this meeting, there was little
inspiration at the Prime Minister's office that evening.[5]

The significance of Ben-Gurion's meeting with the writers (and
a subsequent meeting in October) may be fully appreciated only
from the perspective of political development. The state was only
a few months old, and the legendary leader, who had just won
the War of Independence, called in the nation's writers to reas-
sure them that "nobody would conquer or enslave the human
spirit." Ben-Gurion expressed his trust that the new state would
never become a totalitarian state in which the government determines scientific truth, literary style, or artistic fashion. The intellectual, he said, would have absolute freedom of thought, adding
that this right entails a duty to live up to the responsibilities of
the intellectual. What this meant was for the intellectuals themselves to determine. What role ought they to play in national
integration, cultural growth, and the absorption of immigrants?
How could the writer participate in the overall nation-building
effort, what is his special task, and what role should the state
play in encouraging or rewarding it? Ben-Gurion assumed that
these questions preoccupied the intellectuals as they did the
politicians and called for an open-ended dialogue between the
country's elected representatives and the members of the "free
republic of Jewish spirit, literature and science."

This event, described in the first section of this chapter, was of
course, unusual. An intellectual elite was approached to determine its cultural and political role in a new state.[6] This was not
an attempt by the statesman to recruit support or legitimize his
own political position; given Ben-Gurion's messianic notions and
his fears regarding the cultural character of the new state, it is
safe to assume that he deemed the meetings important as part of
his nation-building efforts. The Prime Minister was receptive,
but the intellectuals had little to say. All options regarding the
cultural formation of the state were perceived as open, but the
writers showed little initiative. As the foremost novelists, poets,
and other persons of letters rose one by one to make long
speeches in response to Ben-Gurion's challenge, they did not
veer from a narrow range of conceptions about society, culture,
and their role in it, and they hardly challenged the Prime Min-

ister's own view of this role. There was some of Panichas's "concern, candor, courage," but the writers showed no willingness to make a difference in the "charismatic center of society."

And yet they did. In spite of the reluctance by the writers' elite in 1949 to play an independent societal role and the admiration many of them felt toward the charismatic leader, important tensions had evolved on the level of ideas. These tensions, described in the second section, had little to do with personal inclination and political affiliation. On the contrary, they were apparent mainly in those instances in which writers—such as Yizhar, Hazaz, and Alterman—had relatively close contacts with the Prime Minister. These were conflicts of principle which were in some ways beyond politics, resulting from what Glicksberg characterized as the writer's concern with "life as a whole."[7] The evolvement of these conflicts, despite the writers' greater commitment to mainstream values even in comparison with other intellectuals, supports the assumption underlying this study: that the relationship revealed here reflects a general conflict between knowledge and power. The political manifestations of this took place only in the early 1960s when Ben-Gurion ceased to play his charismatic role. The final section describes one example—the public reaction to Ben-Gurion's comment in 1961 that he read no fine literature. Only when The Affair was at its climax did the writers raise the simple question never raised before: "So what?"

The Meetings of 1949

The first meeting with the writers was opened by Ben-Gurion with the suggestion that the formation of the cultural and moral character of the state cannot be carried out by government, although the government is not wholly a stranger to matters of the spirit. The government tends to devote resources to tasks such as security, housing, taxing, services, international relations and so forth, yet the ultimate historic test of a nation lies in the sphere of culture. The writer's involvement in the cultural formation of the state was, to him, crucial. He claimed that government action in public affairs is always bound by legal and other constraints, while the writer is free and may contribute a fresh perspective. Therefore, intellectuals ought to be involved in practical affairs and join in a mutually beneficial dialogue with the men of action.

There was no immediate challenge in Ben-Gurion's words, since the writers had a long tradition of cooperation with politics. As Cordova has shown in his study of the writers' association in pre-state Israel,[8] there had always existed a "modus vivendi" between the political and cultural elites. The ideologists of the Labor movement, who dominated political life in the pre-state society, accepted the cultural elite as carriers of the central values of national revival, and this prevented the development of a critical attitude among the latter toward the nation-building political elites. At the same time, there was no reason to assume that this tradition of cooperation between the writers and the pre-state movements would automatically be carried over to the state. Writers could be expected to align as an institutionalized cultural center with political forces but not necessarily with those supporting "statism." Many writers were members of the pre-state political movements that called for the preservation of the spontaneous, voluntary (and partisan) nature of society with the formation of the state. But, in spite of this affiliation, the writers were enthusiastic supporters of the principle of "statism" in one of its extreme expressions—admiration for Ben-Gurion. While no generalization of the attitude of writers can be accurate, letters received by the Prime Minister from writers were often very laudatory. He was always the "great man," or "the redeemer."[9] An open letter to Ben-Gurion during The Affair seemed to typify many writers' feelings:

♦ ♦ ♦

We prayed for your well-being and were proud of you. We saw you as the symbol of redemption and independence, and decorated our homes and schools with your picture, pointing to you as the carrier of the flag of independence and liberation. We told legends about you to our children, we presented you as an example of devotion, justice, and fairness, self-sacrifice, purity and faith, and now the soil under our feet, which was stable and strong, quakes and shakes.[10]

♦ ♦ ♦

The language used in the meetings of 1949 was no less grandiloquent, yet behind that language three very earthly trends can be identified: formalism, elitism, and a tendency to place cultural activity under the umbrella of the state.

Formalism

$f$or a group considered repre-
sentative of the free human spirit, an unusual number of formal
institutional proposals were raised in the meetings. True, the
writers raised their formal proposals only after they had clarified
that the great change in the life of the nation could not be directly
reflected in literature. "After all," an old poet complained, "it is
impossible to come and tell us, especially at our age: 'try to write
so and so.'" The events associated with the formation of the
state were so incomprehensible, another novelist said, that the
epic of the times cannot be written by order from above, although, when the time comes, great literary works will be produced. "Let's be practical," he said, and ventured to discuss what
practical ways ought to be taken in order to "blow winds of
change into the nation." First, a special public office must be
instituted to provide new immigrants with periodical literature.
Second, a "forum for the voice of the people," composed of writers and scientists, should be instituted to serve as a channel for
the public's complaints about the state authorities.

At least three writers proposed the institutionalization of a
parliament of writers which would serve as the spiritual equivalent of the political parliament in existence. One writer labeled
it "the central army of the men of the spirit," another preferred
the historic title "Sanhedrin," referring to the ruling committee
of sages in ancient Israel, and yet another talked about a simple
committee, whose structure, however, was far from simple.

◆ ◆ ◆

*I consider the "Committee for Spiritual Culture" to be a group
nominated by you and by the Minister of Education, from among
the outstanding members of the following professions: literature,
philosophy, history, education and the arts (theater, music,
painting and sculpture), composed of:*

4 writers (because literature	*1 educator*
involves many kinds and types	*1 actor*
of writers)	*1 musician*
2 philosophers	*1 painter*
2 historians	*1 sculptor*

Altogether 13, and with representatives of the prime minister and the minister of education a total of 15 members.

♦ ♦ ♦

The senior writer submitted an elaborate proposal to the Prime Minister outlining the authority of this government-nominated committee, its role in the service of national and societal goals "in their widest and deepest sense," its budgetary sources (entirely from the government), and, of course, its major expenses. Such formalism by intellectuals is common in intellectual life today. One only has to open a mainstream literary or scholarly journal to learn about the institutional arrangements, committees, dignitaries, awards, travel funds, or relations with the government. But the meetings described here took place in 1949, in an atmosphere of a new beginning and within a society rewarding the man of letters in less formal ways. The tendency to formalize the intellectual's contribution to society is, therefore, hard to understand. Part of it was, no doubt, the urge to translate an intellectual contribution into an immediate and practical one. It leads one to consider whether any attempt to turn the intellectual's contribution into practical language may not turn him into his own caricature.[11]

This is what happened to the "Sanhedrin" proposal. The proposal to establish a supreme body of sages like the Sanhedrin which regulated spiritual and material life in ancient Israel was raised by an outstanding scholar and author named Eliezer Steinman. It was based on Steinman's conviction that the writer ought to refrain from political action. He claimed that a distance between art and the state must be kept and that the writer should never become a public servant but only reflect his individual feelings in literature. Steinman, in contrast to other writers at the meeting, was worried about the potential power of the state to suppress the individual. This is where the Sanhedrin proposal came in. It was not intended to be another governing body or a committee of consultants to the government. Steinman tried to institutionalize the idea of the intellectual as a sage whose authority in matters of spiritual and moral life is derived not from the state but from the people. He believed that intellectuals who possess power and who carry titles not given by the state could enlighten political life. However, it was the attempt to put this belief into a proposal that turned it into a caricature. In the Prime

Minister's office, Steinman detailed at length the structure and function of spiritual rule by writers. The Sanhedrin would study the nation's historical heritage and write a new guide for the disoriented souls of the times. It would also set cultural standards. Upon reading the account of this meeting, one wonders yet again why those renown for their conscientious societal critique were demanding "mind control." Steinman, who once wondered why the devil is being paid his dues in every human affair, [12] was now paying him more than his dues. The Sanhedrin, he said, would rubber stamp good taste; and its eye would observe all channels by which culture, education, and art are being transmitted to the people, in order to prevent their contamination.

The formalism detected here sheds light on a difficulty that arises whenever the intellectual gets involved in public affairs. The common demand for his involvement recognizes the unique nature of his occupation, but to be involved demands skills that he does not necessarily possess. Furthermore, the contribution of the intellectual qua intellectual cannot be formally defined and even the most modest attempt to draft a constitution for him becomes ridiculous or dangerous. In 1949, the writers felt that action had to be taken to mold the cultural character of the new state. They shared Ben-Gurion's feeling that this required serious attention to the soul as well as to the body. But in matters of the soul, there are, it seems, no short cuts.

Elitism

In 1948, the young state of Israel began one of the most immense tasks ever undertaken by a new nation: the housing and cultural absorption of thousands of new immigrants from 70 exiles. As is well known, the effort was made possible by Ben-Gurion's effective leadership. He defined the new nation's broad goals and insisted upon their pursuit, in spite of great obstacles and the shortage of material resources. To Ben-Gurion, the ingathering of the exiles constituted the essence of nation building and the true fulfilment of the messianic dream. The Jews returning to their homeland fulfilled a historical imperative, and everyone was to take part in the process by which "human dust," contaminated by 2,000 years of artificial existence in the Diaspora (yet never abandoning the messianic faith), was to become a nation.

The second meeting between Ben-Gurion and the writers in October was devoted to the question of the role of the intellectual in the cultural absorption of these new immigrants. The meeting was inspired again by Ben-Gurion, and the writers have merely reflected his notions on this matter. This was particularly apparent in regard to the elitist view of new immigrants implied by the notion of "human dust."[13] Cultural absorption was defined, after Ben-Gurion, as a process of the dissemination of existing values and ways of life to an amorphous mass of newcomers. The writers had not given any hint about the cultural heritage these masses might have or about the contribution they could be expected to make to the cultural formation of the state. As one poet stated, the newcomers need to be given a moral imperative to guide them. The intellectual's role was thereby defined in terms similar to those describing missionary work. The writers shared the common notion that "relevant" values are those developed in modern Palestine. The newcomers were perceived as preoccupied merely with material needs. The light hidden in the Labor movement, it was said, must be shown to them; the writer must "lower himself" to the masses. "We should all become social workers now," it was declared; "the writers must generate a moral aim in the heart of those newcomers, and we have, thank God, many supreme aims with which to nourish the generation." Another writer objected to the proposal to go and mingle with the newcomers as being too unambitious. He claimed that greater action was needed, such as the creation of a parliament of intellectuals. If such a parliament existed, it would inspire the newcomers like a ray of sun.

Professor Ben-Zion Dinaburg, a historian and at one time Minister of Education, who lectured to the writers in the October meeting, provided an interesting perspective. His lecture reflected the dilemma a nation-building elite faces as it meets social groups who did not take part in the struggle for independence and who do not share its ideology and feeling of unity.[14] According to Dinaburg, the new immigrant "has not experienced our spiritual development which has brought about the building of the land of Israel." Absorption, to him, meant a process by which "the newcomer changes in spirit and gradually begins to resemble the settlers, adopting their ways of reacting, thinking, relating to each other, dressing and their values." Economic absorption unaccompanied by spiritual absorption, he claimed, may lead to a wholly different society, one which does not resemble the society that fought hard for independence. Dinaburg supported the Prime Minister's call for organized activity by the intellectuals, but, in contrast to Ben-Gurion, he considered that activity part of the responsibility of the government.

In the long protocols of the two meetings it is possible to detect only two deviations from the elitist point of view. The first was by Moshe Shamir, a young writer affiliated with the Marxist Mapam party at the time. Shamir was the only participant who questioned the notion of a select elite of old-timers absorbing the newcomers. The spirit of a nation, he said, cannot be planned, and there is no reason why those living in the land should determine the cultural patterns for all others. The ingathering of the exiles, Shamir claimed, requires a truly populist movement; he warned of turning the writer into a "bureaucrat of the spirit" if only because his bureaucratic skills are limited. Another deviation was by Rachel Shazar, a long-time activist in the Women's Labor movement. She called on the writers to abandon the mystical assumption that the newcomers constituted a different breed of human beings and demanded they be given better housing, work, and education. All the rest, she said, would follow naturally.

The Government Umbrella

According to Raymond Aron, "the tendency to criticize the established order is, so to speak, the occupational disease of the intellectuals."[15] Such statements are usually made without considering the actual behavior of intellectuals in a political context. There is generally little correlation between the common portrayal of intellectuals as creative, free, or restless[16] and the behavior one observes behind closed doors. Aron hinted at this contradiction when he wrote that "when one observes the attitudes of intellectuals towards politics, one's first impression is that they are very similar to those of non-intellectuals. In the opinions of teachers or writers there is the same mixture of half-baked knowledge, of traditional prejudices, of preferences which are more aesthetic than rational, as in those of shopkeepers or industrialists."[17] But the literature on intellectuals did not generally stress their reluctance to play a significant social role nor the demand that the government assume responsibility for cultural development.

It is perhaps unfair to demand that a group of poets and novelists at a late night meeting with the Prime Minister should represent the image of the restless intellectual. But it does seem significant that one by one the country's writers defined their role as the voice of the government. An important exception has already been discussed—Steinman's attempt to institutionalize a role for the writer who is unsubordinated to the state. But the common view was reflected in one poet's definition of the state as the "backbone" of the writers' association. She admitted that no external "backbone" could be significant were there no talent and creative ability. But since these exist, the writer's creative work should be "handed over" to the state so that it "grows and flourishes and becomes an expression of our vision and spirit." She called for a "writers' constitution" which would outline their rights and duties. While objecting to the Soviet example, in which the writer is the servant of the state, she contended that in moments of great national need the writer must put himself in the service of the state and serve as its spokesman.

It also seems significant that the relationship between the writer and the state was conceived by many participants as reciprocal. Some were very explicit, calling for state subsidies for chosen writers or demanding that the writers' association be invited to take part in official state ceremonies more often. The wish to have the state as sponsor and patron was expressed by both young and old writers. The request for state patronage was understandable in the context in which it was made. The state had barely been established, and its role in cultural life was still conceived as open to a variety of definitions. The state's image as Leviathan was still inconceivable, although there were already signs of dissatisfaction with the anonymity of state activity. The writers' hope that the state would devote resources and efforts to encourage their field of activity is also understandable. The question, however, is why their adjustment to the concept of statism was so smooth and why it preceded for at least a decade their self-consciousness as intellectuals. To some extent, the answer was provided by the writer and poet Avigdor Hameiri, who expressed everybody's fascination with the fact that for the first time in 2,000 years the Jewish intellectual lived in his own state.

Hameiri's argument throws light on what may be the major reason for the strong commitment of the writers to the state:

◆ ◆ ◆

Tragedy is a soul without a body, and comedy, a body without a soul. King Lear in the forest, who used to have a body: throne, followers, sceptre, a red robe on his shoulders and a crown on his head, and lost that body—he is tragic. And on the other hand, when the clown comes on stage and puts on a royal body, but inside remains what he was—this is comedy. So far we have been tragedy, an abstract soul without a body. And the state— this is the form, the body we put on.[18]

◆ ◆ ◆

In 1949, the writers' relationship with power was marked by an unquestionable commitment to the state. Not only did the writers have strong links to the mainstream ideological movements of the pre-state period, they had little difficulty in adjusting to the authority of the new state. They identified it with messianic values, and many of them admired the messiah at the top. The tensions that nevertheless evolved between Ben-Gurion and the writers on the level of ideas are, therefore, worthy of examination.

From Commitment to Conflict

The writers' commitment to mainstream political values had deep roots in Hebrew literature. As literary critics have often argued, Hebrew literature has, since ancient times, reflected the religious, social, and political environment in which it flourished: "It has generally emerged from the people and been directed at them as a collective entity."[19] The modern Hebrew writer's commitment to the collective entity was analyzed by Halkin in his 1950 essay on "New Directions in Palestinian Literature" in which he suggested that "all of Jewish history, as it were, strives in Palestinian literature to sanction the efforts which present-day Jewry is making to find salvation in its ancestral homeland."[20] Halkin hinted at the messianic overtones of this literature. The effort to build a new society in Palestine was interpreted as part of a broader national and universal mission, and aspects of national life which had not been part of that effort were considered tragic: "In Hebrew fiction today every

hue and shade of Jewish martyrdom, individual as well as collective, is traceable to Jewish homelessness as its prime cause."[21]
Poetry, Halkin wrote, whether describing times of relative peace
or times of strife and struggle, seeks chiefly to express the essence of group life in the reviving country. And since the love of
the country is so elementary a concept in Jewish tradition,
Halkin expected its new manifestations in Palestinian verse to
lose their distinctiveness if only because they may have been
interpreted as the traditional messianic yearnings of Jewish
literature.

In what turned out to be an original but inaccurate prophecy,
Halkin proposed that "as long as the young Palestinian product
could be compacted into the messianic vision, the newness of his
personality, the difference between him and his grandfather
could be overlooked. Now that he has become an Israeli, the
forger of a civilization in keeping with his own native propensi-
ties, the question as to his kinship with his antecedents must
begin to obtrude itself more persistently."[22] Halkin and other
critics wrongly believed that the search for new ways, which was
no doubt coming, would consist of a return to national and religious roots.[23] The question of the writer's kinship with his antecedents indeed preoccupied him, but the answer was sought in
universal-humanistic thinking rather than in national-messianic
ideology.

Nothing indicates better the writer's escape from his commitment to the messianic notion of the state than Aharon Meged's
novel *The Living on the Dead*, the story of a writer facing trial
for not completing the epic of Davidov, a legendary founding
father. Meged's novel expresses the tormented conscience of a
generation haunted by its own commitment to its social and ideological roots. This generation fulfills the mission set up by its
forefathers but fails to read the messianic message involved.
Meged's heroes are anti-heroes in a true sense. They are everyday citizens whose behavior, like that of Hameiri's clown, is
comic due to the normative burden they carry. Here are the
closing lines of *The Living on the Dead*:

◆ ◆ ◆

*If you find the torn and crumpled pages of the Book of Davidov
scattered about here and there over the face of the land—a page
caught in a bush, a page fluttering from rock to rock, a page
stuck to a stone dike, or drifting over the sand or fluttering by*

the roadside—do not bring them back to me. Better that they should disappear into oblivion than that I should ever see them again. I do not want an ambush in my home, a nest of rustling memories under my bed, eyes observing my thoughts! I want to be my own master. I want rest.[24]

• • •

Meged's novel was interpreted by Yudkin and others as the modern writer's attempt to carve out an identity for himself, to be freed of the imposition of the past. But this is only part of the story. In fact, the individual's search for his own identity in the face of group traditions was always a strong motive in Hebrew literature. Even Yizhar Smilanski (known as S. Yizhar), whose bond to the pioneer tradition with its outstanding tendency to sympathize with the broad, public interest has often been noted, portrayed in his stories a hero who never exercises his latent wish to leave the group, yet never forgets this wish in his psychic world.[25] A truly new dimension, however, was introduced into Hebrew literature in the consideration of man as neither a social animal nor an individual but, rather, as a metaphysical condition.[26] Israeli literature in the 1950s stripped the individual of his social and psychological context and began to deal—first reluctantly, then explicitly—with the condition of man in the universe. This trend aroused inevitable tensions.

The Tension over the Tragedy of Human Existence

Like all generalizations, the attempt to identify literary trends is dangerous. Obvious exceptions to the literature of commitment in Israel, like the writings of Agnon and Brenner, make it almost impossible to discuss changes from "social" to "metaphysical" or from "messianic" to "universal" literature. The terms themselves pose severe problems since a messianic outlook incorporates, for example, a universalist notion. As Halkin noted, the literature of commitment to the collective effort written in Palestine in the 1930s and 1940s was itself "the expression of the bewilderment of Jewish existence in the world rather than a conscious glorification of an idea set up as a guiding principle."[27] Furthermore, literary works, unlike ideological manifestos, reflect varied individual impressions which often do not fall into clear patterns, and, even when they do, they do not necessarily parallel ideological ones.

At the same time, it is possible to identify changes in literary style and content which, as they accumulate, represent turning points in outlook. Gershon Shaked, in his study of a "new wave in Israeli literature" singled out the year 1958 as one such turning point.[28] In that year Yizhar's novel *The Days of Ziklag*, in which fundamental values of social collective life were questioned by the writer who was perhaps most associated with them, came out. This novel was interpreted by Shaked as the first to cast doubt on the value of collective existence and its replacement by stress on human existence as such. This motive appears in the novel in elementary form when compared to later works by such authors as Sadeh or Yehoshua, but the underlying tension found in Yizhar's earlier stories between the individual and the group turns into a conflict in *The Days of Ziklag*. Yizhar became the spokesman of a generation of writers committed to the social order yet in search of the meaning of every social order in a turbulent world.

This outlook was articulated by Yizhar in a lecture on "Literature in a Turbulent World" in 1958.[29] This lecture was devoted to a comparison of nineteenth-century and twentieth-century literature. Although critical of the social order, nineteenth-century literature was always optimistic, he said. One hundred years ago, the writer observed injustice, inequality, and greed; but there was belief, there was hope for a world order in which, if only implemented, greed would be abolished. This was a world view that believed in solutions. It was expected that the solution would come, however slowly. Whether it lies in one social theory or in another, progress is assured. In contrast to this world view, Yizhar put forth the twentieth-century view expressed in Agnon's *Book of Deeds*.[30] Each of the short stories composing the book describes a set of situations that express man's position in a turbulent world. Each begins with a simple, clear, good and necessary task, yet the task is never accomplished. As an example, Yizhar quotes the beginning of Agnon's short story "The Candles":

◆ ◆ ◆

I finally took time to go to the sea. All the six days of Creation I was busy and had not time to bathe. On Friday afternoon I freed myself of all my affairs, took white garments with me, and went to bathe.

♦ ♦ ♦

As in all the stories in *The Book of Deeds*, there comes a distraction, in this story in the form of Mr. Haim Apropos, a short, potbellied man with an eternal smile on his face. The narrator of the story follows Apropos into a house he did not intend to visit, does things he did not intend to do, and then Mr. Apropos disappears. The narrator then notices that four white candles are about to tip over, and as he grasps them, they melt and twist in his hands. The more he fusses with the candles, the more they twist and melt, and he becomes consumed by remorse. He finally arrives at the sea but feels a sudden embarrassment and fears he will not be able to recognize which shirt to put on after bathing, which one is dirty and which is clean. Before he plunges into the sea, the water rises and covers his feet. Frightened, he jumps upon a bridge that juts out into the sea, and the bridge begins to quake and vibrate.

Yizhar's interpretation of "The Candles" in his 1958 lecture is itself a literary work. The man intended to bathe in the sea, he said, a deed which in principle could not be simpler, clearer, and more defined. And yet that pure, simple aim cannot be fulfilled. At the hands of an incomprehensible force, what was meaningful in the simplest sense became devoid of meaning. Yizhar interpreted the short story as a manifesto on the condition of Man who is afraid when there is nothing to be feared, who flinches for no apparent reason. "He takes the shadow of mountains for the mountains, is ground between them, fails to evaluate things in their true proportions, and, his sense of balance distorted, sees no way to proceed. Man becomes rootless. Nameless. A grain among grains. Just one man in a crowd. Lost in the crowd and fearful in his anonymity."

Yizhar emphasized that when the anonymous, nameless person in the story arrives at the beach, he does not know how to approach the sea. And instead of entering the water, as he intended, he climbs up, escapes to a bridge, "the last promontory of the solid soil that invades the oceanic existence, the other, infinite world of the insubstantial." And even as he stands on the bridge, the haven of solidity, it begins to tremble under his feet, and everything is a maelstrom. Security has gone; terra firma, every piece of ground, is no longer firm, nothing left to stand on. The link between man and things has been lost—like the link between man and man and the link between man and time. A lonely man stands on a bridge over the sea, and the bridge shudders and quakes under his feet.

Yizhar, the spokesman for a society returning to the soil to build a new building, was now questioning the existence of all soil, of every building. The author who was the closest among the modern Hebrew writers to writing an epic of the collective effort in Palestine, who composed the tale of "midnight convoy," a convoy always pushing forward for there is "no time to flirt with the willful and whimsical road nor to play catch with the dust for an itinerary is an itinerary,"[31] now doubted whether human effort had any meaning at all. Most significantly, Yizhar, who shared the dominant ideology of the pre-state society, was now considering ideology an unstable bridge over troubled waters. Yizhar referred to ideology in his 1958 lecture as an anachronism (although his claims were in no way unideological) posing the dilemma of what comes first, "man or man's flags," and noting the tragedy of the person lifting a flag whose color has faded and whose meaning is gone.

Unintentionally, Yizhar became a critic of the adherence to existing doctrines as an ultimate solution to the condition of man. Observing the human condition and considering it one of vulnerability, danger, and aimlessness, referring to modern man as a child who lost the "big, confident, guiding hand of Dad," Yizhar could no longer accept simple doctrinary substitutes. He remained the ideologue in calling for a new vision but turned into social critic not recognizing that vision among existing inventories. Yizhar refused to be considered a modern nihilist: "The song I am singing today is no heresy, except in the eyes of fools." He realized the demand from his generation of writers, and from himself in particular, to write an epic, to express positive values, to lead the way. But he could not do this because the old ideological statements had lost their meaning. It is understandable why Yizhar's position in 1958 was criticized as not being genuine.[32]

The committed writer had never abandoned his fascination with the collective effort as he observed it in the 1930s and 1940s and was searching for its equivalent. Yet no replacement could be found. Loyal to his self-image as a writer, Yizhar claimed he could not write lullabies for children falling asleep in a fools' paradise. The writer must stand bare on cold ice, he declared, as Socrates did in Alkibidas' description. In his lecture he quoted:

◆ ◆ ◆

There was a severe frost, for the winter in that region is really tremendous, and everybody else either remained indoors, or if they went out had on no end of clothing, and were well shod, and had their feet swathed in felt and fleeces: in the midst of this, Socrates, with his bare feet on the ice, and in his ordinary dress, marched better than any of the other soldiers who had their shoes on. . . .

◆ ◆ ◆

It is significant that Yizhar omitted the closing line of this quotation: "And they looked daggers at him because he seemed to despise them." The writer turned critic by the dynamics of his work and depth of observation could not yet consider himself in 1958 as a young rebel.

One month later, Prime Minister Ben-Gurion, who received a copy of the lecture from Yizhar, wrote him the following letter:[33]

◆ ◆ ◆

Dear Yizhar:

I read your lecture in Eilat on a turbulent world with much interest—and with no little fear. True, the title of your lecture diminishes the turbulence. You supposedly talk not about a turbulent world but about "literature in a turbulent world." I must admit that I have not read most of the books, if any, which are quoted in your lecture and I am ready to accept in advance your interpretation of the extracts from prose and poetry which indicate turbulence. But in the second paragraph of your lecture you begin with a turbulent statement: "The world is turbulent indeed," and you exempt yourself even from the need to prove this. Permit me to doubt whether this adjective adequately epitomizes and defines the nature of the contemporary world.

One should, of course, not ignore the turbulence in the world. And I am ready to admit one big and terrible "turbulence": the fear of atomic war that carries the danger of the destruction of mankind. The danger may be exaggerated, but it exists. Yet in your talk you hardly touch upon this fear, and the turbulent world, as it seems to you, or rather as it is reflected in literature and the press (oh, what a worthless press) is a world devoid of faith, truth, purpose, desires, mission, values and vision. I do not accept this general definition. And if the novels and poems you have read portray contemporary man in this way, the portrayal is ill-intentioned, distorted, one-sided and misleading.

You quote with justified fascination Alkidibas' description of Socrates, but you forget Socrates' description of Athenian life at the time, the description of its sages, leaders, governors, artists and poets. I believe Socrates exaggerated the negative side of his descriptions, and the people of Athens, its sages and leaders, were not as negative as he implied, just as Jerusalem was no harlot full of murderers, and the whole Jewish nation was no sinful nation of people laden with iniquity, a seed of evil doers, children that are corrupters as Isaiah overstated in his holy rage. But even today, all is not lost, and if there is no Isaiah around, there is many a Socrates who in their wisdom, sense of justice and striving for the sublime, the good and the beautiful do not fall short of Plato's great teacher.

You would not disagree with me—there is no hint that you would in your lecture—if I said that conditions, not only material ones (and these should not be underestimated) in a great part of the world are better now than they were in the 19th century or even in the first half of the 20th century. There are those who belittle the change in material conditions but this can be done only after they have been improved. . . . But if you remember Dickens' tales of horror about the disgraceful poverty of early 19th century England—and we have no better criterion than that for comparison, you must admit that our world to-day—at least in part—is now free of some of the malignant evils and disgraceful inequalities and all this due to the spirit of man which moves upward.

But I doubt if we are any poorer today even in spiritual life than in former years.

It is all too easy to dismiss the wondrous, majestic development of science today. And it is true that the tree of knowledge is not necessarily the tree of the knowledge of good and evil.

*But aren't the great "men of knowledge" in our days intellectual
giants who inspire wonder and admiration as Socrates, Gior-
dano Bruno, and Spinoza did in their day? Scientific development should not be considered merely as material development;
it is the rise of the human spirit and its advance towards the
hidden and mysterious infinity which we shall never reach. The
more science exposes the secrets of the microcosm and macrocosm—the deeper and wider the infinite mystery of the cosmos
and every peak we reach will reveal to us new peaks beckoning
from beyond, with higher and yet sublimer peaks still undis-
closed. And if there are people today who have been emptied of
any spiritual, moral, divine content, and who live in an empty
space of "eat, drink and be merry . . ." wrapped in boredom
and emptiness, such people always have existed, whether or not
described by novelists and poets.*

*But I have gone on for longer than intended when I began
writing, and still feel I have told you hardly nothing of what
may be said on this matter, so I shall put an end to words.*

Yours,

D. Ben-Gurion

◆ ◆ ◆

In the correspondence that followed,[34] the statesman and the
writer talked across each other. Yizhar tried to support the points
he made in his lecture by citing the obvious evils apparent in the
modern world. Ben-Gurion responded by citing the achievements—past and future. The initial intellectual conflict between
them was not, however, over the evaluation of temporary phenomena but rather over the level on which such evaluation ought
to be made. In his lecture, the writer observed, on a general
level, the "condition of man." To Yizhar there existed an individual beyond his historic manifestations, a metaphysical individual
whose relationship to the world is affected by temporal events
but is not identical to them. Ben-Gurion's thinking was not at all
metaphysical. Thus, when Yizhar talked, for example, about
"war," to Ben-Gurion wars were the function of spatial and temporal conditions, and a concept like "the atomic age" was meaningless. Ben-Gurion's monistic outlook was apparent in his
correspondence with Yizhar. He saw no distinction between ma-

terial progress and spiritual satisfaction. Yizhar, the novelist, tried to identify the "way of God" beyond world events. Ben-Gurion, the politician, replied that he was unfamiliar with the "way of God." To him, not everything God does is clear, acceptable, and reasonable. Sometimes he even does shocking, horrifying, and disappointing things, "but the struggle, on the whole, is positive." Ben-Gurion left no doubt that the struggle of the human race is the struggle of millions of individuals, not of metaphysical "man," or, for that matter, of God.

The intellectual conflict between the statesman and the writer over the level on which the human condition ought to be analyzed was reflected in a short letter to the editor Ben-Gurion wrote at the time his correspondence with Yizhar took place. The letter was a response to a short obituary written by Hugo Bergman, the philosopher, praising the late Joseph Sprinzak, Speaker of the Knesset (Israel's parliament) as one who remained a human being at a time in which the human aspect of public life had been lost. Instead of human beings, Bergman wrote, Kafka's castle dominates public life with its anonymous, faceless administration, its clerks and secretaries, and its functional roles.[35] When he wrote the somewhat routine obituary Bergman most probably did not expect this response from an angry Prime Minister:

◆ ◆ ◆

I am not a literary critic and I do not know whether Kafka's stories are "prophetic" visions or horror stories produced by the hysterical imagination of a highly skilled writer. . . . But Bergman, no doubt, does not write flippantly, and without weighing every sentence and word he is writing. How did he allow himself to put on paper the terrible, senseless words that "the human being is gone, here, and in other countries, and a nightmare has taken over?" Every reader would of course accept Bergman's evaluation of [Speaker] Sprinzak as a human being, but is there the slightest truth in the awful saying that "the human in man had departed the land?" We can ask Professor Bergman whether he knows the billions of people who live in our time and whether he knows they are not human, but we do not have to go that far. Isn't there a human being among the hundreds of thousands of workers who work productively in industry, or are artisans and establish families and help each other and contribute to society, to the state and to the whole era? Has the human in man de-

parted among the tens of thousands of settlers, old and new, who cultivate the land, and make the desert blossom, and form advanced social ways of life, and educate their sons to cherish work and vision? Has the human image, which is the image of God, departed from the thousands of teachers and educators who teach wisdom to babies, children and adults, and shape the future pioneers and scientists and developers of the land, its culture, and literature? Is there really no human being among the teachers at the Hebrew University in Jerusalem?

The "prophets" of doom in our times only consider the product of their own stormy and sick minds if they generalize from outrageous phenomena which do exist, although no more, and in my opinion even less, than in previous periods—and turn them into the image of man today. There is no greater distortion of the truth than the implication that dissolute persons in the country and the world constitute the norm.[36]

◆ ◆ ◆

The Tension over the Organic Nature of History

"**t**he Sermon," a famous short story by Israel's writer Hazaz,[37] has proved difficult for literary critics. "Yudka was no speaker" it states at the outset of the story, and yet Yudka, the trembling and stumbling Kibbutz member appearing before a committee of sorts, ventures into a long speech over the meaning of Jewish history. The difficulty with the story lies in the apparent simplicity of the sermon. Although placed in a fictional framework, there is a great temptation to view its short, clear, straightforward sentences ("Boys, from the day we were driven out from our land we've been a people without a history. Class dismissed. Go out and play football.") as an expression of Hazaz's political message. Yet any attempt to read a clear message is doomed to failure. Somewhat like Plato's *Pytagoras*, the sermon leads one through what seems a logical discourse only to reveal in the end that the wrong path had been taken. The skilled artist has hidden a complex dialectic behind simple statements. This becomes clear only in the end when Yudka begs his listeners for just a few more minutes of patience to come to the point. "Say what you want," he is being told, "and let's see if we can't do without the philosophy."

In order to make sense of "The Sermon," Dan Miron, a literary

critic, proposed to view it as part of a larger philosophical system
developed by Hazaz.[38] The story can, however, be understood as
an individual unit once it is realized that it is not Yudka's stumbling that serves as fictional background to the content of the
sermon. It is the sermon that is fiction; the stumbling is real.
Yudka does indeed present a political manifesto—one which differs from that of the politician. The difference was once defined
by Yizhar: "The statesman chooses between the 'either' and the
'or.' He eliminates one, and the other is automatically eliminated
too and turns from a choice into a decision. Yet the philosopher
lives in the tension between the 'either' and the 'or.' . . . Where
the statesman's mind comes to rest, and he relaxes, the intellectual's begins to storm."[39] A different perspective is therefore
needed to reveal the writer's political message. This holds true
not only when the message is hidden behind the lines of a novel
but also when the writer comes up with an explicit political statement. The intellectual who speaks up in matters of politics does
not necessarily become a politician.

This was apparent in 1962 when Hazaz was chosen to give the
central speech in the annual conference of the writers' association. It was a complex speech lamenting the destruction of authentic Jewish life in Eastern Europe and discussing the tragic
implications of this destruction to the modern state of Israel.
Shortly after the speech, a well-publicized debate between
Hazaz and Ben-Gurion was finagled by the secretary general of
the Labor party.[40] Not only was Hazaz uninformed in advance
about the purpose of the meeting with the Prime Minister, but
he was expected to reproduce in political terms a set of ideas
which were in essence literary. In the heated atmosphere of
The Affair, Hazaz was later accused of trembling and stumbling
in the presence of the leader rather than transmitting a clear
message.[41] But the message was there. Hazaz, like Yudka, "was
no speaker," and yet he spoke. His sermon was fiction; the stumbling was real.

The intellectual tension between Hazaz and Ben-Gurion concerned their interpretation of the historical process. To the statesman, especially the messianic statesman, history is continually
being "made." Hazaz searched for an organic historical process,
one which is not formed by grand actions or decisions but by the
gradual evolvement of human, cultural, and political life. "Nation-building," to Hazaz, was an impossible concept. He ob-

served the destruction of Jewish cultural life in modern history ("The Sermon" had been written in 1942) and could not accept man-made substitutes, including the Zionist effort to which he was committed.

Hazaz found himself in a dilemma. He played a major role in the historical process of the national-cultural revival and at the same time doubted the authentic nature of this process. He admired the nation-builder, sang his praises (Hazaz continued to support Ben-Gurion even during The Affair), and yet recognized that the effort was, in a sense, ahistorical. To Hazaz, the small Jewish town (*stettl*) in Eastern Europe, with its little glory, was history. The attempt to revive a biblical past was not; it was just an artificial, political event in Jewish life. This impossible position for the author is what makes Yudka stumble; the more committed he is and the more he participates in the collective effort, the harder it is for the intellectual to admit his own skepticism, his fate as an intellectual:

◆ ◆ ◆

Yudka drew himself up stiffly, looking harried and confused, so much did he have to say and so little did he know how to begin.

It was shocking, how confused and how harried he was! This quarryman, who split rocks and rent mountains, and went out fearlessly on night patrols, no sooner had to speak publicly before his comrades, than he completely lost himself from fright.

When Yudka finally speaks, he states, in the language of the confused quarryman, what may be the greatest dilemma of the intellectual in history:

I didn't come here to make a speech, only to say something important. . . . Really, I shouldn't say anything at all. . . . Do you know what it is to speak when it's best for you to be still?

◆ ◆ ◆

Yudka insists that he is "opposed" to Jewish history because "we didn't make our own history." He lists a number of events and people considered "historical," such as bold deeds, heroes, great fighters, and fearless conquerors and concludes that "Jewish history is dull, uninteresting. It has no glory or action, no

heroes or conquerors, no rulers and masters of their fate." Many
literary critics have overlooked the irony involved here; in the
end, it turns out that Yudka is opposed to the very effort to revive
the glory and action, heroes and conquerors. For what is Zionism
if not an effort by the modern Jew to become the master of his
own fate? But Yudka considers this effort ahistorical too:

♦ ♦ ♦

One thing is clear. Zionism is not a continuation, it is no med-
icine for an ailment. That's nonsense! It is uprooting and destruc-
tion, it's the opposite of what has been, it's the end. . . . Zionism,
with a small group at its head, is the nucleus of a different people
. . . Please note that: not new or restored, but different.

♦ ♦ ♦

It seems that Israeli critics during the early years of the state
were so impressed by Yudka's rejection of the Diaspora that they
missed the dialectics involved. Yudka's "objection" to Jewish history applies to the lack of "organic" heroes in the Diaspora as well
as to their apparent formation, or revival, in modern Israel. True,
in "The Sermon" Hazaz wrote a strong exposé of the artificial
nature of the messianic ideal in Jewish history. But if one follows
Hazaz's logic, political messianism, that is, the consideration of
present deeds as the fulfilment of messianic yearnings, is no less
superficial. No wonder Yudka stumbles when he tries to express
his thinking before a committee of tough, self-confident, unques-
tioning participants in the nation-building effort. Had he really
been critical only of the passivity involved in Jewish history and
its messianic ideal, he could have stated it in the same confident
manner with which the committee treated him. Here is his view
of messianism:

♦ ♦ ♦

How, how can men who are by no means simple, who are no
fools at all; on the contrary, very shrewd men, men with more
than a touch of skepticism, men who are practical, and maybe
even a bit too practical; how can they believe something like that,
a thing like that—and not just believe, but trust it, pin their
whole life upon it, the whole substance of their life and survival,
their national, historic fate?

♦ ♦ ♦

This critique does not oppose a specific historical ideal but any historical ideal that replaces an organic, daily, "normal" history. Thus considered, "The Sermon" is not inconsistent with Hazaz's speech of 1962 in which he praised life in the small Jewish settlement of Eastern Europe. That earthly life was an antithesis, in Hazaz's thinking, to life by an ideal, be it the messianic ideal of the past or its modern version. In his speech he was explicit, objecting to such concepts as "Chosen People" or "light unto the nations" as national ideals. He also contended that in the setting of a nation's goals, the Bible could be of little help. To Hazaz, the history of a people comes before a book, and preoccupation with the Bible as a symbol of cultural revival is a poor substitute for true renaissance. In the subsequent debate with Ben-Gurion, Hazaz was even more explicit:

◆ ◆ ◆

You created in your imagination a reality which does not exist in fact. It is in the politician's nature to cover up things, maybe in order not to despair or neglect his work. The writer is different, it is in his nature to reveal things, otherwise he would not be loyal to his work.

Hazaz was right, but so was Ben-Gurion in his answer:

You do not evaluate correctly the facts of our life. The Jewish nation is going through a revolution. We shall not return to what we were.

◆ ◆ ◆

The two statements, that by the writer feeling modern reality is breaking away from authentic Jewish life and that by the statesman realizing the break is irreversible, represent the same dialectical thought which Yudka, in his stumbling sermon, tried to convey to the committee.

Epic as Critique

An interesting source of tension between the writer and the statesman lies in the very fact that politics becomes a subject for literature. The writer committed to reflecting upon the great moments of history be-

T H E   W R I T E R S : 143

comes a witness to its tragic moments as well, and the poet singing a leader's praises often finds himself singing a requiem when fortunes change. Even if it is presumed to be otherwise, politics is never "greater than life," and its observation from a literary point of view puts it in an overall human perspective. Seen in this perspective, even the messianic leader is found to be determined by the forces that distinguish man from God.

This section tells the story of the relationship between the poet Nathan Alterman and Ben-Gurion. Alterman, known as Ben-Gurion's "court poet," never failed to reflect on the greatness of the days. Yet when the days got gloomy—it was all there, in his beautiful poetry.[42]

Although Alterman never wrote in order to please a "court," his poetry (or rather part of it) was, as Moshe Dayan labeled it, "Ben-Gurionistic." Wrote Dayan: "Nathan Alterman, in his special 'Altermanism' educated the nation to 'Ben-Gurionism.'"[43] Dayan, who was close to both men, characterized Alterman as he who disseminated Ben-Gurion's message to the people. To Alterman, the role implied giving up what Yizhar considered the essence of intellectual life: the doubt. "Both avoided them, the 'but' and the 'perhaps,' not because they were not aware of them, but because they were above them, on a level above them, above doubts."[44]

Alterman not only put his pen, so to speak, in the service of current affairs, he sang the praises of the leader as only poets can do. In his poetry, Ben-Gurion was always the sage surrounded by amateurs, or the lonely hero carrying the burden unaided. Whenever Ben-Gurion resigned, or threatened he would, Alterman was ready with the (usually premature) lament. In Alterman's political poetry Ben-Gurion was the man destined by history to lead, to build, to serve. "There exists no greater force in the nation's modern history," sang Alterman, "let God be with him, as he stands in front of the red shining candle of the nation's life."[45]

Alterman's reputation as "court poet" was enhanced by an incident that occurred in 1956. On the eve of the Sinai War, Alterman joined the Prime Minister, the chief of staff, and the French ambassador to watch the unloading of heavy military equipment shipped from France. The cabinet was only informed of the event three months later when Ben-Gurion, on the stand in Parliament, read Alterman's poem "One Night" describing his impres-

sions. The poem ended with the words: "If only the people knew
how many thanks they owe to the few who initiated the task."[46]

Ben-Gurion, like many Israelis, had a special affection toward
Alterman, whom he considered a committed poet. Alterman was
often critical but always involved, very artistic and very political
at the same time. Ben-Gurion's greetings to Alterman on his 50th
birthday reveal his affection:

♦ ♦ ♦

*You disproved the view that pure literature and poetry cannot
accompany current events and that literature and poetry which
deal with current affairs are only . . . journalism in rhymes. . . .*

*I do not belong to those who despise art for its own sake. In
my opinion, everything in the world is for its own sake, and not
merely a means to something else (although everything is a link
in a chain and hence a means), because only that which is worthy
in itself is truly valuable. Man is an end in himself. Every good
deed is an end in itself. Every true idea is an end in itself and
every literary and poetic expression is an end in itself. But having
said that, I do not believe the world is composed of separate
atoms with no link between them, on the contrary—I visualize a
supreme cosmic unity everywhere, and there is nothing big or
small which is not part of this unity, for better or worse.*

*But there was, and is, a theory, that pure literature and poetry
are not concerned with daily events—only with love, the sun, the
stars, destiny, sorrow, joy, life and death in their abstract form.*

*I consider it an illustration of your greatness as a writer that
you deal with current affairs and succeed in giving them clear,
poetic, enchanting and inspiring meaning as no other of our
poets has done (as far as I know). In my opinion, the true and
lasting beauty, delicacy and lyricism of your poems is not dimin-
ished by the close and immediate influence of current events or
phenomena which you transform by the mysterious magic of the
poet's pen into literary masterpieces. This requires not only
unique poetic skills, but a supreme human quality.*[47]

♦ ♦ ♦

Alterman's "committed" poetry was widely criticized. Doubt
was cast on the ability to keep being inspired once that inspiration is "called upon to work extra hours in the workshop filling

social orders."[48] Critics argued that Alterman's "committed" poetry was less genuine than his earlier poems. In a review written
in 1965, Kidan noted the major change in Alterman's poetry
which occurred during the struggle for independence and the
establishment of the state.[49] Alterman's skeptical humanism
turned into a messianic belief which ignored all gaps between
vision and reality, or dismissed social ills by expressing hope for
the future. According to Kidan, this stemmed from Alterman's
fascination with the establishment of the state and from his
perception of it as an expression of messianic redemption, a phenomenon above and beyond the laws of history. In the first years
of nation-building, Kidan noted, Alterman could maintain his
messianic view in spite of his observation of gaps between the
vision and reality because there were very real factors bridging
the gap. Prominent among these factors was the personality of
Ben-Gurion, who symbolized for Alterman the transcendental
bridge between daily life and the divine.

But then, wrote Kidan, came the "morning after," and Alterman could no longer ignore the gap. Messianic ideology still
prevailed in his poetry of the 1960s, but the poet was forced to
admit underlying problems and to reveal that his poems dealt
with only a limited aspect of life. "Not all that is being told,"
Alterman wrote, "is important, and a lot of that which is important is missing." Alterman recognized that the picture he portrayed was only partial. "Another man, another evening, will
have to return,"[50] one of his poems said.

Thus, Alterman, whose artistic skills led him to look beyond
history, was forced, by the same skills, to face history. The writer
who committed his whole being to the national effort now had to
admit he was writing only part of the story. He continued to
follow the nation-building effort, but that effort became increasingly an episode within a broader historical reality which seemed
less and less glamorous. Alterman continued to reflect the mood
of the times, but the times had changed. He continued to praise
Ben-Gurion but the praises of the 1960s turned into a requiem.
Ben-Gurion's loneliness after The Affair was too real to be heroic.
In 1947, after a scandal concerning the use of undiplomatic language by Ben-Gurion, Alterman described the outspoken leader
as besieged by his gray colleagues who learned to "speak like
ministers."[51] When Ben-Gurion resigned in 1953, he was the
lonely hero in the desert where "a light-beam of anxiety and

anticipation shines over the whole landscape."[52] In 1961, however, it all sounded different:

◆ ◆ ◆

It is night now. All is quiet. The guests have gone. I, too, say good-bye to you and turn to leave. I am the seventy-fifth year of your life. You do not even raise your head to say good-bye. Fine, so be it. I have already been told you do not care for birthday celebrations. Fine. I know it is wrong to disturb you at this hour of night. And still, I have a desire to say something to you. It is my desire to tell you that I feel I am part of a great and rare life-story. I have the urge to tell you that you are entitled to look back over your life with a feeling of satisfaction and gratitude.[53]

◆ ◆ ◆

In this birthday greeting, Alterman still hints at the fighting spirit of the past, but it is now the spirit of an old, if never tired, soldier. Alterman could not escape the sadness involved in the beautiful picture he described—the elder statesman sitting at his desk, or falling asleep, after the guests have gone:

◆ ◆ ◆

I am certain you cannot hear what I am saying, since had you heard me, you would have jumped up to correct some mistake or wrongdoing of mine, and you would have probably insisted upon it with full vigor. Perhaps I would have left you in anger. I shall therefore only say this to you: I am glad I leave you healthy in body and strong in spirit, with all your great attributes and faults at their peaks, alert and sprite as always.[54]

◆ ◆ ◆

The Great Battle

the great battle between Ben-Gurion and the writers began in October 1961, coinciding with The Affair. In the 12 years that had passed since the writers first assembled in the Prime Minister's office and expressed their commitment to the state, great changes had taken place in society. The turn of the new decade marked the end of the messianic period, and the nation-building effort was now routine. The 12 years that had passed since 1949 were a period of maturity in the life of the nation as well as in literature, and the intellectual tensions that evolved in those years between the statesman and the writers now came to the fore. The political debate discussed in this section was not necessarily a "result" of The Affair, but coincided with it. The time was ripe for a whole different set of relations between the statesman and the writers.

The first bullet in the battle was shot in an interview the Prime Minister gave to a major newspaper on the eve of the Jewish new year.[55] Ben-Gurion was asked what his feelings were regarding fine literature. "Fine literature?" he responded, "I have not read fine literature for several years now." "No Hebrew, not even Greek literature?" he was asked. "No, really. A few days ago someone wrote that I do not read Hebrew short stories. The truth is I do not read stories at all." "For lack of time or for lack of interest?" "Both," he replied.

The volume and intensity of the response to Ben-Gurion's statement indicate that in 1961 the stage was set for a new knowledge-power relationship. The first major response came from the novelist Moshe Shamir, who published an open letter to the Prime Minister in which he claimed that just as Ben-Gurion's devotion to the Bible is a blessing, his disregard of contemporary Hebrew literature is a disaster.[56] This letter caused no less fury than Ben-Gurion's original statement, for writers had now begun to realize that they did not need approval by the government. Shamir's style was considered shameful, for it did not treat the writer as the statesman's equal. An article by Hanoch Bartov, another young writer, indicated this new dimension introduced into intellectual life since the meetings of 1949. Bartov blamed the intellectuals themselves for the disregard Ben-Gurion expressed toward them. It lay, he wrote, in their failure to play the role of social critics. An enlightened ruler, wrote Bartov, is a blessing to himself and to his country, but there is no connection whatsoever between the preferences of the ruler and the "way of the spirit." The writer does not need the Prime Minister's approval to write a book. He considered Shamir's concern with approval as inviting astonishment and pity. "Why does he care?"[57]

If anyone needed an answer it came within a week. Ben-Gurion, in full fighting spirit, leaked to the press a letter he had received from Shamir half a year earlier.[58] In this letter, which accompanied a collection of essays he sent to the Prime Minister,

Shamir wrote that although he often found himself at loggerheads with Ben-Gurion, his writing was inspired by his knowledge that Ben-Gurion might read it, as if some secret conspiracy between the writer and statesman existed. When this letter appeared in the press, the intellectual community was outraged; Shamir dropped out of the debate, but the battle had only begun. There was enormous surprise over Shamir's perception that the writer maintains a secret conspiracy with the ruler, especially in the light of Shamir's former image as a young rebel. But there was more. Shamir's letter symbolized a relationship that no longer had a place in Israeli intellectual life. A new model of the relationship between the ruler and the writer now prevailed—one of equal status and open conflict. One newspaper expressed the transformation clearly: "Ben-Gurion," it reacted to his leaking of Shamir's letter, "decided to respond to him like a ruler."[59]

Significantly, it was none other than Benjamin Michaly, the head of the writers' association, an association long connected with mainstream politics, who clarified the new mode.[60] While he still expressed concern over why Ben-Gurion did not patronize or "encourage" writers, he portrayed a new relationship. In an article published on October 12, 1960, he considered the ruler and writer as being in perpetual conflict. Times change; regimes come and go, but the conflict persists. In periods of great change or danger the ruler and writer come closer, but even then the tension is only shelved temporarily. Michaly explained this conflict by great differences in outlook. First, the ruler, even when he strives for a better future, is, unlike the writer, concerned only with the present. Second, the ruler, in contrast to the writer, overlooks the failures of his regime. Michaly did not really think in terms of the conflictual model he himself stated. Had he done so, he would not have been as concerned with Ben-Gurion's preferences regarding fine literature. But in two ways his essay spoke a new language: First, in its concern over Ben-Gurion's inability to enjoy fine literature as such (in the meetings of 1949, little was said about literature for its own sake), and second, Michaly raised for the first time the possibility that an open conflict between the ruler and the writers may lead to better and richer literature.

A letter to the editor on October 28, written by three Leftist authors, made clear that a political conflict existed between Ben-Gurion and the writers. The letter complained about "politicians"

preaching "pseudo-prophetic morality to writers and intellectuals," which constitutes a "semi-official" intervention in their
affairs. They called upon the intellectuals to reverse the process
and speak up on matters of public concern.[61]

But the generation of writers represented in the 1949 meetings
had no easy time in adjusting to their new role. Their confusion
was expressed in *Moznayim*, a periodical published by the writers' association. In the November issue, for example, the poet
Shin Shalom explicitly lamented the old relationship between
the writer and the ruler which had collapsed.[62] Shalom admitted
that he and his colleagues "spoiled" the leadership to the extent
of being labeled "court poets." "This voluntary surrender of ours
to the heads of the tribes of Israel gave us pride. We wanted to
see the laying of the foundation of the kingdom of Israel, hence,
we have given up our pride." Shalom complained that the rulers
had not fulfilled their part of the deal. It is the way of the ruler
not to share power. Committed poetry had granted them power,
and as they reached the throne they betrayed those who lifted
them to it.

A response to Shalom by a young poet expressed more pity
than anger. He mocked Shalom for his desire to renew a golden
age of close relations between rulers and poets. "Should Ben-
Gurion perhaps declare he loves poetry and thus open the new
golden age?" he asked.[63] Nathan Alterman was also critical of
Shalom but from a different perspective: "The true writer is the
first to inquire around whom the world revolves, but the last to
answer: 'around me.' "[64]

The debate continued for weeks, with bystanders, as well as
participants, wondering over the fury stirred up by a short remark by the Prime Minister. One newspaper ironically asked
whether anybody knew what President Eisenhower felt about
the American literary heritage, what General de Gaulle thought
about the French novel, or whether Mr. Macmillan, England's
prime minister, loved poems by Byron and Keats.[65] But in a
historical perspective, the debate was significant. The new relationship between the writer and power was part of the process
by which the nation-building era ended and a new era began.

During the debate with the writers, Ben-Gurion expressed
himself in Parliament and in public.[66] He also published a
lengthy article in response to Shalom.[67] However, his point of
view, and for that matter the core of the debate, was expressed

in a letter he wrote six months before his initial statement. In an answer to Shamir's letter of February (which he also leaked and which was published alongside Shamir's), he wrote:

◆ ◆ ◆

I know it is dangerous to make such a heretical statement to a devoted writer, but perhaps you too would admit that life—when it is rich and meaningful—is more important than the books attempting to reflect it. . . . The great and loud song I hear—is the song of our young men of might and feat. They create our great new literature—on the mountains and in the valleys, in the workshop and factory, in the air and on the sea, in the laboratory and in the university, in the army barracks and in the police (yes, in the police, too), and I have no doubt that this "living literature" would receive its appropriate expression in stories, poems, and plays. The writers who will create (or perhaps have already created) this work of art are perhaps already walking among us, but whether they do or not, this is not going to diminish the greatness of the generation, the period and the days. The epic by Aeschylus was also not written during his hero's lifetime. Let the great deeds be done—the books will be written, and if they are late to arrive, I shall not be bored in the meantime.[68]

◆ ◆ ◆

Ben-Gurion never changed his notion of literature as the reflection of actual deeds. But society had changed, literature had changed, and the writer abandoned his initial commitment to the collective group. National revival was increasingly considered within the overall development of human history, and doubts were cast over whether immediate heroic deeds constituted true history. The writer, willingly or not, became an observer of gaps between vision and reality. The new generation of writers could not write the epic Ben-Gurion waited for, as Meged had shown in *The Living on the Dead*. Daily life in the 1960s did not seem messianic; it seemed routine, and the general condition of man seemed tragic. As a young student of philosophy wrote in a letter to Ben-Gurion during the great debate over literature, common man "is none but a cog in the wheels of history." While the Prime Minister, he wrote, envisages great acts of building and conquering, the builders engage in a continuous process of routine, daily

work. To them, he added, literature fulfills an important function, one of directing man toward his own self where he finds his
happiness and satisfaction.[69]

This was a new line of thinking, and the Prime Minister treated
the letter very seriously. He answered that although he usually
saw the full range of things more than others, he was not the
only one to apply vision to reality. He insisted, as he always had,
that great visionary deeds were done by many people,
each of whom played a part in the farm settlements, in industry,
in the army, in education, and in science. Ben-Gurion saw in
those daily, routine deeds the epic of the times, which waited
for its reflection in literature. He wrote that he did not ignore the value of fine literature but that he believed more in
"the living example by the model person." Living people, he
felt, were sometimes more capable of serving as models and
guides for life than were books.[70]

The Emerging Philosopher·King

In the previous chapters, 12 debates between Ben-Gurion and the intellectuals were discussed. These debates concerned a variety of issues faced by Israeli society in its "nation-building" era, but they include a common denominator. In all 12 debates, the intellectuals advocated restraint on the uses of knowledge as it combines with action. The intellectuals who were part of the system combining the two also became the guardians of knowledge against its abuse, playing both the bride and the chaperon during its 12-year honeymoon with political messianism. This dual role of the intellectual in the charismatic center of society makes him a most interesting phenomenon.

"Charismatic centers" have been defined, according to Shils, Eisenstadt, and Geertz, as the loci of important acts in society, where institutional and cultural reality is being formed and orderly social change assured. The collaboration between knowledge and power, including the tensions involved in that collaboration, were expected to play an important role in society. The intellectuals' perception of the statesman as endowed with charisma is an important element to consider in explaining the degree to which intellectuals play a significant role in the collaboration. From this perspective, Ben-Gurion's relationship with Israel's intellectuals, a relationship characterized by the evolvement of tension within the context of political messianism, must be considered. In this special context a close collaboration between knowledge and power is expected, since political messianism is a condition in which those in the charismatic center search, find, and revise the tie between social action and its divine symbolic meaning. The intellectuals, because of their concern with symbols, are naturally called upon to engage in political symbolism as well.[1]

What characterized the messianic period in Israel was the dominance of the statesman in defining the parameters of the sociocultural dialogue and in attributing meanings and norms to reality. The intellectuals—some consciously, some not—became legitimizers of a messianic interpretation of social and political reality. At the same time they played a restraining role concerning the utilization of knowledge.[2] The scientists' objection to Ben-Gurion's extension of the concept of "truth" limited the statesman's ability to define moral statements as natural laws and consider a specific set of norms as derived from the eternal harmony of nature.[3] The philosophers were explicit as to the boundaries of knowledge, limiting the scope of the symbolic meanings which can be attributed to the political state.[4] The biblical scholars, in a very straightforward manner, restricted the ways and means by which knowledge ought to be acquired. And the writers objected to the one-dimensional observation of reality implied by the notion of political messianism.[5] The intellectuals were a diverse group in their social affiliations and political preferences, but in their concern with knowledge they formed a unified group in a very real sense. It was a "guild of knowledge," concerned with its extension, that confronted Ben-Gurion during The Affair.[6]

"Guilds of knowledge" are never formed simply because some groups in society are preoccupied with knowledge. This preoccupation may be a necessary condition for the formation of group consciousness over questions of societal knowledge but not a sufficient one. It had often been assumed that intellectuals, by nature of their activities, represented specific interests. This led to their public image as proponents of the expansion of knowledge and its uses[7] and, subsequently, to demands for controls over this expansion.[8] The 12 debates discussed here prove this image to be inaccurate, since it was the intellectuals who played a restraining role. This leads me back to the belief, expressed in the introduction, that our predictive power regarding the political behavior of intellectuals may be enhanced by a more dynamic concept of their societal role. The findings of my study are consistent with such a concept—Ben-Gurion's challenge had an enormous impact on the formation of a group consciousness by intellectuals and perception of his charisma on its political saliency. Were it not for his lively mind and passionate interests, or his brashness in challenging anyone in the fields of knowledge in which he was self-taught, the intellectuals may never have concerned themselves with the nature of their collaboration with power. Were it not for the fading of his charisma, their concerns would have probably remained on the level of "court politics." But Ben-Gurion's challenge to the intellectuals had more than an episodic element to it. He did not simply activate a response from the intellectuals; his model of leadership constituted a profound challenge which exceeded its time and place. An analysis of this challenge allows, I feel, for a general explanation (or theory) of the tension between knowledge and power.

The Model

In a speech given on the third anniversary of Ben-Gurion's death, the writer Yizhar labeled him the "philosopher-king."[9] This Platonic image of Ben-Gurion is useful because it puts him in a long tradition of Jewish leadership. As Segre had shown, Jewish leadership in its most varied institutional form was always the expression of the "best" who judged, ruled, guided, and educated in the name of the divine authority. This certainly did not envisage a combination of power, of "mixed rule" similar to the one suggested by Aristotle or followed by modern representative democracy, although it was a system allowing the spirit of criticism to develop due to the idea that the whole nation can attain the spiritual-moral perfection of what Segre calls the "genuine aristocrat."[10] But, the Platonic image locates Ben-Gurion not only in a tradition of the past but also in the future. His model of leadership had been, in a very real sense, an early manifestation of "technostructure," that is, a system of societal decision-making in which knowledge and power are strongly interwoven.[11] Such a system is attributed—in different versions—to the emerging technological society that implies, as Toffler has characterized it, a massive transformation of society while it searches for a balance between advanced science and technology and the "Gandhian vision."[12] By referring to the decision-making system of the future as "Gandhi with satellites," Toffler pointed to the usefulness of searching for the model of "technostructure" in the visionary leaders who led massive nation-building efforts in the 1950s and 1960s. In fact, Toffler's "third wave" resembles these massive efforts guided by leaders who demanded a commitment to the transformation of society through planned, systemic change. At one point he was explicit: "Tomorrow's 'development' strategies will come not from Washington or Moscow or Paris or Geneva but from Africa, Asia and Latin America. They will be indigenous, matched to actual local needs. They will not overemphasize economics at the expense of ecology, culture, religion, or family structure and the psychological dimensions of existence."[13]

The model of Ben-Gurion's leadership was characterized by the effective utilization of knowledge and manipulation of power in the service of an encompassing vision of social transformation. His qualities as a man of spirit and action combined to form, in the words of one disciple, "a chariot covering vast new distances when harnessed to the horses of vision."[14] Vision, it will be recalled, has been defined in this study as a set of goals exceeding obvious parameters of resources. Indeed, the setting of such goals was the cornerstone of Ben-Gurion's leadership, but his biographers were right to note that it had never been distinct from considerations of power and knowledge.[15] Ben-Gurion's daring goals were always accompanied by a strong sense of reality and his far-reaching dreams were based on detailed analysis of the components of reality. He was a modern prophet, Bar Zohar wrote, but one equipped with a slide rule.[16] The bonding of knowledge and power with vision had important implications for both, since vision hardly tolerates controls over the manipulation of power nor on the utilization of knowledge. The visionary statesman is one whose concern with knowledge, like his concern with power, is intended above all to overcome constraints posed by its nature, traditions, or practices.[17]

The underlying issue in Ben-Gurion's debates with the intellectuals was the latter's resistance to their leader's attempt to overcome the constraints of knowledge as part of his wish to overcome the boundaries of reality. The statesman whose vision reached the land and the sea, the earth and the sky, terra firma

and the stratosphere[18] could hardly accept the hypothetical nature of science, the destructive potential of technology, the distinction between facts and values, or the rules of historiography.
In fact, he could hardly tolerate knowledge at all unless harnessed to the horses of vision. He is, to use a common typology,
a man of intelligence, not of intellect. In Hofstadter's words, his
mind seeks to grasp, manipulate, re-order, adjust rather than to
examine, ponder, wonder, theorize, criticize, or imagine.[19] Ben-
Gurion himself had often made the distinction between knowledge for action and knowledge for its own sake. He admired both
but resented knowledge when not connected to a broader purpose or act. His political secretary, Yitzhak Navon, provided a
useful example. Despite Ben-Gurion's deep involvement in philosophy, Navon wrote, he negated the use of theoretical philosophical systems which could not withstand the test of
application, viewing them as sterile. Thus, he had little patience
for the polemic as to "whether ideological struggle derives from
economic, social and political discordance, or whether the struggle gives rise to it." The essential thing was to comprehend the
practical significance of such struggles and their place in the "flux
of history." Navon noted that for Ben-Gurion, the "flux of history"
enabled man to change his fate, to influence events and his life.
Therefore, although there were, in his opinion, "ideas which
have changed economic and political regimes, there have also
been regimes which have revived ideas and granted them
sway."[20]

The attempt to link knowledge with action implies, as this
quotation reminds us, a need to adjust knowledge to fit the needs
of the state. Interestingly, however, even those intellectuals who
were most fiercely opposed to Ben-Gurion's use of knowledge
could not resist their admiration for his diligence, his avid reading, his incredible memory, great curiosity and thoroughness in
the search for truth. All these had made him a great student, but
no intellectual. What distinguished him from an intellectual was
his refusal to accept the constraints inherent in knowledge or
rather those put on knowledge and its uses by the intellectual.
Israel Kolatt noted Ben-Gurion's refusal to discipline his scientific
thinking.[21] Ben-Gurion admired the scientist's drive for research
which he considered the link between man and the world but
refused to accept the boundaries to which this drive must be

confined. Kolatt further claimed that despite his cautious realism, Ben-Gurion had no empirical mind. Facts and values were interwoven, and the heterogeneity of human and social experience was ignored. He refused to subject his thinking to the lessons of experience. The past, he insisted, teaches us a lesson about the past but not about the future.

Shimon Peres, who worked closely with Ben-Gurion for many years, provided important insights on the nature of knowledge when related to action. According to Peres, Ben-Gurion, who on one hand never satisfied his thirst for knowledge, was not capable of learning anything without later forming a distinct opinion about it. Sometimes his opinions preceded his knowledge, and then he sought corroboration in his studies; sometimes his knowledge preceded his opinions, and then he would attempt to formulate new conclusions. In either case, neither knowledge nor opinion was isolated.[22]

A more systematic analysis of Ben-Gurion's practices of knowledge acquisition and utilization reveals his attempt to overcome the constraints of knowledge and put it in the service of action. A review of these practices provides a rather comprehensive model of the philosopher-king. Endowed with vision, the philosopher-king searches for knowledge to fulfill his extraordinary goals when professional expertise falls short. His criteria of choice of relevant knowledge are strictly derived from his goals, and he inspires the production of knowledge that would fit these criteria. He also utilizes knowledge in order to achieve a burning commitment to the goals by both elites and the masses. These practices, revealed in Ben-Gurion's files, require greater study not only because they throw light on the concept of philosopher-king but because they seem to have become functional prerequisites of the modern technostructure.

Knowledge Acquisition

Ben-Gurion's files are characterized by the great amount—and variety—of information with which he concerned himself. One finds in them intelligence briefings, political memos, technical reports, legal documents, newspaper clips, scientific manuscripts, and, above all, letters, letters, letters:

♦ ♦ ♦

Dear Mr. Prime Minister:

*I am writing to you as a writer and as a Prime Minister who
cherishes the national heritage on the following matter—the
moth that damages our books. I am afraid that in thirty to fifty
years no remains will be left of the books printed in the country
today.*

*I, for one, have a large library which includes 100- to 150-year-
old books which are in very good shape; not one mark by moths
can be found on them. On the other hand, I own books which
were published in Israel as late as 1960 (including a book by my
wife printed in Jerusalem) and they are already affected by
moths and damaged. . . .*[23]

♦ ♦ ♦

Ben-Gurion's attention to this letter provides an example of his
practice of knowledge acquisition. While every statesman re-
ceives dozens of similar letters, the philosopher-king is distinguished by his genuine concern with the information involved.
For Ben-Gurion, there was no matter classified a priori as trivial.
While large bureaucracies in developed societies supposedly
know in advance what is trivial and what is not, or what input is
worth listening to,[24] Ben-Gurion never took the sources of relevant input for granted. He often contended that a new nation
must search for solutions to its problems in unconventional
sources. For instance, restoring the symbol of "People of the
Book," he believed, may be of great practical value. Thus, the
world statesman, the strategist, the shrewd politician concerned
himself with details regarding moths damaging books in much
the same way as he listened to proposals concerning weapons
systems or energy. He did not leave it to a public relations officer
to politely respond to a letter of this kind but considered it his
role as Prime Minister to check some of his own thousands of
books to compare the damage done by moths to old vs. new ones.
"I have checked a few new books in my Jerusalem apartment,"
he responded, "which were printed since 1955 and after—and
haven't found a single damaged one. Yet my having not seen one
is no proof and the matter still requires checking. I shall ask the
Minister of Commerce and Industry to commission one of his

deputies in charge of printers and binders to look into your claim, and I shall let you know the results."[25]

It has become so common for politicians to cite correspondence of this kind as a sign of responsiveness that it is hard to distinguish between genuine and feigned concern. The issue dealt with here, however, is not a politician's responsiveness but rather his broad search for appropriate information.[26] Thus, while Ben-Gurion had regular contact with scientists of note, he also searched for scientific solutions to national problems in what was considered the periphery of science at the time. Deeming, for instance, the search for alternative energy sources important long before mainstream science concerned itself with the problem, Ben-Gurion initiated research into solar energy, even dragging his whole coalition cabinet to an abandoned British military camp to show the bored ministers a successful solar energy installation. This trip had more than a symbolic function; it was one of Ben-Gurion's many attempts to overcome the tendency by the modern bureaucracy to ignore information seemingly irrelevant at first sight.[27] His correspondence with his own bureaucracy was filled with reminders to pay attention, to look around, not to ignore "trivial" information. Here are two typical notes to the Minister of Agriculture:

◆ ◆ ◆

Dear Moshe: *August 8, 1960*

I hereby enclose Holzman's letter about the grapefruit which can grow in salty water. By coincidence I met the chief gardener of Tel Aviv after I received the letter. He also knows about this fruit and he confirmed Holzman's claim to me. Anyway, it is worthwhile paying attention to the matter and trying to grow that fruit around Eilat and Ashkelon which are close to the sea where it is not difficult to use sea water with no great expense involved.

With the growing shortage of water in the country, no chance should be missed to expand agriculture which needs no sweet waters.

Yours,

D. Ben-Gurion

To: *Minister of Agriculture*   *August 14, 1960*
From: Prime Minister

It turned out that Holzman's letter had been sent to you and was received in your office immediately, but your secretary saw fit to delay submitting it to you for all kinds of reasons. It is appropriate for you to instruct her not to delay things next time I send them to you.

Cordially,

D. Ben-Gurion

And to the minister's secretary:

Don't delay this little note—submit it immediately to the Minister of Agriculture.

♦ ♦ ♦

Ben-Gurion's willingness to listen to proposals rejected by the bureaucracy brought an influx of esoteric proposals such as that by the night watchman who found a way to solve the country's water shortage by bringing clouds down to earth. At the same time, however, it opened an important channel for creative information. Scientists involved in conflicts over research and development or inventors whose contributions were rejected often turned to Ben-Gurion for help. For instance, in 1954, a fundamental debate took place over the development of natural resources. The National Scientific Council, favoring the coordination of production of potash, copper, and Dead Sea minerals, called for the Prime Minister's intervention against his own bureaucracy's vested interests.[28] Individual scientists often turned to Ben-Gurion when the government he headed, or one of its ministries, seemed to operate against the national interest. When the Minister of Agriculture, faced with a problem of milk surplus, decided to reduce milk production, Ben-Gurion was impressed by a letter he received from a professor of parasitology claiming that the problem consisted not of an overproduction of milk but rather of a lack of awareness among the poor regarding its value. The solution to the problem of surplus, the letter said, lay not in economics but in education.[29] This was a classical argument often

rejected by bureaucracies as "academic." Indeed, when Ben-Gurion referred the letter to the Ministers of Finance and Agriculture, they were much less impressed.[30]

But even the philosopher-king cannot avoid having to choose
between relevant and irrelevant information. What distinguishes
his choice process is the lack of random considerations. Consist-
ency can be partly assured when decisions as to what reaches
one's desk or what should be acted upon are made less on the
basis of bureaucratic politics than on the basis of political vision.
Ben-Gurion was known for his ability to grasp information relevant to his visionary goals. This had both positive and negative
consequences. On the one hand, important information was
sometimes disregarded. For instance, in 1959, a group of students called upon him to recognize as independent a university
in Tel-Aviv. The time seemed ripe for a second university in the
country, yet Ben-Gurion was so preoccupied with the notion of
the Hebrew University in Jerusalem as a spiritual center and
with the role of Jerusalem in international politics that he ignored
the substantive problem.[31] Also, the absorption of information in
the light of a broad vision often resulted in the neglect of details.
While frequently referring to the country's limited resources,
Ben-Gurion often paid little attention to considerations of cost.[32]

On the other hand, Ben-Gurion's consideration of information
in the light of its contribution to a broader vision opened an
important channel for citizens with good ideas but no authority
or status. Many were surprised to find that a point they made
had reached the Prime Minister. For example, the professors of
botany who complained about inaccuracies in pictures of flowers
appearing on stamps could not predict the Prime Minister's
prophetic rage against the post office: "We are beginning to become familiar with the country's plants and we want to disseminate this familiarity to a nation returning to its homeland," he
wrote, "and the Post Office should not encourage the ignorant."[33]

Ben-Gurion's broad goals not only served as criteria for the
choice of relevant information but also as guidelines for the production of knowledge. Scientists were often inspired by him to
turn to applied fields, and persons of letters were stimulated to
pursue new paths. In their memoirs, intellectuals often referred
to Ben-Gurion's influence upon their career decisions.[34] Letters
he received on such questions as demography, energy, science
policy, education, industrial development, etc., usually referred

to some previous statement by him on these matters; for example, the above-mentioned professor of parasitology, commenting
on the milk industry, referred in his letter to the Prime Minister's
frequent mention of "a land of milk and honey." Ben-Gurion not
only created a symbolic frame of reference, he played a concrete
role in pointing out the social problems to be considered. For
instance, the chairman of a department at Tel Aviv University
admitted in a letter to Ben-Gurion that he was inspired by the
Prime Minister's declarations concerning mass education for
adults and accompanied his statement by a detailed proposal on
this matter.[35] He received a detailed response by the Prime Minister in which the inspiration he himself got from the proposal
can be detected.[36] While this correspondence was preliminary
and the programs dealt with in the proposal were carried out
only several years later, one cannot escape the feeling that mutual inspiration was involved which, although impractical at first,
was a necessary condition for nation-building. Literature on expertise describes attempts in modern developed societies, especially during the 1960s, to institutionalize knowledge-based input
as having often lacked this element of genuine, mutual
stimulation.[37]

The established community of knowledge certainly did not
contact Ben-Gurion only on the level of genuine societal concerns. The philosopher-king received many requests to intervene
in matters of concern to that community. The associate dean
asking for resources, the researcher asking for army helicopters
to help carry out his research, the university president asking the
Prime Minister to intervene in an intra-university dispute over
the distribution of funds, the request to aid a colleague who was
denied tenure, or the request to help persuade foreign scholars
to make a contribution to a local symposium are all part of the
relationship between knowledge and power. This is also where
the real test of the philosopher-king lies. It is to be expected that
close contact between knowledge and power would lead to requests by intellectuals on particular matters and that such requests would open up the gate to authoritarian control over the
intellectual community, especially over academia. Ben-Gurion
showed little interest in exploiting such loopholes and infringing
upon academic freedom, which helped promote his image as
philosopher-king.

Knowledge Utilization

The position that Ben-Gurion held as world statesman, national leader, and effective politician was enhanced by his concerns with intellectual affairs. This went beyond his ability to quote Greek or Buddhist thinkers on diplomatic occasions. He was well read; his interests were wide and so were his activities in the cultural sphere. He was very active, for instance, in a committee sponsoring translations of scientific literary treasures into Hebrew. Members of the committee admired his familiarity with literary works, as did the public. While on vacations, Ben-Gurion always carried with him books in various languages and often expressed his frustration that he could not read Indian philosophy in the original. During a visit to Burma he spent three days in a monastery. And although critics charged that this was too obvious an attempt to improve relations with Burma's U Nu or India's Nehru, it was not merely politics. Ben-Gurion was one of a generation of master statesmen whose nationalist interests were in no contradiction to an open, global mind. But Ben-Gurion's intellectual skills often became political tools in purely partisan affairs. Spinoza, Plato, or Buddha provided a unique language in which friends and foes alike could be addressed. One incident was fascinating. Appearing before Parliament to explain one of his most controversial decisions, the decision to retreat from Sinai, conquered by Israel in 1956, Ben-Gurion attacked the right-wing opposition for what he considered its unsubstantiated pride regarding the country's military strength. "I learned from one ancient sage what courage is," he declared. "That sage said that courage is a kind of knowledge; the knowledge to fear that which is to be feared, and not to fear that which is not to be feared." "Spinoza thinks differently," Yohanan Bader, a Right-wing leader, interrupted. "No, my learned friend, I did not quote Spinoza this time," Ben-Gurion answered.[38]

A day later, the Prime Minister, still facing a serious international crisis, wrote a letter to Bader:

Dear Dr. Bader: ◆ ◆ ◆ *November 15, 1956*

I did not hear your interruption correctly, but when I read the minutes I saw that you said that Spinoza's opinion is different. I

believe that you were mistaken in your understanding of Spi-
noza. Actually, Spinoza does not deal with the question of what
courage is, but with man's passions, and he notes that different
people's passions towards the same thing are different. One
man's meat is another man's poison, but Spinoza does not deter-
mine which of them is right. Spinoza also notes that one fears
what the other does not fear, but he passes judgment neither on
the "courageous" nor on the "coward". . . .

◆ ◆ ◆

Bader, the fierce political opponent who confronted the Prime
Minister over a major foreign policy question, now found himself
deeply engaged in a philosophy lesson. He wrote:

◆ ◆ ◆

Very respectable Mr. Ben-Gurion: *November 21, 1956*

. . . As often happens in parliamentary interruptions, I did not
exactly dwell on the essence of Spinoza's remarks on passions,
especially since dozens of years have passed since the good old
days when I was deeply engaged in the study of philosophy.

Generally speaking, I believe Spinoza's psychological approach
is more correct than Plato's rationalist approach, as expressed in
"Protagoras." You have probably paid attention to the conclud-
ing paragraph of the dialogue in which Plato himself recognizes
the doubts raised by his own approach: is it really clear knowl-
edge, or reason, that distinguishes courage from lack of cour-
age? It goes without saying that a person familiar with
something will not be frightened of it . . . but in the most cru-
cial decisions faced by an individual or group, even the most
detailed knowledge and best analysis would not excuse one from
having to make a decision with courage, and courage is no mere
reflection of knowledge. . . .

Dear Mr. Bader   *November 26, 1956*

I am afraid you were wrong about Plato, as you were about
Spinoza—and probably for the same reason—that you have not
dealt with him for many years.

It is not true that Plato recognized "the doubts raised by his
own approach: is it really clear knowledge, or reason, that dis-

*tinguishes courage from lack of courage?" Plato had no such
doubts. . . . At the end of the dialogue (Protagoras) doubt is
cast on an entirely different matter: not on what courage means
but on whether excellence can be granted by learning or not,
and it is this question which remains open at the end of the
dialogue, but as far as courage is concerned, Plato is explicit
beyond doubt. Nobody, of course, is obliged to accept Plato's
opinion, and you have every right to oppose him. The decision I
made was also not made on the basis of Plato's statements, but
on the basis of an analysis of the situation and circumstances; I
would have done it even if Plato had not written* Laches *and*
Protagoras. *I do not hold the Athenian philosopher responsible
for my deeds. But since I know you as a "lover of wisdom"—and
according to Socrates (Plato) one is no "lover of wisdom" unless
he loves the truth—and I wholeheartedly agree with him on
that—I wanted to make you aware of the mistake you made in
your parliamentary interruption regarding Spinoza, and in
your letter of November 21, 1956—regarding Plato.*

Sincerely,

D. Ben-Gurion

♦ ♦ ♦

There is no greater knowledge expressed in this correspondence than that used in letters by students trying to impress the
Prime Minister with quotations from the classics. But the use of
the same quotations by Ben-Gurion must be seen in a different
perspective. It set the stage for a unique political culture, one in
which even a partisan debate becomes somehow fundamental.
Ben-Gurion's concern with knowledge and his symbolic argu-
mentation were an aspect of political messianism—the consideration of earthly deeds in the light of divine ideas. It brought the
messianic style into the political system; it made politics part of
the process of "redemption." A political process in which the
aging head of the political center must admit that "my knowledge
of Greek has faded tremendously after fifty years, but Latin I still
comprehend"[39] is not a "normal" political process. By using
knowledge, the philosopher-king helps maintain a certain intellectual tension which in turn translates into political vitality,
helping to sustain his position as national figure despite his clear
partisan affiliation.

An example can be found in Ben-Gurion's effectiveness in solving labor disputes. Israel's professionals—teachers, engineers, journalists and others—were frequently engaged in labor disputes with the government. In his meetings with their unions, Ben-Gurion was at his best. There was always the indication at the outset that he was speaking not as Prime Minister but as citizen. There was always the reminder that he was not a teacher, engineer, or journalist but also some hint that he had experience in the field. "Comrades, this time I can refer to you as comrades in the simplest sense of the term."[40] And after the credentials had been established modestly but firmly there came the speech regarding the historic mission of the professional. In 1960, the teachers' union agreed to renew its cooperation with the Ministry of Education, after a year and a half of turmoil and strikes, following a speech by the Prime Minister before the union's central committee. "The teachers were taught a lesson in Zionism by Ben-Gurion," one newspaper announced the next morning.[41]

Ben-Gurion's symbolic role as representative of the state, the nation, and perhaps of all Jewish history created difficulties for his political foes. One of the reasons why they had difficulty in coping with his symbolic role was its unconventional knowledge-base. The incorporation of world classics into the symbolic system of the Jewish state, even the incorporation of biblical studies as a secular activity, was hard to deal with. Other politicians were often intelligent, well-read persons, but no other figure was as able as Ben-Gurion to combine power with knowledge. Religious politicians, for example, were aware of the political implications of Ben-Gurion's call in 1953 to restore the injustice done to Spinoza by the rabbis of Amsterdam in 1656, but it was not a political argument the modern rabbis of Israel were used to.[42] The philosopher-king was no expert on such issues, but he was a master in their utilization in political—especially parliamentary—debates. He always caught political opponents by surprise, as when after a long summer recess of Parliament, when the whole nation was expecting to hear a political statement summarizing the summer events, the Prime Minister declared that "undoubtedly, the most important event which took place during the recess was the successful launching of an artificial satellite into orbit by Russian scientists to an altitude of over 500 miles, moving around the earth with a velocity of five miles per second or 18,000 miles per hour."[43] When old-timers, such as Peretz Bernstein, head of the

General Zionist party, questioned the appropriateness of the statement, Ben-Gurion's parliamentary battle had already been won:

♦ ♦ ♦

Mr. Bernstein wonders why the artificial satellite had to be mentioned at the beginning of the government's statement after a long summer. Mr. Bernstein probably thinks that the most important event during summer recess was the election of the presidency and executive board of the centrist party also known as the General Zionists.[44]

♦ ♦ ♦

The Intellectuals' Response

The visionary leader attempts to overcome the boundaries of reality in order to achieve a better future for his people even if the list of existing, or expected, resources does not bear much promise. It is this list which he then ventures to alter. Knowledge, defining the parameters of action—its possibilities and impossibilities—becomes a hindrance to visionary politics.[45] The scientist, investigating available means of action, the philosopher defining available normative paths, even the writer who legitimizes them may ultimately provide too narrow a set of options. The intellectuals may be ignored, but not for long. The visionary leader recognizes that vision must be harnessed to reality, and reality is confined by man's knowledge about it. The model of leadership discussed in this study is one of the "philosopher-king" who recognizes the combined role of knowledge, power, and vision in the process of social transformation. He may be as skilled as other leaders in building for himself the image of an intellectual, surrounding himself with academic "yes men," or exploiting conditions of "conflicting expertise" in order to legitimize previously made decisions.[46] But in essence this leadership type cannot be satisfied with these practices. The philosopher-king, who by definition is aware of limited resources and great hardships to overcome, can be expected to concern himself with the acquisition and utilization of knowledge in some "real" sense. To him, this requires the extension of knowledge so as to serve visionary goals.

Ben-Gurion, the philosopher-king, was never satisfied with

common sources of knowledge and constantly sought to expand
the range of information from which solutions to national problems could be derived. In his choice of relevant knowledge he
refused to limit himself to criteria defined by the scientific or
other professional establishments. A famous legend relates that
when Ben-Gurion was once informed that experts had claimed
the Negev desert could never be developed, no matter how
much water was brought south, he snapped: "Let's look for another set of experts."[47] This story is instructive because, contrary
to the way it has been interpreted, it indicates no despite of
expertise. It meant that while Ben-Gurion sought the intellectual's participation in the nation-building process, the latter, to
be of use, had to abandon old professional traditions (many of
which developed in the Diaspora Ben-Gurion abhorred) and be
endowed with messianic ideals and a sense of vision. Only then
would the intellectual called upon to provide expertise approach
the problems with a mind open to the tasks at hand and would
the man of letters make a contribution and flourish. Ben-Gurion
made claims upon persons of knowledge even in fields like law
or medicine, which were most associated with professionalism in
its rigid sense. He demanded that lawyers form new legal codes
that would "forward our physical and moral healing and the
cleansing of our lives from the trivia and dross which gathered
upon us in dependence and exile."[48] Similarly, the practitioners
of medicine "must not be confined to cure of the sick, but by
prophylaxis find ways of fortifying the health of our youth and
grown, nature-born and newcomer, of invigorating their muscles
and minds."[49] Ben-Gurion opposed the confining of intellectual
activity into specialized fields and traditions. He objected to
scholarship as a "closed province of eclectic specialists,"[50] propos-
ing that every farmer or tradesman can and must contribute to
the enrichment of the science nearest his craft. This required,
above all, that the man of letters abandon his specialized language and thought and engage in the spiritual and physical tasks
of nation-building. The greatest charge in this regard was laid on
the writer. "If spirit be not patrimony of all, of people and youth,
the Hebrew writer labors in vain. [He is] to give faithful expression to it, to magnify and ennoble it by the power of his inspiring
and fertile imagery."[51]

The writers who met Ben-Gurion in 1949 had not, however,
been aware of the extent of his demands until much later. The

intellectual was not asked to contribute his free afternoons to social service activities. Intellectual activity itself was challenged by the philosopher-king. Ben-Gurion demanded its transformation as part of the process of social change. If nation-building were to succeed, the knowledge base of society had to be expanded; intellectual activity had to become a source of new insights and truths as well as a source of messianic inspiration. Ben-Gurion was aware of the limits of knowledge which traditionally did not allow the intellectual to play such roles but he hoped that, with the right set of attitudes, they could be removed. For instance, he had a very good understanding of the concept of scientific truth as interpreted in the 1950s. He was well aware that science, especially physics, denied the notion of "absolute truth" which he himself declared to be impossible to reach. But Ben-Gurion developed a "religion of science" as part of his hope that the scientist make every effort to reveal the secrets of nature and put them to technological use rather than engage in a fruitless game in which hypotheses are devised only to be rejected later. Ben-Gurion definitely had great sympathy for the philosophers' preoccupation with universal normative questions. He himself was preoccupied with Buddha and Plato, and the ancient biblical prophets were, after all, universalist philosophers too. But he hoped that the philosopher—in a new state of mind— would confirm the tie he saw between universal norms and concrete reality in the new state of Israel. Ben-Gurion's own scholarship was devoted to this task. It is possible to take care of the future, he declared, only if we examine the ever-changing realities, not with the eyes of yesterday and the day before, but with an insight into the winds of change.[52] Ben-Gurion's scholarship was an attempt by a highly creative mind to apply his insight to the world of letters and inspire it to do the same.

But the world of letters objected. Permeating all 12 debates between Ben-Gurion and the intellectuals was the latter's insistence upon the boundaries of knowledge which ought to be recognized. To the intellectuals, this recognition constituted a restraint never to be lifted. Whatever the degree of their involvement in the nation-building process or of their acceptance of the messianic interpretation of the state, the intellectuals' preoccupation with knowledge led them to recognize its constraints and the dangers facing their profession once these limits are ignored. The "trade unionist" aspect of the intellectuals' response must be stressed. Their objection to Ben-Gurion's extension of knowledge did not stem from an intellectual tradition into which they were socialized; there hardly existed a consistent tradition of intellectuality in the Israel of the 1950s.[53] It arose because of their concern with knowledge that the intellectuals developed a group consciousness which then turned into a societal force. The restraining role of the intellectuals vis-à-vis the philosopher-king, a role of great significance in the process of Israel's social transformation in the early 1960s, originated from the nature of this preoccupation with knowledge.

The response to the philosopher-king by different intellectual groups was, of course, varied. The scientists were more explicit on the hypothetical nature of knowledge, while the philosophers were more radical when this point became politically salient. The biblical scholars were more conscious about the autonomous character of learning, while the writers were more skilled at maintaining it. But all groups examined here shared a belief in three constraints of knowledge which, they demanded, ought to be recognized. First, knowledge is always hypothetical; any notion may be found to be wrong, and any truth should, therefore, remain open to scrutiny. Second, knowledge is always partial; any cognition is part of a larger context and should never be mistaken for it. And third, knowledge is the product of the autonomous mind free from guidelines as to the truth to be found and may only flourish if kept this way. The role of the intellectuals consisted of constantly reminding the philosopher-king that these restraints must be applied when knowledge is put in the service of action. As revealed in the age-old myth of the Tower of Babel, there exists a profound tension between man's desire to extend the scope of human knowledge and his admission that there exist limits to the extension. This tension lay at the core of the relationship between Ben-Gurion and the intellectuals.

In each debate there were demands to control the extension of knowledge. For example, in the debate over science and truth, it was stated that ideas must always be reevaluated in light of experience. In the debates over values in their relationship to science, or on the use of force by the state, the interpretation of truth as absolute and normative was further restrained. Norms, the intellectuals claimed, being derived from experience cannot be attributed an additional ontological status. Demands for autonomy of knowledge were expressed in all debates touching upon the norms of inquiry, but even in the debate over the organic nature of history, a limit was put on politicians' attributing a messianic meaning to historical processes. In the debate over science and societal self-control, scientists demanded greater autonomy in determining the consequences of science. A third set of debates exposed the partiality of the notion of political messianism. Debates with philosophers stressed the broader societal context of the political state, and debates with writers, the universal, human context. Many writers, it will be recalled, were devoted to the notion of political messianism, yet through the writer's observation, they ultimately put reality in its human, and hence nonmessianic, context.

The scientists, philosophers, biblical scholars, and writers shared the belief that no single cognition of reality exists which represents an absolute grasp of reality. Living in the post-war, post-holocaust world, they could not accept the notion that human cognition is capable of grasping more than fragments of the world or that any one perception, belief, or theory could be so encompassing as to have all others derived from it.[54] The truths of yesterday, they realized, may be refuted by today's events, and new perspectives may reveal new paths to be explored. They also realized that an open empirical mind can lead to great achievements. The physicists and biologists had all the proof they needed that development—for better or worse—depends on an autonomous science engaged in experimentation.[55] Other intellectuals—notably the biblical scholars—had also just realized the importance of a modest empirical approach to the acquisition of knowledge in lieu of grand frames of thought. Popper's *Open Society* had a great impact on Israeli scholarship, and few scholars had patience for Platonic notions in any field of knowledge.[56] This was illustrated in monumental works by scholars like Kaufmann and Talmon, who provided not only intellectual frames of reference but also new social guidelines and ultimately played a significant role in the process of social transformation in which political messianism gave way, in the early 1960s, to a new model of social relations.

Yehezkel Kaufmann's work serves as an example of the inconsistency between political messianism and intellectuality as interpreted at the time. His many volumes on *The Religion of Israel*,[57] published in Israel from 1937 on, had an enormous impact on Ben-Gurion, who frequently mentioned his work as a symbol of scholarship endowed by a messianic spirit. It provided Ben-Gurion with the proof of a link between the normative environment in which the scholar operates and his ability to grasp the truth, for Kaufmann, living in the land of the Bible during its era of redemption, came up with a refreshing interpretation of the origins of the Jewish people's faith. It was easy to agree with Ben-Gurion on this point. Biblical scholars and historians of antiquity in general tended to interpret the Israelite religion as an organic outgrowth of the ancient orient's religious milieu. Some scholars discovered the origins of biblical faith in the monotheistic tendencies of the religions of the ancient Near East; others pointed to pagan elements in the religion of Israel. Kaufmann vigorously presented an opposite thesis that the Israelite religion was an original creation of the people of Israel, something absolutely different from anything the pagan world ever knew. Israel's world, Kaufmann wrote, was its own creation, notwithstanding its utilization of ancient pagan material. He explained, and Ben-Gurion concurred, that "to fathom the meaning of this world, we must interpret its symbols from within; the attempts to explain it in the light of pagan models only obscure its real character and bar the way to a true appreciation."[58] But what did such an interpretation imply? It was the beginning of a new tradition of biblical research which contrasted with Ben-Gurion's symbolic uses of the Bible, a tradition insisting on the testing of hypotheses and on their rejection if the facts so demanded, on the consideration of biblical events in their historiographical context, on the selection of areas of research other than those called for by political ideology, and on a whole set of norms of inquiry. Kaufmann's thesis was a main cornerstone of political messianism, but at the same time Kaufmann and many of his disciples demanded that it not be founded on the testimony of obscure passages, on ingenious combinations of isolated "hints" and "clues" scattered here and there throughout the Bible, or on learned conjectures supported by little real evidence. It is no wonder that political messianism would soon fall prey to this set of demands.

It is, of course, impossible to establish a clear link between intellectual trends and historical developments. What role did the dialogue over knowledge, or the tension over its expansion, play in the decline of political messianism in Israel? How did the demand to recognize the constraints of knowledge inspire the specific model of the "open society" emerging in the early 1960s?

It is possible to point at inconsistencies between intellectual approaches but not at their societal impact. One is tempted to link the intellectuals' demands described here with the political demand for greater plurality in social relations; the empirical, experimental approach to knowledge had often been associated with the decline of absolutism and the rise of democracy.[59] The intellectuals, it could be argued, came up with a set of guidelines to replace those declining with the fading of Ben-Gurion's charisma. Before such an argument can be given, however, a word of caution is needed. The fact that at a certain point intellectuals derive from their concept of knowledge a model of societal relations, e.g., the model of an open, pluralistic society, does not mean that they willingly join the political forces advocating it. They may still be prepared to play a nominal role in the charismatic center of society. Much of the literature claiming the "betrayal" of the intellectuals refers to this incompatibility between the intellectuals' models of social relations and their actual political behavior.

Karl Popper's accusations on this count are well known. In *The Open Society and Its Enemies*, Popper examined a moment of enlightenment in world history—the fifth century B.C.—when the closed, magical, tribal, collectivist society was challenged by the open society, a new form of life in which individuals are confronted with personal decisions, and a social system characterized by reason and responsibility prevails. Published in 1945, *The Open Society* expressed a widespread recognition that the open society stood little chance as man's yearnings for tribal collectivism and messianic salvation were stronger than his willingness to take responsibility and face an unknown, self-made future. Popper attacked intellectuals like Plato, who, unwilling and unable to help mankind along its difficult path into an unknown future that it had to create for itself, tried to make mankind turn back to the past. Incapable of leading a new way, they could only make themselves leaders of what Popper saw as a "perennial revolt against freedom."[60]

Why was this option not chosen by Israel's intellectuals in the early 1960s? Why did they quite spontaneously abandon their nominal role in the charismatic center and begin to define the parameters of the "open society" with full fervor? The answer seems to lie on both the intellectual and the political levels. On the intellectual level, the model of the open society, derived from their approach to knowledge, included a role for the intellectuals just as the model of political messianism had. This can best be demonstrated with reference to Talmon's work on *The Origins of Totalitarian Democracy*.[61] Talmon distinguished between two schools of democratic thought. The liberal school assumes politics to be a matter of trial and error and regards political systems as pragmatic contrivances of human ingenuity and spontaneity. It also recognizes a variety of levels of personal and collective endeavors which are altogether outside the sphere of politics. The totalitarian democratic school, on the other hand, is based upon the assumption of the sole and exclusive truth in politics. It may be called political messianism, wrote Talmon, in the sense that it postulates a preordained and perfect scheme of things to which men are irresistably driven and at which they are bound to arrive. It recognizes ultimately only the political plane and includes in the scope of politics the whole of human existence.

Talmon's work attempted to show human civilization as the evolution of a multiplicity of historically and pragmatically formed clusters of social existence and social endeavor, not as the achievement of the abstract individual man on a single level of existence. He insisted that the idea of an all-embracing and all-solving creed is incompatible with liberty. The two ideals—the messianic ideal and the liberal ideal—correspond to the two instincts most deeply embedded in human nature: the yearning for salvation and the love of freedom. Attempts to satisfy both at the same time, he claimed, are bound to result, if not in unmitigated tyranny and serfdom, at least in the monumental hypocrisy and self-deception of totalitarian democracy where political messianism replaces empirical thinking and free criticism with reasoning by definition, based on a priori collective concepts which must be accepted, whatever the evidence of the senses.

Here lay the important role of the intellectual. Although Talmon realized that the power of the latter to influence events is strictly limited, he believed that, like the psychoanalyst whose treatment makes the patient aware of his unconscious, the social analyst may be able to cure the human urge for totalitarian democracy, namely the longing for a final resolution of all contradictions and conflicts into a state of total harmony. The intellectual could drive home the truth that human society and human life can never reach a state of repose, that all that can be done is to

proceed through trial and error. Thus, the intellectual, by nature
of his own methods of trial and error, of his doubting mind and
empirical-pragmatic approach to reality, becomes, in Talmon's
thinking, a political actor. He exposes the impossibilities of political messianism, its contradictions and difficulties. He objects to
the absolutist rules it imposes on reality and reveals its draw-
backs. By detailed analysis or delicate observation, he shows the
many facets hidden in an apparently one-dimensional world. The
man of knowledge who, like Hazaz or his hero Yudka, tries to
join in with the collective effort, soon realizes that he hampers
that effort. He reveals that concepts holding together the collective, messianic group (such as "Chosen People") are at best problematic and that all-embracing creeds are incompatible with
other cherished creeds, like liberty.

Yet, even the intellectual who is aware of such incompatibilities may not be willing to become a political actor. He may prefer
to overlook built-in inconsistencies rather than expose them. He
may simply apply a different set of rules and norms to learning
and politics. Even if political suppression does not exist where
he lives, he may be worried by the cost he would have to bear if
he were to take on Yudka's role. Applying his skeptical mind to a
set of socio-cultural truths held by a self-confident laity engaged
in fulfilling ancient messianic dreams is no pleasant role. In order
to explain why this role is, nevertheless, adopted, one must return to the second level of analysis—that of politics.

Although a variety of political factors may be involved, the
story of Ben-Gurion and the intellectuals confirms that charisma
is a major intervening variable to be considered. What activated
the intellectuals' political response and accounted for their societal impact was their perception of Ben-Gurion's fading charisma
in The Affair. Their conscious hypothetical, partial, autonomical
approach now became a model for the open society emerging out
of the messianic condition. And the intellectuals, for their part,
were willing to supply the norms because of their recognition
that the same bond between knowledge and power which they
eagerly accepted when Ben-Gurion dominated the scene as a
symbol of national unity became abusive in conditions of power
politics. The messianic myth of science and technology, tolerated
when used to serve the nation-building effort, was intolerable
when it became a political asset in an election campaign. Legit-

imizing the socio-cultural value system of a party boss is hardly the same as singing the praises of a leader personifying the national revival.

The political role of the intellectuals in this story may thus be characterized as a dual one. While attracted to charisma and enhancing political messianism, they provided a societal alternative because of their preoccupation with knowledge. And if this story has a lesson for the modern intellectual, it is that his societal contribution depends on his ability to overcome the fascination with charisma and to state—confidently and creatively—the case of knowledge as it combines with power to serve national goals.

Notes

Introduction

1. Haim Hazaz, "Beyom Tzah," *Davar*, February 3, 1961.
2. On The Affair see Peter Medding, *Mapai in Israel: Political Organization and Government in a New Society* (Cambridge, Eng.: Cambridge University Press, 1972).
3. On the political implications of The Affair see Rael Jean Isaac, *Party and Politics in Israel: Three Visions of a Jewish State* (New York: Longman, 1981).
4. *Davar*, January 11, 1961.
5. See David Ben-Gurion, *Devarim Kahawayatam* (Tel Aviv: Am-Hassefer, 1965). (In Hebrew.)
6. Eliahu Hassin and Dan Horowitz, *Haparashah* (Tel-Aviv: Am-Hassefer, 1961). (In Hebrew.)
7. For instance, Nathan Yanai, *Qera Batzameret* (Tel-Aviv: Levin-Epstein, 1969). (In Hebrew.)
8. See, for example, J. L. Talmon, "Haparashah: Parashat Derakhim," *Ha'aretz*, February 17, 1961.
9. Edward Shils, "The Intellectuals and the Powers: Some Perspectives for Comparative Analysis," in *On Intellectuals*, ed. Philip Rieff (Garden City, N.Y.: Doubleday, 1970), pp. 27–51.
10. This definition is consistent with that of Robert Merton, *Social Theory and Social Structure* (New York: Free Press, 1957; rpt. 1968), p. 263; and Seymour M. Lipset, *Political Man* (New York: Doubleday, 1963), p. 333. For a survey of definitions see Ray Nichols, *Treason, Tradition and the Intellectuals: Julien Benda and Political Discourse* (Lawrence, Kansas: The Regents Press of Kansas, 1978).
11. See Alvin Gouldner, *The Future of Intellectuals and the Rise*

of the New Class (New York: Seabury, 1979); and George Konrad and Ivan Szelenyi, *The Intellectuals on the Road to Class Power* (New York: Harcourt Brace Jovanovich, 1979).

12. J. P. Nettl, "Ideas, Intellectuals and Structures of Dissent," in *On Intellectuals*, pp. 57–134.

13. The recent scholarly attention to such conditions is reflected in Robert Rich, ed., *The Knowledge Cycle* (Beverly Hills, Calif.: Sage, 1981); and Carol Weiss, ed., *Using Social Research in Public Policy Making* (Lexington, Mass.: Lexington Books, 1977).

14. See, for example, Thomas Molnar, *The Decline of the Intellectual* (New York: World Publishing, 1965).

15. See Lewis Feuer, *Ideology and the Ideologists* (Oxford: Blackwell, 1975).

16. Nettl, "Ideas, Intellectuals and Structures of Dissent," in *On Intellectuals*, p. 60.

17. See, for instance, Harold Wilensky, *Intellectuals in Labour Unions: Organizational Pressures on Professional Roles* (Glencoe, Ill.: Free Press, 1956). Also Robert Wood, "Scientists and Politics: The Rise of an Apolitical Elite," in *Scientists and National Policy-Making*, ed., Robert Gilpin and Christopher Wright (New York: Columbia University Press, 1964), pp. 41–72; S. P. Barnes, "Making Out in Industrial Research," *Science Studies*, 1 (January 1971):157–75; and Henry Aaron, *Politics and the Professors: The Great Debate in Perspective* (Washington, D.C.: Brookings Institution, 1978).

18. Karl Mannheim, *Ideology and Utopia* (New York: Harcourt, 1936).

19. Talcott Parsons, "The Intellectual: A Social Role Category," in *On Intellectuals*, pp. 3–26.

20. Suzanne Keller, *Beyond the Ruling Class* (New York: Arno, 1979).

21. Robert Brym, *Intellectuals and Politics* (London: Allen, Unwin, 1980).

22. See S. M. Lipset and Asoke Basu, "The Roles of Intellectuals and Political Roles," in *The Intellegentsia and the Intellectuals*, ed. Alexander Gella (Beverly Hills, Calif.: Sage, 1976), pp. 111–50.

23. Edward Shils, "Intellectuals, Tradition and the Traditions of Intellectuals: Some Preliminary Considerations," in *Intellectuals and Tradition*, ed., S. N. Eisenstadt and S. R. Graubard (New York: Humanities Press, 1973), p. 23.

24. Ibid., p. 29.

25. Ibid., p. 30.

26. Ibid.

27. Edward Shils, "Charisma, Order and Status," *American Sociological Review*, 30 (1965):201.

28. S. N. Eisenstadt, "Intellectuals and Tradition," in *Intellectuals and Tradition*, p. 4.

29. Clifford Geertz, "Centers, Kings and Charisma: Reflections on the Symbolism of Power," in *Culture and Its Creators: Essays in*

Honor of Edward Shils, ed. Joseph Ben-David and Terry Nichols Clark (Chicago: University of Chicago Press, 1977).

30. Raymond Aron, *The Opium of the Intellectuals* (Garden City, N.Y.: Doubleday, 1957), p. 215.

31. Robert Brym, *Intellectuals and Politics*, p. 68.

32. David Apter, "Nkrumah, Charisma and the Coup," in *Philosophers and Kings: Studies in Leadership*, ed. Dankwart Rustow (New York: Braziller, 1970).

33. Avraham Avi-hai, *Ben-Gurion: State-Builder* (New York: Wiley, 1974), p. 289.

34. See Michael Bar Zohar, *Ben-Gurion* (London: Weidenfeld and Nicolson, 1978).

35. David Ben-Gurion, "The Call of Spirit in Israel," in *Rebirth and Destiny of Israel*, ed. David Ben-Gurion (New York: Philosophical Library, 1954).

36. Ibid., p. 403.

37. Although no systematic studies on the political sociology of intellectuals in Israel are available, important clues are provided in S. N. Eisenstadt, *Israeli Society* (London: Weidenfeld and Nicolson, 1967), chap. 10.

38. On such conditions see, for example, Charles Kadushin, *The American Intellectual Elite* (Boston: Little, Brown, 1974).

39. On the relationship between the political and intellectual elites in Israel see Reuven Kahane, "Emdot Haideologiah Hadominantit Kelapey Mada," in *Revadim Beyisrael*, ed. S. N. Eisenstadt, R. Bar-Yossef, R. Kahane, and A. Shelach (Jerusalem: Academon, 1968). (In Hebrew.)

40. Ben-Gurion, "The Call of Spirit in Israel," p. 427.

41. Shlomo Avinery, "Israel in the Post Ben-Gurion Era: The Nemesis of Messianism," *Midstream*, 11 (September 1965):20.

42. Protocol of meeting with Professors Urbach, Bergman, Talmon, Katz, Rotenstreich, Scholem, Jerusalem, March 28, 1961. (The meeting was organized by the writer Yizhar, who was also present.)

43. Talmon, "Haparashah: Parashat Derakhim."

44. See John Kenneth Galbraith, *The New Industrial State* (New York: New American Library, 1962); Daniel Bell, *The Coming of Post-Industrial Society: A Venture in Social Forecasting* (New York: Basic Books, 1973); and William Evan, *Knowledge and Power in a Global Setting* (Beverly Hills, Calif.: Sage, 1981).

··· ℵ ···

The Scientists

1. Jean-Jacques Salomon, *Science and Politics* (Cambridge, Mass.: MIT Press, 1973), pp. 179–80.

2. See Don K. Price, *Government and Science* (New York: New York University Press, 1954); J. S. Dupré and S. A. Lakoff, *Science*

and the Nation: Policy and Politics (Englewood Cliffs, N.J.: Prentice-Hall, 1962); Robert Gilpin and Christopher Wright, eds., *Scientists and National Policy-Making* (New York: Columbia University Press, 1964); Sanford A. Lakoff, ed., *Knowledge and Power* (New York: Free Press, 1966); Joseph Haberer, *Politics and the Community of Science* (New York: Van Nostrand, 1969); and Dean Schooler, *Science, Scientists and Public Policy* (New York: Free Press, 1971).

3. Salomon, *Science and Politics*, p. 188.

4. See Spencer R. Weart, *Scientists in Power* (Cambridge, Mass.: Harvard University Press, 1979).

5. *Davar*, July 7, 1961.

6. *Herut*, July 6, 1961.

7. Yud-Yud, "Teguvot," *Davar*, July 7, 1961.

8. *Davar*, July 16, 1961.

9. Letter from Benjamin Rosenblat, July 5, 1961.

10. Letter to Israel Lifshitz, July 16, 1961.

11. Yaacov Hazan, "Hama'agal Hashalem," *Al-Hamishmar*, July 21, 1961.

12. Report on intellectuals' conference, *Al-Hamishmar*, July 23, 1961.

13. See also Jean-Jacques Salomon, "Public Reactions to Science and Technology: The Wizard Faces Social Judgement," in *Science, Technology and Human Prospect*, ed. Chauncey Starr and Philip Ritterbush (New York: Pergamon, 1980).

14. Shimon Peres, *From These Men* (London: Weidenfeld and Nicolson, 1981), p. 27.

15. Letter to Rina Katzir and her three children, June 22, 1972.

16. Note from Aharon Katzir to Yitzhak Navon, May 19, 1958.

17. Letter to Michael Shimshoni, July 27, 1959.

18. Letter to Ernst Bergman, March 12, 1966.

19. Letter to Renana and Dulik, January 13, 1959.

20. Letter to Renana, November 21, 1962.

21. Letter to Paula, November 27, 1933.

22. *Look*, 26(January 16, 1962), 20.

23. On science and fascination see Charles B. Paul, *Science and Immortality: The Eloges of the Paris Academy of Sciences, 1699–1791* (Berkeley: University of California Press, 1980).

24. Address to the International Conference on Nucleus Structure, Rehovot, September 8, 1957.

25. Ibid.

26. Ibid.

27. Address to the International Symposium on Functional Components of Carcinogenesis, Rehovot, September 9, 1959.

28. Speech before the Third Convention of the Students' Union, Tel-Aviv, January 12, 1944.

29. Ibid.

30. Address to the Symposium on New Perspectives in Biology, Rehovot, June 10, 1963.

31. Address to the Conference on Science in the Advancement of New States, Rehovot, August 15, 1960.

32. "Science and Ethics: Contribution of Greece, India and Israel," lecture at Brandeis University, March 9, 1960.

33. Speech before the Third Convention, January 12, 1944.

34. Letter to Ehud Avriel, March 4, 1948.

35. See Shimon Peres, *David's Sling* (London: Weidenfeld and Nicolson, 1970).

36. For example, see letter from Shmuel Sambursky, August 17, 1958.

37. D. Dyoknay, "David Ben-Gurion," *Ma'ariv*, August 5, 1955.

38. Ben-Gurion, "Science and Ethics."

39. Ibid.

40. See Ernst Gellner, *Spectacles and Predicaments: Essays in Social Theory* (Cambridge, Eng.: Cambridge University Press, 1979).

41. Ben-Gurion, "Science and Ethics."

42. Protocol of the first general meeting of the National Academy of Sciences, Jerusalem, February 23, 1960.

43. Ben-Gurion, "Science and Ethics."

44. Expressed in Ben-Gurion's diary, entry for June 3, 1959.

45. Ben-Gurion, "Netaken Hame'uvat," *Davar*, December 25, 1953.

46. See Michael Polanyi, *The Tacit Dimension* (Garden City, N.Y.: Doubleday, 1966).

47. Ben-Gurion, "Ma'or Ledorot," *Davar*, March 12, 1954.

48. Ben-Gurion, "Science and Ethics."

49. Speech at the opening of the Nuclear Physics Institute, May 20, 1958.

50. Ben-Gurion, "Science and Ethics."

51. Ibid.

52. Ibid.

53. Ibid.

54. Ibid.

55. Ben-Gurion, "Torah Umalkhut," *Hazon Vaderekh* (Tel-Aviv: Mapai, 1951), pp. 313–14. (In Hebrew.)

56. Joseph Schaechter, "Hipus Derakhim shel Ha'adam Ben Zemanenu," *Niv Hakevutza*, 7(May 1957):211–16.

57. Letter to Joseph Shaechter, June 20, 1957.

58. Letter to Joseph Schaechter, September 2, 1957.

59. Ibid.

60. Don K. Price, *The Scientific Estate* (Cambridge, Mass.: Harvard University Press, 1965), especially chap. 4.

61. Greeting to the Fifth International Conference on Biological Standardization, Jerusalem, September 14, 1959.

62. Ibid.

63. Ibid.

64. Price, *The Scientific Estate*, p. 83.

65. Letter from Amos Deshalit, January 26, 1960. This was also expressed in various interviews.

66. Amos Deshalit, untitled and unpublished manuscript dated February 1960, found in Ben-Gurion's files.

67. Lecture at the First World Ideological Conference, Jerusalem, August 11, 1957.

68. Letter from Amos Deshalit, February 3, 1957.

69. Amos Deshalit, untitled manuscript, as in n.66.

70. Ben-Gurion's diary, entry for January 4, 1957.

71. Letter to Amos Deshalit, January 13, 1957.

72. Marcus C. Goodall, *Science, Logic and Political Action* (Cambridge, Mass.: Schenkman, 1970), p. 17.

73. Ibid., p. 65.

74. Aaron Sloman, *The Computer Revolution in Philosophy: Philosophy, Science and Models of Mind* (Sussex, Eng.: Harvester, 1978), p. 272.

75. Letter from Amos Deshalit, February 3, 1957.

76. Letter to Hans Kreitler, February 17, 1963.

77. Letter to Amos Deshalit, June 10, 1959.

78. Letter from Amos Deshalit, July 3, 1959.

79. Letter to Amos Deshalit, July 27, 1959.

80. Moshe Pearlman, *Ben-Gurion Looks Back: In Talks with Moshe Pearlman* (New York: Simon and Schuster, 1965), p. 200.

81. Letter to B. Barshay, February 13, 1962.

82. Moshe Pearlman, *Ben-Gurion Looks Back*, p. 197.

83. Ibid., p. 198.

84. Langdon Winner, *Autonomous Technology: Technics Out of Control as a Theme in Political Thought* (Cambridge, Mass.: MIT Press, 1977).

85. See Albert H. Teich, ed., *Technology and Man's Future* (New York: St. Martin's Press, 1981).

86. Aharon Katzir, Lecture in *Be'ayot Kelaliot Bahinukh Hayisraeli*, Ministry of Education and Culture publication, December 1958. (In Hebrew.)

87. Protocol of the first general meeting of the National Academy of Sciences, Jerusalem, February 23, 1960.

88. Letter from Hugo Bergman, February 26, 1960.

89. Ibid.

90. Letter to Hugo Bergman, March 29, 1960.

91. Letter from Hugo Bergman, April 21, 1960.

92. Abba Eban, "Science and National Liberation," in *Science and the New Nations*, ed. Ruth Gruber (New York: Basic Books, 1961).

93. See Ralph Lapp, *The New Priesthood: The Scientific Elite and the Uses of Power* (New York: Harper and Row, 1965).

94. Speech before the Third Convention.

95. Ibid.

96. See Guy Benveniste, *The Politics of Expertise* (Berkeley, Calif.: Glendessary, 1972); and Harold Wilensky, *Organizational Intelligence: Knowledge and Policy in Government and Industry* (New York: Basic Books, 1967).

97. Letter to E.I.J. Poznanski, November 7, 1962.

98. Letter to E.I.J. Poznanski, November 22, 1962.

99. Letter from E.I.J. Poznanski, December 14, 1962.

100. Letter to E.I.J. Poznanski, December 20, 1962.

101. See Aaron Wildawsky, *Speaking Truth to Power: The Art and Craft of Policy Analysis* (Boston: Little, Brown, 1979).

102. Hans Kreitler, "Yahasso shel Hano'ar Hayisraely Le'idealim," unpublished manuscript sent to Ben-Gurion on July 4, 1963.

103. *Davar,* July 5, 1963.

104. Letter to Hans Kreitler, July 7, 1963.

105. Moshe Czudnowski, "Doh Preliminary Al Yelidey 1945," unpublished study sent to Ben-Gurion, September 22, 1963.

106. Letter to Moshe Czudnowski, September 30, 1963.

107. Letter from Moshe Czudnowski, November 25, 1963.

108. Letter to Moshe Czudnowski, December 2, 1963.

109. All of the correspondence between Akzin and Ben-Gurion was published by Professor Akzin in *Ma'ariv,* December 23, 1959.

··· ב ···

The Philosophers

1. J. L. Talmon, *Utopianism and Politics* (London: Conservative Political Centre, 1957).

2. Lewis Feuer, *Marx and the Intellectuals: A Set of Post-Ideological Essays* (Garden City, N.Y.: Anchor Books, 1969).

3. J. L. Talmon, *Political Messianism: The Romantic Phase* (New York: Praeger, 1960), p. 88.

4. Letter from J. L. Talmon, June 3, 1960.

5. See S. N. Eisenstadt, *Israeli Society* (London: Weidenfeld and Nicolson, 1967).

6. Marie Syrkin, "Out of Zion: A Report of the Ideological Conference," *Midstream,* III (Autumn 1957):28.

7. Ben-Gurion, speech at the Ideological Conference, Jerusalem, August 8–15, 1957.

8. Avraham Avi-hai, *Ben-Gurion: State Builder* (New York: Wiley, 1974).

9. Moshe Pearlman, *Ben-Gurion Looks Back: In Talks with Moshe Pearlman* (New York: Simon and Schuster, 1965), p. 230.

10. Protocol of a private meeting with 11 intellectuals in Aharon Katzir's home, July 4, 1961.

11. Pearlman, *Ben-Gurion Looks Back,* p. 231.

12. "Divrey Sofrim," protocol of a meeting with writers at the Prime Minister's office, October 11, 1949.

13. Speech at the Ideological Conference.

14. David Ben-Gurion, "In Defense of Messianism," *Midstream,* XII (March 1966):63–68.

15. Speech at the Ideological Conference.

16. Dan Segre, *A Crisis of Identity: Israel and Zionism* (Oxford: Oxford University Press, 1980).

17. Shlomo Avinery, "Israel in the Post Ben-Gurion Era: The Nemesis of Messianism," *Midstream*, XI (September 1965):16–32.

18. David Ben-Gurion, "Words and Values," *Jewish Frontier*, 24 (December 1957):11.

19. Ibid.

20. Ibid., p. 13.

21. Ibid., p. 14.

22. Letter to Nathan Rotenstreich, March 28, 1957.

23. Ben-Gurion, "Words and Values," p. 15.

24. Harold Fisch, *The Zionist Revolution: A New Perspective* (London: Weidenfeld and Nicolson, 1978).

25. Dan Segre, *A Crisis of Identity*, p. 94.

26. Harold Fisch, *The Zionist Revolution*, p. 107.

27. Dan Segre, *A Crisis of Identity*, p. 95.

28. David Ben-Gurion and Nathan Rotenstreich, "Israel and Zionism: A Discussion," *Jewish Frontier*, 24 (December 1957):17.

29. Ibid.

30. Ibid.

31. Ibid.

32. This letter and parts of the following correspondence between Ben-Gurion and Rotenstreich appeared in English in *Jewish Frontier*, 24 (December 1957) and in Hebrew in *Hazut*, 3 (1957).

33. Ben-Gurion, "In Defense of Messianism," p. 68.

34. Shlomo Avinery, "Israel in the Post Ben-Gurion Era," p. 20.

35. Letter from Shlomo Avinery, August 13, 1957.

36. Amos Elon, *The Israelis: Founders and Sons* (London: Weidenfeld and Nicolson, 1971), p. 288.

37. Talmon, *Political Messianism*, p. 514.

38. Martin Buber, *To Hallow This Life: An Anthology*, ed. Jacob Trapp (New York: Harper, 1958), p. 138.

39. Martin Buber, "Biblical Leadership," in *Biblical Humanism*, ed. Nahum Glatzer (London: Macdonald, 1968).

40. Ibid., p. 144.

41. Ibid., p. 148.

42. Ibid.

43. Ibid.

44. Ibid., p. 150.

45. "Zionism True and False: Interview with Professor Mordechai Martin Buber," in *Unease in Zion*, ed. Ehud Ben-Ezer (New York: Quadrangle Books, 1974).

46. From Buber's speech at the Ideological Conference in 1957. The text of the speech was published in English as part of the interview cited in n.45 and in Hebrew in *Davar*, October 4, 1957.

47. Ibid.

48. Ben-Gurion, Letter to the editor, *Davar*, October 9, 1957.

49. Martin Buber, "The Man of Today and the Jewish Bible," in *Biblical Humanism*, p. 2.

50. Ernst Simon, "Buber or Ben-Gurion?" *New Outlook*, 9 (February 1966):9–17.

51. Letter from Martin Buber, January 30, 1961.

52. Letter to Martin Buber, February 5, 1963.

53. Letter from Martin Buber, February 21, 1963.

54. David Ben-Gurion, "Uniqueness and Destiny," in *Ben-Gurion Looks at the Bible*, trans. Jonathan Kolatch (London: W. H. Allen, 1972).

55. Ibid., p. 37.

56. Yeshayahu Leibowitz, "Le'ahar Kibbya," in Yeshayahu Leibowitz, *Yahadut, Am Ye'hudy Umedinat Yisra'el* (Tel-Aviv: Schoken, 1976), pp. 229–34. (In Hebrew.)

57. Yeshayahu Leibowitz, "Jewish Identity and Israeli Silence" in Ben-Ezer, *Unease in Zion*, pp. 195–96.

58. Leibowitz, "Le'ahar Kibbya," p. 233.

59. Pearlman, *Ben-Gurion Looks Back*, pp. 149–50.

60. Rotenstreich, personal interview, March 2, 1981.

61. Ben-Gurion, *Davar*, March 5, 1954.

62. Nathan Rotenstreich, "Shilton, Hevrah Utehumeyha," in *Beyn Am Limedinato*, ed. Nathan Rotenstreich (Tel-Aviv: Haqibbutz Hameuhad, 1965). (In Hebrew.)

63. Buber, *To Hallow This Life*, p. 139.

64. Ben-Ezer, *Unease in Zion*, p. 108.

65. Buber, *To Hallow This Life*, p. 123.

66. Ben-Ezer, *Unease in Zion*, p. 118.

67. Yariv Ben-Aharon, "Nesheq Mikol Maqom," *Baqibbutz*, No. 613, June 16, 1963.

68. Matti Meged, "Hagevul Ha'aharon," *Lamerhav*, July 7, 1959.

69. Letter to Yariv Ben-Aharon, July 3, 1963.

70. Letter from Yariv Ben-Aharon, July 9, 1963.

71. Letter to Yariv Ben-Aharon, July 14, 1963.

72. From Werner Manheim, *Martin Buber* (New York: Twayne, 1974).

73. See Ben-Gurion, "Hamedina Vehama'amatz Haruhany," *Molad*, 7 (April-May 1951):3–11.

74. Protocol, July 4, 1961.

75. See Dennis Palumbo, "Introduction," *Policy Studies Journal*, 8 (1980):1037–42.

76. This was expressed in Ben-Gurion's lecture at the first meeting of the clerks' union as early as May 5, 1928.

77. Letter to Renana, October 15, 1958.

78. *Knesset Record*, Fifth Knesset, Session 222, February 20, 1963.

79. *Ha'aretz*, March 8, 1963.

80. *Ha'aretz*, March 10, 1963.

81. *Min Hayessod*, March 14, 1963.

82. Letter from Shmuel Sambursky, March 10, 1963.

83. Letter to Shmuel Sambursky, March 17, 1963.

··· ג ···

The Biblical Scholars

1. *Jerusalem Post*, May 13, 1960.
2. Maurice Cranston, *The Mask of Politics and Other Essays* (London: Allen Lane, 1973), p. 1.
3. See Kenneth Hudson, *The Language of Modern Politics* (London: Macmillan, 1978); A. F. Davies, *Skills, Outlooks and Passions: A Psychoanalytic Contribution to the Study of Politics* (Cambridge, Eng.: Cambridge University Press, 1980); and Murray Edleman, *The Symbolic Uses of Politics* (Urbana: University of Illinois Press, 1964).
4. Alvin Gouldner, *The Future of Intellectuals and the Rise of the New Class* (New York: Seabury, 1979), p. 28.
5. David Ben-Gurion, ed., *Ben-Gurion Looks at the Bible*, trans. Jonathan Kolatch (London: W. H. Allen, 1972), pp. 113–25.
6. Ibid, p. 113.
7. This thesis can be found in almost every essay in the work cited in n. 5.
8. Speech before the Second Jewish Studies Conference, Jerusalem, July 28, 1957.
9. Ben-Gurion, *Ben-Gurion Looks at the Bible*, p. 55.
10. Ibid., pp. 57–59.
11. See Bernard Lewis, *History: Remembered, Recovered, Invented* (Princeton: Princeton University Press, 1975).
12. Ben-Gurion, *Ben-Gurion Looks at the Bible*, p. 60.
13. Ibid.
14. See, for instance, Yigael Yadin, *The Art of Warfare in Biblical Lands in the Light of Archaeological Study* (New York: McGraw-Hill, 1963).
15. Lecture before the Military High Command, March 27, 1953.
16. Protocol of a lunch meeting at the Press Club, December 2, 1960.
17. Letter to S. Grodjenski, October 28, 1951.
18. Ibid.
19. *Ma'ariv*, May 12, 1959.
20. *Ma'ariv*, May 20, 1960.
21. Letter from E. Elinar, Y. Elitzur, F. Meltzer, November 11, 1959.
22. Shlomo Grodjenski, *Davar*, May 19, 1960.
23. Letter from Yaacov Goren, November 9, 1960.
24. *Knesset Record*, Fifth Knesset, Session 97, May 18, 1960.
25. See Ervin Birnbaum, *The Politics of Compromise: State and Religion in Israel* (Rutherford, N.J.: Fairleigh Dickinson University Press, 1970).
26. Social Science Research Council, *Theory and Practice in Historical Study: A Report of the Committee on Historiography* (New York: Social Science Research Council, undated).

27. Ibid., p. 5.

28. See R. F. Atkinson, *Knowledge and Explanation in History* (London: Macmillan, 1978); and Frederick Olafson, *The Dialectic of Action* (Chicago: University of Chicago Press, 1979).

29. Martin Buber, *Biblical Humanism*, ed. Nahum Glatzer (London: Macdonald, 1968), p. 5.

30. Yehuda Elitzur, "Yetziat Mitzrayim Nosah Ben-Gurion," *Ha'aretz*, June 13, 1960.

31. Lewis, *History: Remembered, Recovered, Invented*, p. 54.

32. Baruch Karu, *Haboker*, May 18, 1960.

33. Shlomo Grodjenski, *Davar*, May 19, 1960.

34. Israel Eldad, "Ben-Gurion Bepardes Hamiqra," *Haboker*, May 20, 1960.

35. Kenneth Hoover, *The Elements of Social Scientific Thinking* (New York: St. Martin's, 1980).

36. See Leonard Marsak, ed., *The Nature of Historical Inquiry* (New York: Holt, Rinehart, and Winston, 1970).

37. Edward Hallett Carr, *What is History?* (New York: Knopf, 1962), p. 35.

38. Letter to M. Beit-David, May 22, 1960.

39. *Hazofeh*, May 22, 1960.

40. Dickinson McGaw and George Watson, *Political and Social Inquiry* (New York: Wiley, 1976), p. 421.

41. See Dorothy Nelkin, "Scientists and Professional Responsibility: The Experience of American Ecologists," *Social Studies of Science*, 7 (February 1977):75–95; and Harriet Zuckerman, *Scientific Elite: Nobel Laureates in the United States* (New York: Free Press, 1977).

··· ׀ ···

The Writers

1. George A. Panichas, "The Writer and Society: Some Reflections," in *The Politics of Twentieth-Century Novelists*, ed. George A. Panichas (New York: Hawthorn, 1971), xxxii.

2. See the series on writers and politics in various countries edited by John Flower (London: Hodder and Stoughton, 1977–1981).

3. Panichas, "The Writer and Society," xxxix.

4. Julien Benda, *The Betrayal of the Intellectuals* (Boston: Beacon Press, 1955), p. 32.

5. All quotations regarding the meetings of 1949 are from their protocols entitled "Divrey Sofrim" and dated March 27, 1949; October 11, 1949.

6. See Günter Grass, *The Meeting at Telgte* (New York: Harcourt Brace Jovanovich, 1981).

7. Charles I. Glicksberg, *The Literature of Commitment* (London: Associated University Presses, 1976), p. 15.

8. Abraham Cordova, "The Institutionalization of a Cultural Center in Palestine: The Case of the Writers' Association," *Jewish Social Studies*, XLII (Winter 1980):37–62.

9. Letter from Yaacov Fichman, undated; letter from Shalom Ash, March 7, 1957; letter from Anda Amir, June 15,1963.

10. Eliezer Smoly, "An Open Letter to Ben-Gurion," *Davar*, December 30, 1960.

11. See Peter Nettl, "Power and the Intellectuals," in *Power and Consciousness*, ed. C. O'Brien and W. Vanech (London: University of London Press, 1969).

12. Meir Yanai, *Koh Amar Steinman* (Tel-Aviv: Alef, 1975), p. 73. (In Hebrew.)

13. See Myron Aronoff, *Frontiertown: The Politics of Community Building in Israel* (Manchester: Manchester University Press, 1974).

14. See William Zartman, ed., *Elites in the Middle East* (New York: Praeger, 1980).

15. Raymond Aron, *The Opium of the Intellectuals* (Garden City, N.Y.: Doubleday, 1957), p. 210.

16. See James Wilkinson, *The Intellectual Resistance in Europe* (Cambridge, Mass.: Harvard University Press, 1981).

17. Aron, *The Opium of the Intellectuals*, p. 213.

18. "Divrey Sofrim," March 27, 1949, p. 21.

19. Leon I. Yudkin, *Escape into Siege: A Survey of Israeli Literature Today* (London: Routledge and Kegan Paul, 1974), p. 104.

20. Simon Halkin, *Modern Hebrew Literature: Trends and Values* (New York: Schocken, 1950), p. 111.

21. Ibid., p. 115.

22. Ibid., p. 216.

23. See Baruch Kurzweil, *Sifrutenu Ha'hadashah: Hemshekh Omahapekhah?* (Tel-Aviv: Schocken, 1965). (In Hebrew.)

24. Aharon Meged, *The Living on the Dead* (London: Jonathan Cape, 1970), p. 251.

25. Dan Miron, "S. Yizhar: Some General Observations," in S. Yizhar, *Midnight Convoy and Other Stories* (Jerusalem: Israel Universities Press, 1969).

26. Yudkin, *Escape into Siege*, p. 105.

27. Halkin, *Modern Hebrew Literature*, p. 116.

28. Gershon Shaked, *Gal Hadash Bassiporet Ha'ivrit* (Tel-Aviv: Sifriyat Hapoalim, 1971). (In Hebrew.)

29. S. Yizhar, Lecture in *Be'ayot Kelaliot Bahinukh Hayisraeli*, Ministry of Education and Culture Publication (December 1958). (In Hebrew.) All quotations are from this lecture.

30. For excerpts translated into English see Arnold Band, *Nostalgia and Nightmare* (Berkeley: University of California Press, 1968).

31. Yizhar, *Midnight Convoy and Other Stories*, p. 114.

32. Shaked. See n.28 above.

33. Letter to S. Yizhar, January 27, 1959.

34. Letter to S. Yizhar, February 17, 1959. In that letter,

Ben-Gurion quotes excerpts from an answer by Yizhar to his letter of January 27, 1959, which has not been found.

35. S. H. Bergman, "Ha'adam," *Hapoel Hatzair*, 30 (February 1959):5.

36. Ben-Gurion, "Qitrug Shav," *Hapoel Hatzair*, 30 (February 1959):7.

37. Haim Hazaz, "The Sermon," in *Modern Hebrew Literature*, ed. Robert Alter (New York: Behrman House, 1975).

38. Dan Miron, "Al Haderashah," in *Haim Hazaz*, ed. Hilel Barzel (Tel-Aviv: Am Oved, 1978). (In Hebrew.)

39. S. Yizhar, "Melekh Filossof," *Davar*, October 3, 1976.

40. Excerpts from the speech and the subsequent debate were published by the Labor party in a booklet entitled: *Al Ha'medinah Ve'hassifrut*, October 1962. (In Hebrew.)

41. Eliezer Schweide, "Akharitah Shel Tokhehah," *Min HaYessod*, October 1962.

42. Alterman's "political" poems were published in his column in *Davar*.

43. Moshe Dayan, "Omeq Lelo Qetz," *Davar*, May 20, 1980.

44. Ibid.

45. Nathan Alterman, "LeDavid Ben-Gurion," in *Beyn Hameshoror Lamedinay* (Tel-Aviv: Haqibbutz Hameuhad, 1972); Collection of poems by Alterman concerning Ben-Gurion. (In Hebrew.)

46. Nathan Alterman, "Be'ehad Haleylot," in *Beyn Hameshorer Lamedinay*.

47. Letter to Alterman, August 12, 1960.

48. Uri Sela, "Lenatan Alterman Bly Shemen Za'it," *Ya'ad*, August 10, 1960.

49. Aharon Kidan, "Ky Ne'elmah Ilat devarim Va'aharitam," *Molad*, 23 (May-June 1965):63–68.

50. Quoted in ibid.

51. Nathan Alterman, "Ben-Gurion Bematzor," in *Beyn Hameshorer Lamedinay*.

52. Nathan Alterman, "Ben-Gurion Beterem Tza'ad," in *Beyn Hameshorer Lamedinay*.

53. Nathan Alterman, "Hashanah Hashivim Ve'hamesh," in *Beyn Hameshorer Lamedinay*.

54. Ibid.

55. *Ma'ariv*, September 20, 1960.

56. *Ma'ariv*, September 30, 1960.

57. Hanoch Bartov, *Lamerhav*, October 5, 1960.

58. The letter by Shamir and Ben-Gurion's answer, dated February 16, 1960, were published in *Davar*, October 12, 1960.

59. *Al Hamishmar*, October 21, 1960.

60. B. Y. Michaly, "Ben-Gurion Ve'hassofrim," *Lamerhav*, October 12, 1960.

61. *Lamerhav*, October 28, 1960.

62. Shin Shalom, "Ledivrey Rosh Hamemshalah," *Moznayim*, 11 (November 1960):400–401.

63. Haim Gouri, *Lamerhav*, November 8, 1960.

64. Nathan Alterman, *Davar*, November 18, 1960.

65. *Al Hamishmar*, October 21, 1960.

66. *Knesset Record*, 4th Knesset, 161st session, October 31, 1960.

67. Ben-Gurion, "Al Sifrut Ve'hayim," *Moznayim*, 12 (December 1976):7–10.

68. Letter to Moshe Shamir, February 16, 1960.

69. Letter from Ran Sigad, October 13, 1960.

70. Letter to Ran Sigad, November 8, 1960.

··· ה ···

The Emerging Philosopher·King

1. See Murray Edelman, *Political Language: Words That Succeed and Politics That Fail* (New York: Academic Press, 1977); and Doris Graber, *Verbal Behavior and Politics* (Urbana: University of Illinois Press, 1976).

2. On approaches to knowledge utilization see Charles Lindblom and David Cohen, *Usable Knowledge: Social Science and Social Problem Solving* (New Haven, Conn.: Yale University Press, 1979).

3. See Leo Strauss, *Natural Rights and History* (Chicago: University of Chicago Press, 1953).

4. On "impossibilities" see Arnold Brecht, *Political Theory: The Foundations of Twentieth Century Thought* (Princeton: Princeton University Press, 1959).

5. On knowledge and restraint see J. Bronowski, *Science and Human Values* (London: Hutchinson, 1961).

6. See Robert Holt and John Turner, "The Scholar as Artisan," *Policy Sciences*, 5 (1974):257–70.

7. Norman Moss, *Men Who Play God: The Story of the H-Bomb and How the World Came to Live with It* (New York: Harper and Row, 1968).

8. H. L. Nieburg, *In the Name of Science* (Chicago: Quadrangle, 1970).

9. Yizhar Smilanski, "Melekh Filossof," *Davar*, October 30, 1976.

10. Dan Segre, *A Crisis of Identity: Israel and Zionism* (Oxford: Oxford University Press, 1980).

11. See introduction, n.44.

12. Alvin Toffler, *The Third Wave* (New York: Bantam Books, 1981).

13. Ibid., p. 337.

14. Shimon Peres, *From These Men* (London: Weidenfeld and Nicolson, 1979), p. 18.

15. See Michael Bar Zohar, *Ben-Gurion: A Political Biography* (Tel-Aviv: Am Oved, 1977). (In Hebrew.)

16. Ibid., p. 1409.

17. See Sheldon Wolin, *Politics and Vision: Continuity and Inno-*

vation in Western Political Thought (London: Allen and Unwin, 1961), esp. pp. 44–45.

18. See David Ben-Gurion, "The Call of Spirit in Israel," *Rebirth and Destiny of Israel*, ed. David Ben-Gurion (New York: Philosophical Library, 1954), p. 436.

19. Richard Hofstadter, *Anti-Intellectualism in American Life* (New York: Knopf, 1963), p. 25.

20. Yitzhak Navon, "Ben-Gurion: Foreseer of Coming Generations," *Forum*, 34 (Winter 1979):14.

21. Israel Kolatt, "Ben-Gurion: Hademut Vehagedulah," *Bitefutzot Hagolah*, 67/68 (Winter 1973):21.

22. Shimon Peres, *From These Men*, p. 26.

23. Letter from M. Zilberman, November 19, 1962.

24. See, for example, Anthony Platt, ed., *The Politics of Riot Commissions, 1917–1970* (New York: Collier, 1971).

25. Letter to M. Zilberman, November 25, 1962.

26. See Harold Wilensky, *Organizational Intelligence: Knowledge and Policy in Government and Industry* (New York: Basic Books, 1967).

27. See Alexander George, *Presidential Decision-Making in Foreign Policy: The Effective Use of Information and Advice* (Boulder, Col.: Westview, 1980).

28. Letter from Shmuel Sambursky, August 17, 1958.

29. Letter from S. Adler, March 8, 1960.

30. Note from the Prime Minister to the Ministers of Finance and Agriculture, March 29, 1960.

31. Letter to E. Eldar, June 1, 1959.

32. For instance, letter to Dr. Berman and Professor Backi, June 28, 1961.

33. Letter to Professor Evenary and Dr. Sinkron, August 31, 1952.

34. Saadia Amiel, *Ad Kelot* (Tel-Aviv: Ma'ariv, 1979). (In Hebrew.)

35. Letter from A. N. Polak, November 18, 1962.

36. Letter to A. N. Polak, November 23, 1962.

37. See Dorothy Nelkin, *Controversy: Politics of Technical Decisions* (Beverly Hills, Calif.: Sage, 1979); Theodore Lowi and Benjamin Ginsberg, *Poliscide* (New York: Macmillan, 1976); and Peter Szanton, *Not Well Advised* (New York: Russell Sage, 1981).

38. *Knesset Record*, 187th Session, November 14, 1956.

39. Letter from Peretz Bernstein, June 23, 1956.

40. *Haboker*, August 1, 1963.

41. *Ma'ariv*, July 5, 1960.

42. Ben-Gurion's article appeared in *Davar*, December 25, 1953. For citations of reactions to the article see *Hapoel Hatzair*, No. 26, 1954.

43. *Knesset Record*, 3rd Knesset, 341st session, October 21, 1957.

44. Ibid.

45. See Seymour Martin Lipset, "The New Class and the Professoriate," in B. Bruce-Briggs, ed., *The New Class?* (New Brunswick, N.J.: Transaction, 1979).

46. Joel Primack and Frank Von Hippel, *Advice and Dissent: Scientists in the Political Arena* (New York: Basic Books, 1974).

47. Amram Ducovny, *David Ben-Gurion in His Own Words* (New York: Fleet Press, 1968), p. 102.

48. Ben-Gurion, "The Call of Spirit in Israel," p. 419.

49. Ibid., p. 439.

50. Ibid.

51. Ibid., pp. 426–27.

52. Ducovny, *David Ben-Gurion in His Own Words*, p. 24.

53. See Abraham Cordova and Hanna Herzog, "The Cultural Endeavors of the Labor Movement in Palestine: A Study of the Relationship between Intelligentsia and Intellectuals," *YIVO, Annual of Jewish Social Science*, 1978, pp. 238–59.

54. See Paul Obler and Herman Estrin, eds., *The New Scientist: Essays on the Methods and Values of Modern Science* (New York: Doubleday, 1962).

55. See Paul Weiss, "The Message of Science," *Bulletin of the Atomic Scientists* (September 1959).

56. Karl Popper, *The Open Society and Its Enemies* (London: Routledge, 1945).

57. Yehezkel Kaufmann, *The Religion of Israel* (London: Allen and Unwin, 1961).

58. Ibid., p. 3.

59. See Bernard Barber, *Science and the Social Order* (Glencoe, Ill.: Free Press, 1952).

60. Popper, *The Open Society and Its Enemies*, p. 188.

61. J. L. Talmon, *The Origins of Totalitarian Democracy* (New York: Praeger, 1960).

Selected Bibliography

This bibliography lists studies on "knowledge and power" consulted in the preparation of this book, as well as studies, in English, on Ben-Gurion and his era. Ben-Gurion's major books available in English are also listed. For a bibliography of Ben-Gurion's numerous articles and speeches see Samuel Lachover, ed., *The Writings of David Ben-Gurion: A Bibliography, 1910–1959* (Tel-Aviv, Israel: Israel Library Association, 1960).

Aaron, Henry J. *Politics and the Professors: The Great Debate in Perspective* (Washington D.C.: The Brookings Institution, 1978).

Alatas, Syed Hussein. *Intellectuals in Developing Societies* (London: Cass, 1977).

Apter, David E. "Nkruma, Charisma and the Coup," in *Philosophers and Kings: Studies in Leadership*, Dankwart Rustow, ed. (New York: Braziller, 1970).

Archibald, K. A. "Three Views of the Expert's Role in Policy Making," *Policy Sciences* 1 (Spring 1970): 73–86.

Arian, Alan. *Ideological Change in Israel* (Cleveland: The Press of Case Western Reserve University, 1968).

Aron, Raymond. *The Opium of the Intellectuals* (Garden City, N.Y.: Doubleday, 1957).

Aronoff, Myron J. *Power and Ritual in the Israel Labor Party: A*

Study in Political Anthropology (Assen, The Netherlands: Van Gorcum, 1977).

Avi-hai, Avraham. *Ben-Gurion: State-Builder* (New York: Wiley, 1974).

Avinery, Shlomo. "Israel in the Post Ben-Gurion Era: The Nemesis of Messianism," *Midstream* 11 (September 1965): 16–32.

————. *The Making of Modern Zionism: The Intellectual Origins of the Jewish State* (London: Weidenfeld & Nicolson, 1981).

Bacon, Francis. *New Atlantis* (Oxford: Clarendon Press, 1915). First published in 1627.

Bady, Joseph. "The Ben-Gurion Period in the History and Politics of the State of Israel, 1948–1965." Unpublished dissertation, New York University, 1968.

Barber, Bernard. *Science and the Social Order* (Glencoe, Ill.: The Free Press, 1952).

Barnes, S. P. "Making Out in Industrial Research," *Science Studies* 1 (January 1971): 157–175.

Bar Zohar, Michael. *Ben-Gurion* (London: Weidenfeld & Nicolson, 1978).

————. *The Armed Prophet: A Biography of Ben-Gurion.* Trans. from the French by Len Ortzen (London: A. Barker, 1967).

Bell, Daniel. *The Coming of Post-Industrial Society: A Venture in Social Forecasting* (New York: Basic Books, 1973).

————. *The Cultural Contradictions of Capitalism* (London: Heinemann, 1976).

Benda, Julien. *The Betrayal of the Intellectuals* (Boston: Beacon Press, 1955).

Ben-David, Joseph. "Professionals and Unions in Israel," *Industrial Relations* 5 (October 1965): 48–66.

————. *The Scientist's Role in Society: A Comparative Study* (New York: McGraw-Hill, 1971).

Ben-Ezer, Ehud, ed. *Unease in Zion* (New York: Quadrangle Books, 1974).

Ben-Gurion, David. *Ben-Gurion Looks at the Bible.* Jonathan Kolatch, trans. (London: W. H. Allen, 1972).

————. *Ben Gurion Looks Back: In Talks with Moshe Pearlman* (New York: Simon & Schuster, 1965).

————. *Israel: A Personal History.* N. Meyers and U. Nystar, trans. (New York: Funk & Wagnalls, 1971).

————. *My Talks with Arab Leaders.* A. Rubinstein and Misha Louvish, trans. (Jerusalem: Keter Books, 1972).

—————. *Rebirth and Destiny of Israel* (New York: Philosophical Library, 1954).

—————. *The Jews in Their Land* (London: Aldus Books, 1966).

Benveniste, Guy. *The Politics of Expertise* (Berkeley, Calif.: Gledessary, 1972).

Berlin, Isaiah. *The Hedgehog and the Fox: An Essay on Tolstoy's View of History* (London: Weidenfeld & Nicolson, 1953).

Berman, Ronald. *America in the Sixties: An Intellectual History* (New York: The Free Press, 1968).

Bernal, J. D. *Science in History* (Cambridge, Mass.: MIT Press, 1974). First published in 1954.

Bernstein, Marver H. *The Politics of Israel: The First Decade of Statehood* (Princeton: Princeton University Press, 1957).

Birnbaum, Ervin. *The Politics of Compromise: State and Religion in Israel* (Madison, N.J.: Fairleigh Dickinson University Press, 1970).

Blondel, Jean. *World Leaders: Heads of Government in the Postwar Period* (Beverly Hills, Calif.: Sage, 1980).

Bobrow, Davis. "Analysis and Foreign Policy Choice," *Policy Sciences* 4 (December 1973): 437–51.

Boguslaw, Robert. *The New Utopians: A Study of System Design and Social Change* (Englewood Cliffs, N.J.: Prentice-Hall, 1965).

Boorstin, Daniel J. *The Republic of Technology: Reflections on Our Future Community* (New York: Harper & Row, 1978).

Boulding, Kenneth E. *The Image* (Ann Arbor: University of Michigan Press, 1956).

—————. *The Meaning of the 20th Century: The Great Transition* (New York: Harper & Row, 1964).

Brecher, Michael. *The Foreign Policy System of Israel: Setting, Images, Process* (London: Oxford University Press, 1972).

Bronowski, Jacob. *Science and Human Values* (London: Hutchinson, 1961).

Bruce-Briggs, B. ed. *The New Class?* (New Brunswick, N.J.: Transaction, 1979).

Brym, Robert. *Intellectuals and Politics* (London: Allen & Unwin, 1980).

Calder, Nigel. *Technopolis: Social Control of the Uses of Science* (New York: Clarion, 1969).

Carr, Edward Hallett. *What Is History?* (New York: Vintage, 1961).

Caute, David. *The Fellow-Travellers: A Postscript to the Enlight-enment* (London: Weidenfeld & Nicolson, 1973).

Chomsky, Noam. *American Power and the New Mandarins* (New York: Pantheon, 1969).

Comay, Joan. *Ben-Gurion and the Birth of Israel* (New York: Random House, 1967).

Cordova, Abraham. "The Institutionalization of a Cultural Center in Palestine: The Case of the Writers' Association," *Jewish Social Studies* 17 (Winter 1980): 37–62.

————, and Herzog, Hanna. "The Cultural Endeavors of the Labor Movement in Palestine: A Study of the Relationship between Intelligentsia and Intellectuals," *YIVO: Annual of Jewish Social Science* (1978): 238–59.

Coser, Lewis. *Men of Ideas: A Sociologist's View* (New York: The Free Press, 1965).

Cotgrove, Stephen. "Technology, Rationality and Domination," *Social Studies of Science* 5 (February 1975): 55–78.

Cranston, Maurice. *The Mask of Politics and Other Essays* (London: Allen Lane, 1973).

Crick, Bernard. "Writers and Politics," *Critical Quarterly* 22 (Summer 1980): 63–73.

Crick, Malcolm R. "Anthropology of Knowledge," *Annual Review of Anthropology* 11 (1982): 287–313.

Crossman, Richard H. S. *A Nation Reborn: Israel of Weizmann, Bevin and Ben-Gurion* (London: H. Hamilton, 1960).

Debray, Régis. *Teachers, Writers, Celebrities: The Intellectuals of Modern France* (London: NLB, 1981).

DeHuzar, George B., ed. *The Intellectuals: A Controversial Portrait* (Glencoe, Ill.: The Free Press, 1960).

Deshpande, Rohit. "Action and Enlightenment Functions of Research: Comparing Private and Public Sector Perspectives," *Knowledge: Creation, Diffusion, Utilization* 2 (March 1981): 317–30.

Dewey, John. *Freedom and Culture* (New York: G. P. Putnam's Sons, 1939).

Dickson, David. *Alternative Technology and the Politics of Technical Change* (London: Fontana Collins, 1974).

Dickson, Paul. *Think Tanks* (New York: Atheneum, 1971).

Dror, Yehezkel. *Design for Policy Sciences* (New York: American Elsevier, 1971).

Dunn, Edgar S. *Economic and Social Development: A Process of*

Social Learning (Baltimore: Johns Hopkins University Press, 1971).

Dupré, J. Stefan, and Sanford A. Lakoff. *Science and the Nation: Policy and Politics* (Englewood Cliffs, N.J.: Prentice-Hall, 1962).

Edelman, Maurice. *Ben-Gurion: A Political Biography* (London: Hodder & Stoughton, 1964).

Edelman, Murray. *Political Language: Words That Succeed and Politics That Fail* (New York: Academic Press, 1977).

—————. *The Symbolic Uses of Politics* (Urbana, Ill.: University of Illinois Press, 1964).

Eisenstadt, S. N. *Israeli Society* (London: Weidenfeld & Nicolson, 1967).

—————. *Max Weber on Charisma and Institution Building* (Chicago: University of Chicago Press, 1968).

—————, and S. R. Graubard, eds. *Intellectuals and Tradition* (New York: Humanities Press, 1973).

Elkana, Yehuda. "The Historical Roots of Modern Physics," in *History of Twentieth Century Physics*, Charles Weiner, ed. (New York: Academic Press, 1973).

Ellul, Jacques. *The Technological Society* (New York: Vintage, 1964).

Elon, Amos. *The Israelis: Founders and Sons* (New York: Holt, Rinehart & Winston, 1971).

Etzioni, Amitai. *The Active Society: A Theory of Societal and Political Processes* (New York: The Free Press, 1968).

Etzioni-Halevy, Eva. *Political Culture in Israel* (New York: Praeger, 1977).

Evan, William. *Knowledge and Power in a Global Setting* (Beverly Hills, Calif.: Sage, 1981).

Fein, Leonard. *Israel: Politics and People* (Boston: Little, Brown, 1967).

Ferkiss, Victor. *Technological Man: The Myth and the Reality* (New York: Braziller, 1969).

Feuer, Lewis S. *Ideology and the Ideologists* (Oxford: Blackwell, 1975).

—————. *Marx and the Intellectuals: A Set of Post-Ideological Essays* (Garden City, N.Y.: Doubleday, 1969).

Fisch, Harold. *The Zionist Revolution: A New Perspective* (London: Weidenfeld & Nicolson, 1978).

Flower, John, ed. Series on writers and politics in modern

Britain, France, Germany, Italy, Scandinavia, Spain and Nigeria. Published by Hodder & Stoughton, 1977– .

Galbraith, John Kenneth. *The New Industrial State* (New York: New American Library, 1962).

Geertz, Clifford. "Centers, Kings and Charisma: Reflections on the Symbolism of Power," in *Culture and Its Creators: Essays in Honor of Edward Shils,* Joseph Ben-David and Terry Nicols Clark, eds. (Chicago: University of Chicago Press, 1977), pp. 150–71.

————. *Interpretation of Culture* (New York: Basic Books, 1977).

Gella, Alexander, ed. *The Intelligentsia and the Intellectuals* (Beverly Hills, Calif.: Sage, 1976).

Gellner, Ernst. *Spectacles and Predicaments: Essays in Social Theory* (Cambridge, Eng.: Cambridge University Press, 1979).

————. *Thought and Change* (Chicago: University of Chicago Press, 1964).

George, Alexander. *Presidential Decisionmaking in Foreign Policy: The Effective Use of Information and Advice* (Boulder, Col.: Westview, 1980).

Gianos, Philip. "Scientists as Policy Advisors: The Context of Influence," *Western Political Quarterly* 27 (June 1974): 429–56.

Gilpin, Robert. *American Scientists and Nuclear Weapons Policy* (Princeton: Princeton University Press, 1962).

————, and Christopher Wright, eds. *Scientists and National Policy-Making* (New York: Columbia University Press, 1964).

Glicksberg, Charles I. *The Literature of Commitment* (London: Associated University Presses, 1976).

Goldman, Merle. *China's Intellectuals: Advice and Dissent* (Cambridge, Mass.: Harvard University Press, 1981).

Gouldner, Alvin W. *The Dialectic of Ideology and Technology: The Origins, Grammar and Future of Ideology* (London: Macmillan, 1976).

————. *The Future of Intellectuals and the Rise of the New Class* (New York: Seabury, 1979).

Graber, Doris. *Verbal Behavior and Politics* (Urbana, Ill.: University of Illinois Press, 1976).

Graubard S., and G. Halton, eds. *Excellence and Leadership in a Democracy* (New York: Columbia University Press, 1962).

Gross, John. *The Rise and Fall of the Man of Letters* (London: Weidenfeld & Nicolson, 1969).

Gruber, Ruth, ed. *Science and the New Nations* (New York: Basic Books, 1961).

Haberer, Joseph, ed. *Science and Technology Policy: Perspectives and Developments* (Lexington, Mass.: Lexington Books, 1977).

———. *Politics and the Community of Science* (New York: Van Nostrand, 1969).

Habermass, Jurgen. *Knowledge and Human Interests* (London: Heinemann, 1972).

———. *Theory and Practice* (London: Heinemann, 1974).

Halpern, Ben. *The Idea of the Jewish State* (Cambridge, Mass.: Harvard University Press, 1961).

Hofstadter, Richard. *Anti-Intellectualism in American Life* (New York: Knopf, 1963).

Holt, Robert, and John Turner. "The Scholar as Artisan," *Policy Sciences* 5 (September 1974): 257–70.

Isaac, Rael Jean. *Party and Politics in Israel: Three Visions of a Jewish State* (New York: Longman, 1981).

Jones, Thomas E. *Options for the Future: A Comparative Analysis of Policy-Oriented Forecasts* (New York: Praeger, 1980).

Jungk, Robert. *Brighter than a Thousand Suns: A Personal History of the Atomic Scientists* (New York: Harcourt, 1958).

Kadushin, Charles. *The American Intellectual Elite* (Boston: Little, Brown, 1974).

Kariel, Henry S. *Open Systems: Arenas for Political Action* (Itasca, Ill.: Peacock, 1968).

Kautsky, John H. *The Political Consequences of Modernization* (New York: Wiley, 1972).

Keller, Suzanne. *Beyond the Ruling Class* (New York: Arno, 1979).

Keren, Michael. "Science vs. Government: A Reconsideration," *Policy Sciences* 12 (October 1980): 333–53.

———, and Giora Goldberg. "Technological Development and Ideological Change," in *Israel: A Developing Society*, Asher Arian, ed. (Assen, The Netherlands: Van Gorcum, 1980).

Kerr, Steven, Mary Ann Von Glinow, and Janet Schriesheim. "Issues in the Study of 'Professionals' in Organizations: The Case of Scientists and Engineers," *Organizational Behavior and Human Performance* 18 (April 1977): 329–45.

Kinnon, Colette M., ed. *The Impact of Modern Scientific Ideas on Society: In Commemoration of Einstein* (Boston: D. Reidel, 1981).

Kleinberg, Benjamin S. *American Society in the Postindustrial Age: Technocracy, Power and the End of Ideology* (Columbus, Ohio: Merrill, 1973).

Knei-Paz, Baruch. "Academics in Politics: An Israeli Experience," *Jerusalem Quarterly* 16 (Summer 1980): 54–70.

Ladd, Everett Carll, and Seymour Martin Lipset. *The Divided Academy: Professors and Politics* (New York: Norton, 1975).

Lakoff, Sanford A., ed. *Knowledge and Power: Essays on Science and Government* (New York: The Free Press, 1966).

Lapp, Ralph. *The New Priesthood: The Scientific Elite and the Uses of Power* (New York: Harper & Row, 1965).

Lewis, Bernard. *History: Remembered, Recovered, Invented* (Princeton: Princeton University Press, 1975).

Lindblom, Charles, and David Cohen. *Usable Knowledge: Social Science and Social Problem Solving* (New Haven, Conn.: Yale University Press, 1979).

Lipset, Seymour Martin. *Political Man* (New York: Doubleday, 1963).

————, and Asoke Basu. "The Roles of Intellectuals and Professional Roles," in *The Intelligentsia and the Intellectuals*, Alexander Gella, ed. (Beverly Hills, Calif.: Sage, 1976), pp. 111–50.

Litvinoff, Barnet. *Ben-Gurion of Israel* (London: Weidenfeld & Nicolson, 1954).

Lowi, Theodore, and Benjamin Ginsberg. *Poliscide* (New York: Macmillan, 1976).

Lynn, Lawrence E. "Implementation: Will the Hedgehogs Be Outfoxed?" *Policy Analysis* 3 (Spring 1977): 277–80.

Maccoby, Michael. *The Games-Man: The New Corporate Leaders* (New York: Simon & Schuster, 1976).

Machlup, Fritz. *Knowledge: Its Creation, Distribution and Economic Significance* (Princeton: Princeton University Press, 1980).

Macrae, Duncan. *The Social Function of Social Science* (New Haven, Conn.: Yale University Press, 1976).

Mannheim, Karl. *Ideology and Utopia* (New York: Harcourt, 1936).

Marcuse, Herbert. *One Dimensional Man: Studies in the Ideol-*

ogy of Advanced Industrial Society (Boston: Beacon Press, 1964).

Medding, Peter. *Mapai in Israel: Political Organization and Government in a New Society* (Cambridge, Eng.: Cambridge University Press, 1972).

Merton, Robert. *Social Theory and Social Structure* (New York: The Free Press, 1957).

Michael, Donald. *The Unprepared Society: Planning for a Precarious Future* (New York: Basic Books, 1968).

Molnar, Thomas. *The Decline of the Intellectual* (New York: World Publishing, 1965).

Moss, Norman. *Men Who Play God: The Story of the H-Bomb and How the World Came to Live With It* (New York: Harper & Row, 1968).

Navon, Yitzhak. "Ben-Gurion: Foreseer of Coming Generations," *Forum* 34 (Winter 1979): 13–17.

Nelkin, Dorothy, ed. *Controversy: Politics of Technical Decisions* (Beverly Hills, Calif.: Sage, 1979).

———. *Technological Decisions and Democracy: European Experiments in Public Participation* (Beverly Hills, Calif.: Sage, 1977).

———. "Scientists and Professional Responsibility: The Experience of American Ecologists," *Social Studies of Science* 7 (February 1977): 75–95.

Nettl, J. P. "Ideas, Intellectuals and Structures of Dissent," in *On Intellectuals*, Philip Rieff, ed. (Garden City, N.Y.: Doubleday, 1970), pp. 57–134.

Nichols, Ray. *Treason, Tradition and the Intellectuals: Julien Benda and Political Discourse* (Lawrence, Kansas: Regents Press of Kansas, 1978).

Nieburg, Harold Leonard. *In the Name of Science* (Chicago: Quadrangle Books, 1970).

O'Brien, Canor Cruise, and William Dean Vanech, eds. *Power and Consciousness* (London: University of London Press, 1969).

Paige, Glenn F. D., ed. *Political Leadership: Readings for an Emerging Field* (New York: The Free Press, 1972).

———. *The Scientific Study of Political Leadership* (New York: The Free Press, 1977).

Panichas, George A., ed. *The Politics of Twentieth-Century Novelists* (New York: Hawthorn, 1971).

Parsons, Talcott. "The Intellectual: A Social Role Category," in *On Intellectuals*, Philip Rieff, ed. (Garden City, N.Y.: Doubleday, 1970), pp. 3–26.

Paul, Charles B. *Science and Immortality: The Eloges of the Paris Academy of Sciences, 1699–1791* (Berkeley, Calif.: University of California Press, 1980).

Peres, Shimon. *From These Men* (London: Weidenfeld & Nicolson, 1981).

Pipes, Richard, ed. *The Russian Intelligentsia* (New York: Columbia University Press, 1961).

Platt, Anthony M. *The Politics of Riot Commissions, 1917–1970* (New York: Collier, 1971).

Popper, Karl. *The Open Society and Its Enemies* (London: Routledge, 1945).

Price, Don K. *Government and Science* (New York: New York University Press, 1954).

———. *The Scientific Estate* (Cambridge, Mass.: Harvard University Press, 1965).

Primack, Joel, and Frank Von Hippel. *Advice and Dissent: Scientists in the Political Arena* (New York: Basic Books, 1974).

Pye, Lucian W. *Politics, Personality and Nation Building* (New Haven, Conn.: Yale University Press, 1962).

Quade, Edward S. *Analysis for Public Decisions* (New York: American Elsevier, 1975).

———, and Giandomenico Majone, eds. *Pitfalls of Systems Analysis* (New York: Wiley-Interscience, 1980).

Rapoport, Anatol. *Strategy and Conscience* (New York: Schocken, 1964).

Rich, Robert. *Social Science Information and Public Policy Making* (San Francisco: Jossey-Bass, 1981).

———. *The Knowledge Cycle* (Beverly Hills, Calif.: Sage, 1981).

Rothenberg, Marc. "Organization and Control: Professionals and Amateurs in American Astronomy, 1899–1918," *Social Studies of Science* 11 (August 1981): 275–303.

Russell, Bertrand. *Human Knowledge: Its Scope and Limits* (New York: Simon & Schuster, 1948).

Rustow, Dankwart, ed. *Philosophers and Kings: Studies in Leadership* (New York: Braziller, 1970).

St. John, Robert. *Ben-Gurion* (London: Jarrolds, 1959).

Salomon, Jean-Jacques. *Science and Politics* (Cambridge, Mass.: MIT Press, 1973).

Samuels, Warren J. *Pareto on Policy* (Amsterdam: Elsevier, 1974).

Schlesinger, Philip. "In Search of the Intellectuals: Some Comments on Recent Theory," *Media, Culture and Society* 4 (July 1982): 203–23.

Schon, Donald. *Beyond the Stable State* (New York: Norton, 1971).

Schooler, Dean. *Science, Scientists and Public Policy* (New York: The Free Press, 1971).

Segre, Dan. *A Crisis of Identity: Israel and Zionism* (Oxford: Oxford University Press, 1980).

————. *Israel: A Society in Transition* (London: Oxford University Press, 1971).

Seligman, Lester G. *Leadership in a New Nation: Political Development in Israel* (New York: Atherton Press, 1964).

Shapiro, Yonathan. *The Formative Years of the Israeli Labour Party: The Organization of Power, 1919–1930* (London: Sage, 1976).

Shils, Edward. "Charisma, Order and Status," *American Sociological Review* 30 (April 1965): 199–213.

————. "Intellectuals, Tradition and the Traditions of Intellectuals: Some Preliminary Considerations," in *Intellectuals and Tradition*, S. N. Eisenstadt and S. R. Graubard, eds. (New York: Humanities Press, 1973), pp. 27–51.

————. "Knowledge and the Sociology of Knowledge," *Knowledge: Creation, Diffusion, Utilization* 4 (September 1982): 7–32.

————. "The Intellectuals and the Powers: Some Perspectives for Comparative Analysis," in *On Intellectuals*, Philip Rieff, ed. (Garden City, N.Y.: Doubleday, 1970).

Simon, Ernst. "Buber or Ben-Gurion?" *New Outlook* 9 (February 1966): 9–17.

Skinner, B. F. *Beyond Freedom and Dignity* (New York: Bantam Books, 1971).

Snow, C. P. *Science and Government* (Cambridge, Mass.: Harvard University Press, 1960).

————. *The Two Cultures and the Scientific Revolution* (Cambridge, Eng.: Cambridge University Press, 1962).

Starr, Chauncey, and Philip Ritterbush, eds. *Science, Technology and Human Prospect* (New York: Pergamon, 1980).

Steinbruner, John. *The Cybernetic Theory of Decision* (Princeton: Princeton University Press, 1974).

Stromberg, R. N. "Redemption by War: The Intellectuals and 1914," *The Midwest Quarterly* 20 (Spring 1979): 211–27.

Szanton, Peter. *Not Well Adviced* (New York: Russell Sage, 1981).

Teich, Albert H., ed. *Technology and Man's Future* (New York: St. Martin's Press, 1981).

Toffler, Alvin. *Future Shock* (New York: Bantam Books, 1970).

———. *The Third Wave* (New York: Bantam Books, 1981).

Tucker, Robert C. "The Theory of Charismatic Leadership," in *Philosophers and Kings: Studies in Leadership*, Dankwart Rustow, ed. (New York: Braziller, 1970).

Unger, Roberton Mangabeira. *Knowledge and Politics* (New York: The Free Press, 1975).

Vickers, Jeoffrey. *The Art of Judgement* (New York: Basic Books, 1965).

———. *Value Systems and Social Process* (New York: Basic Books, 1968).

Watson, George. *Politics and Literature in Modern Britain* (London: Macmillan, 1977).

Weart, Spencer R. *Scientists in Power* (Cambridge, Mass.: Harvard University Press, 1979).

Weber, George H., and George J. McCall. *Social Scientists as Advocates* (Beverly Hills, Calif.: Sage, 1978).

Weiss, Carol H. "Research for Policy's Sake: The Enlightenment Function of Social Research," *Policy Analysis* 3 (Fall 1977): 531–45.

———. *Using Social Research in Public Policy Making* (Lexington, Mass.: Lexington Books, 1977).

———, and Michael J. Bucuvalas. *Social Science Research and Decision-Making* (New York: Columbia University Press, 1980).

Werskey, Gary. *The Visible College* (New York: Holt, Rinehart & Winston, 1978).

Wildawsky, Aaron. *Speaking Truth to Power: The Art and Craft of Policy Analysis* (Boston: Little, Brown, 1979).

Wilensky, Harold. *Intellectuals in Labour Unions: Organizational Pressures on Professional Roles* (Glencoe, Ill.: The Free Press, 1956).

———. *Organizational Intelligence: Knowledge and Policy in Government and Industry* (New York: Basic Books, 1967).

Wilkinson, James. *The Intellectual Resistance in Europe* (Cambridge, Mass.: Harvard University Press, 1981).

Wilson, James Q. "Policy Intellectuals and Public Policy," *The Public Interest* 64 (Summer 1981): 31–46.

Winner, Langdon. *Autonomous Technology: Technics Out of Control as a Theme in Political Thought* (Cambridge, Mass.: Harvard University Press, 1977).

Yanai, Nathan. *Party Leadership in Israel* (Ramat-Gan, Israel: Turtledove, 1981).

Zuckerman, Harriet. *Scientific Elite: Nobel Laureates in the United States* (New York: The Free Press, 1977).

Index